Daylight

THE LIGHT AT THE END OF HISTORY

Reacting to Nuclear Impact

Abbey Hepner

Cofounders: Taj Forer and Michael Itkoff
Creative Director: Ursula Damm
Copy Editor: Gabrielle Fastman

ISBN: 978-1-942084-97-6

Printed by OFSET Yapimevi, Turkey

Daylight Books
E-mail: info@daylightbooks.org
Web: www.daylightbooks.org

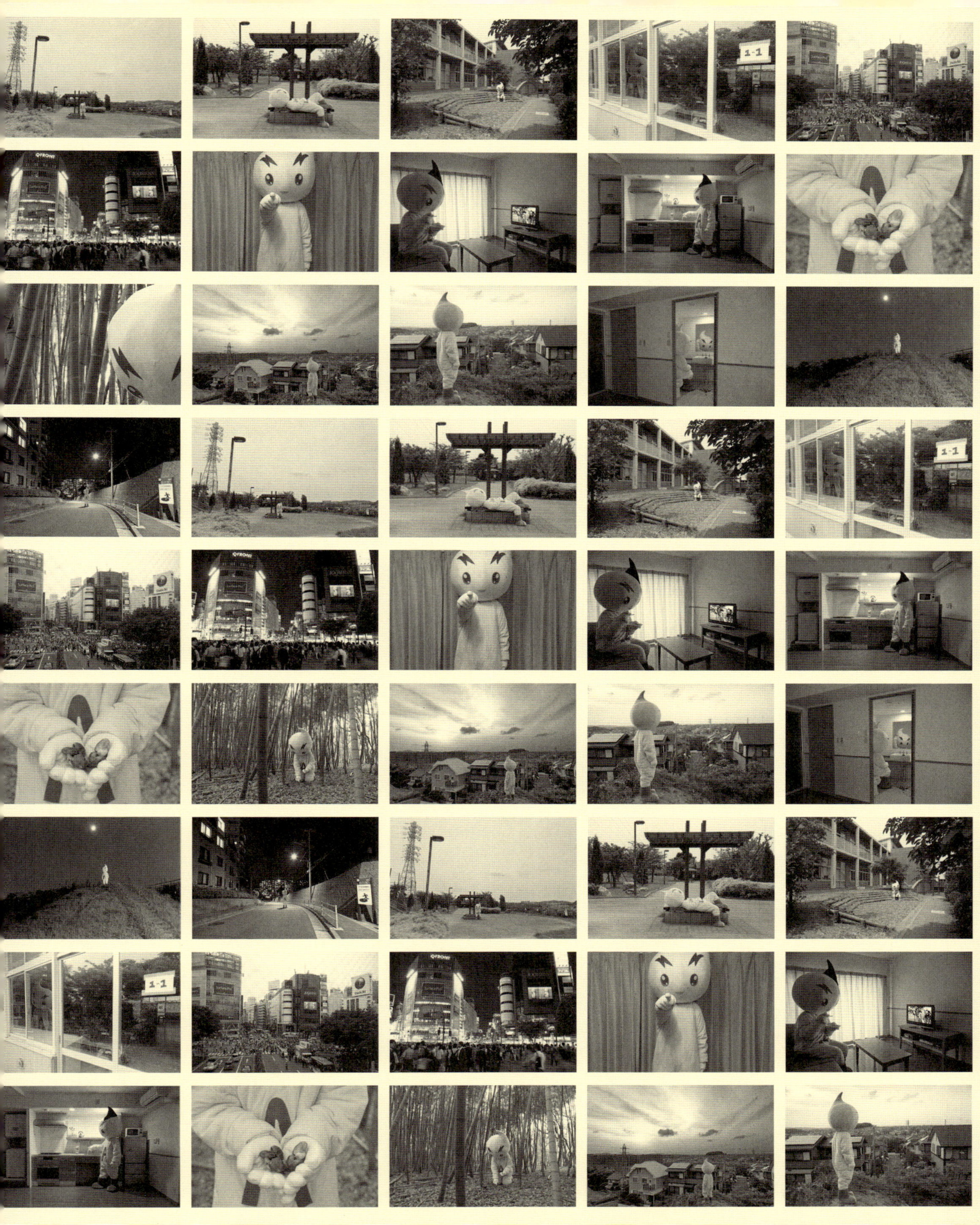

PART

PALINOPSIA

X-ray film images, 16" x 10", 2020

PALINOPSIA

The body was the first site of conquest in the desire to make the invisible visible.[1] X-rays cut through the inner surfaces, turning flesh into a photographic medium that light could penetrate. The dropping of the first atomic bomb was the largest photographic event ever to occur. Inscribed by catastrophic light, Hiroshima and Nagasaki became cameras. Atomic shadow traces appeared throughout the cities—body-shaped black marks where people stood at the time of the detonation. The violent light bleached the buildings and sidewalks except where a body had interrupted it. The shadows were photograms.[2]

Atomic veterans who had watched the tests in Nevada's desert recalled turning away from the bomb's blinding light and covering their eyes with their arms.[3] The flash—an X-ray—rendered their bodies momentarily transparent. They saw through their eyelids, and the bones in their arms became visible. Akira Lippit writes:

> The lethal force of X-rays is recapitulated by the atomic radiation, which echoes the capacity of catastrophic light to penetrate the body and erase the distinction between inside and out, body and environment, images of destruction and unimaginable destruction. X-rays

---

1 Author's note: I am referring to two things: 1) the early history of photography and its relationship to science and medicine, and 2) biopolitics and the idea that controlling bodies is the ultimate form of conquest. Polona Tratnik, *Conquest of Body: Biopower and Biotechnology* (Dordrecht: Springer, 2017), xiii.
2 Akira M. Lippit, *Atomic Light (Shadow Optics)* (Minneapolis: University of Minnesota Press, 2015), p. 48.
3 Author's note: "Downwinder" refers to individuals and communities living in the intermountain area who were exposed to radioactive contamination during atmospheric and underground nuclear weapons testing and nuclear accidents. "Atomic veteran" refers to individuals who were exposed to ionizing radiation while present at the site of a nuclear explosion during active duty in the US military.

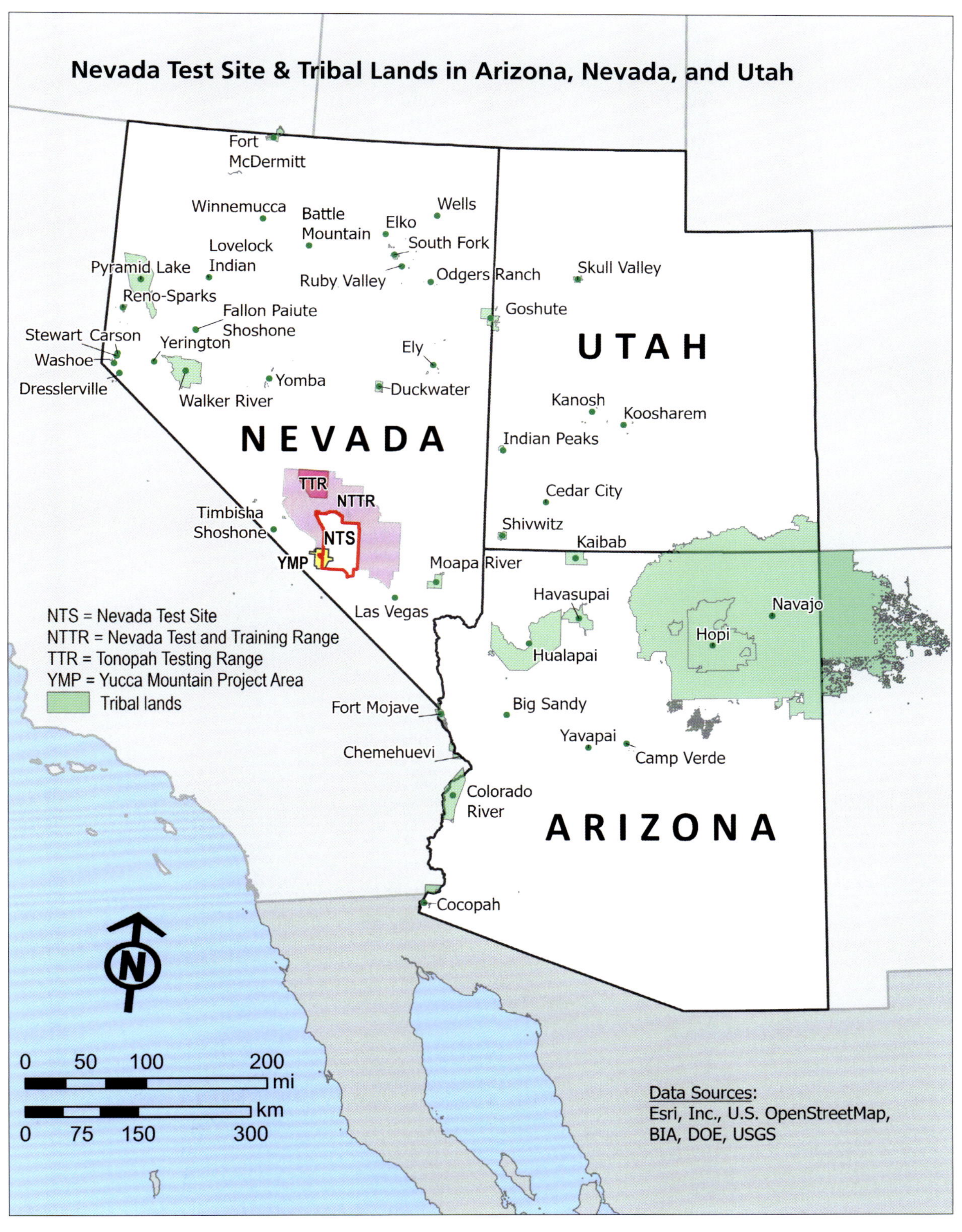

Nevada Test Site & Tribal Lands in Arizona, Nevada, and Utah
Fort McDermitt
Winnemucca
Battle Mountain
Wells
Elko
South Fork
Lovelock Indian
Pyramid Lake
Ruby Valley
Odgers Ranch
Skull Valley
Reno-Sparks
Goshute
Fallon Paiute Shoshone
Stewart Carson
UTAH
Yerington
Ely
Washoe
Dresslerville
Yomba
Duckwater
Kanosh
Walker River
Koosharem
NEVADA
Indian Peaks
TTR
NTTR
Cedar City
Timbisha Shoshone
NTS
Shivwitz
YMP
Kaibab
Moapa River
Havasupai
Las Vegas
Navajo
NTS = Nevada Test Site
Hopi
NTTR = Nevada Test and Training Range
TTR = Tonopah Testing Range
Hualapai
YMP = Yucca Mountain Project Area
Tribal lands
Big Sandy
Fort Mojave
Yavapai
Chemehuevi
Camp Verde
Colorado River
ARIZONA
Cocopah
N
0   50   100   200
mi
km
0   75   150   300
Data Sources:
Esri, Inc., U.S. OpenStreetMap,
BIA, DOE, USGS

and atomic radiation are lined in a secret narrative, bound by a logic that is historical, overdetermined, and destined—and, at the same time, incidental, accidental, and arbitrary.[4]

X-rays and gamma rays are known cancer-causing agents.[5] The generation of atomic veterans and downwinders X-rayed by atomic weapons testing gave birth to the generation X-rayed by medical technology. For the future generations

Thyroid Internal Dose-Map[6]

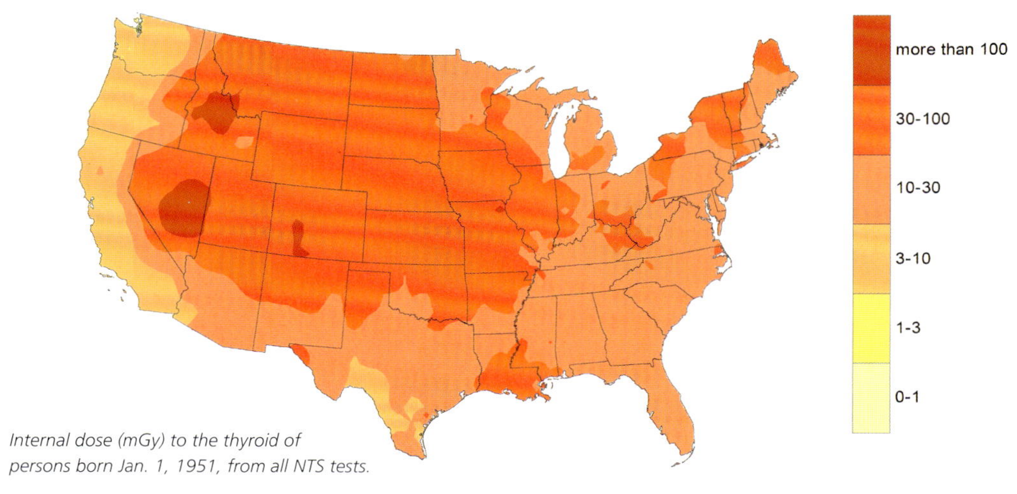

Internal dose (mGy) to the thyroid of persons born Jan. 1, 1951, from all NTS tests.

4   Lippit, *Atomic Light*, p. 84.
5   National Toxicology Program, NTP 11th Report on Carcinogens, *Rep Carcinog*, 2004, vol. 11, 1-A32.
6   "A report on the feasibility of a study on the health consequences to the American population from nuclear weapons tests conducted by the United States and other nations." National Cancer Institute and the US Department of Health and Human Services, Prepared for the US Congress. Washington, DC: US DHHS; 2005, Accessed 1 August 2020, Available at http://www.cdc.gov/nceh/radiation/fallout/default.htm.

afflicted by genetic mutations, childhood cancer, or the fear of either, the connection between the technological and corporeal is used to reduce social tensions (for example, with X-rays, MRIs, or fetal ultrasound images). Simultaneously, it creates an interdependence that is only mitigable with the use of more technology. Radiation, like the nuclear industry, is involved in an interesting paradox: the seductive use of civilian nuclear power plants allows for the continued production of weapons-grade plutonium; the compounds used to cure cancer are also the ones that create it; and the effect of radiation, rendering the body's interior visible, can also create illness that makes it taboo—secret. And that which is secret is socially invisible.[7]

I created *Palinopsia* by photographing a computer screen displaying Google Earth satellite images of bomb craters at the Nevada Test Site. The X-ray film captures an inverse of the image, filling the absent cavity with visible light. It creates an illusion of matter where the matter was removed, reflecting radiation's introduction into the atmosphere. My appropriation of these images is an act of counter-surveillance and provides commentary on image consumption and the inaccessibility of these places and their history.

Platelist:

---

7   Lippit, *Atomic Light*, p. 89.

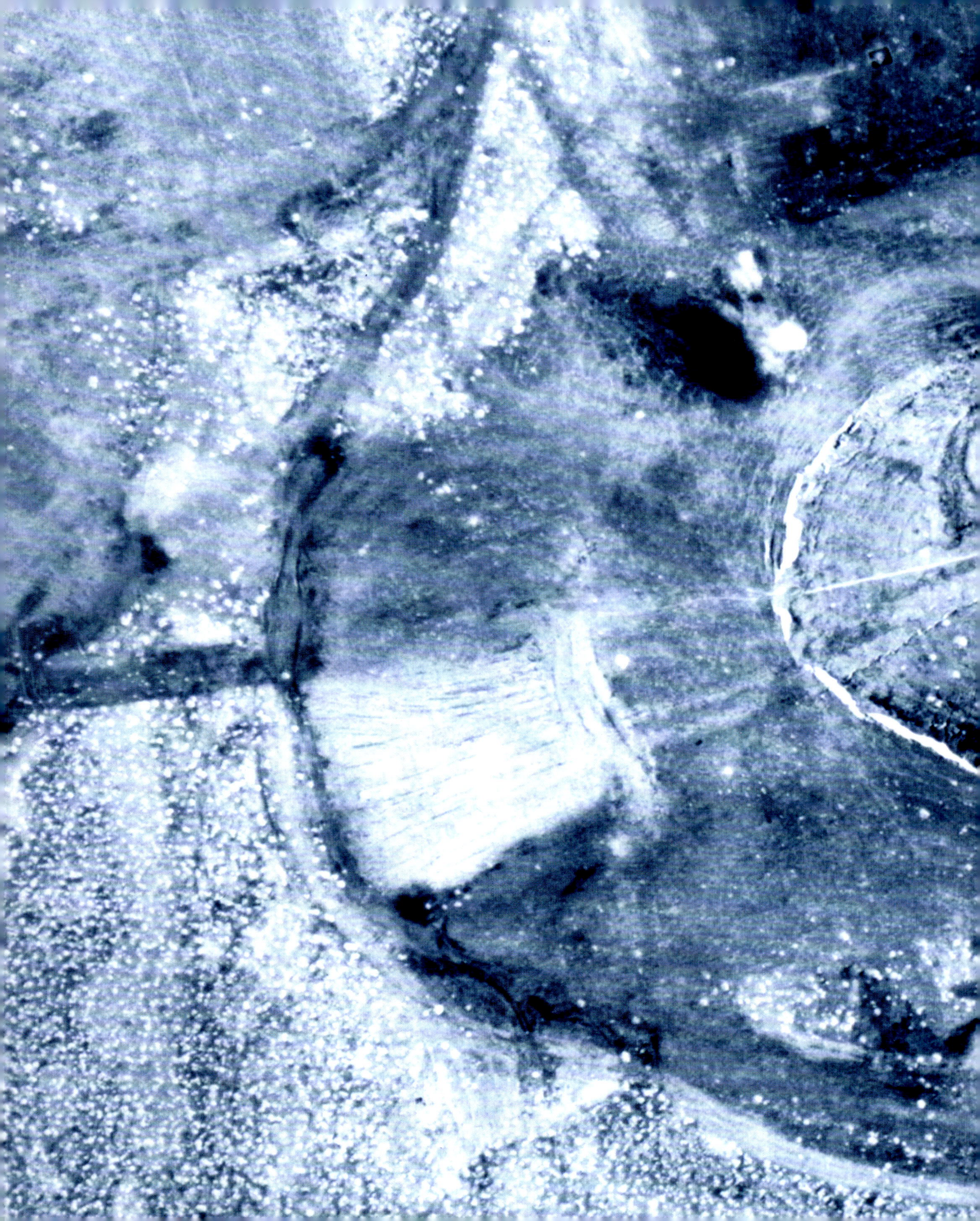

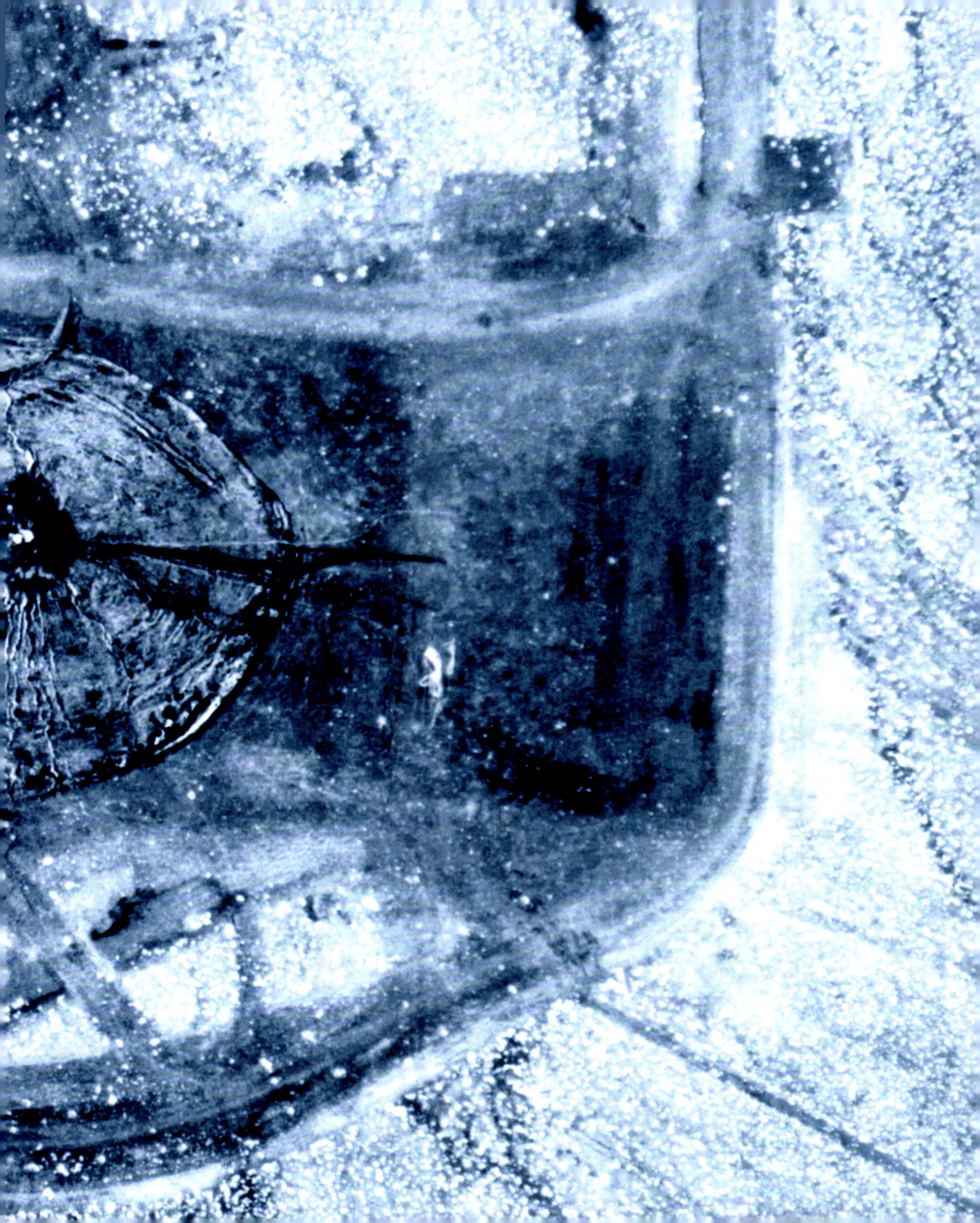

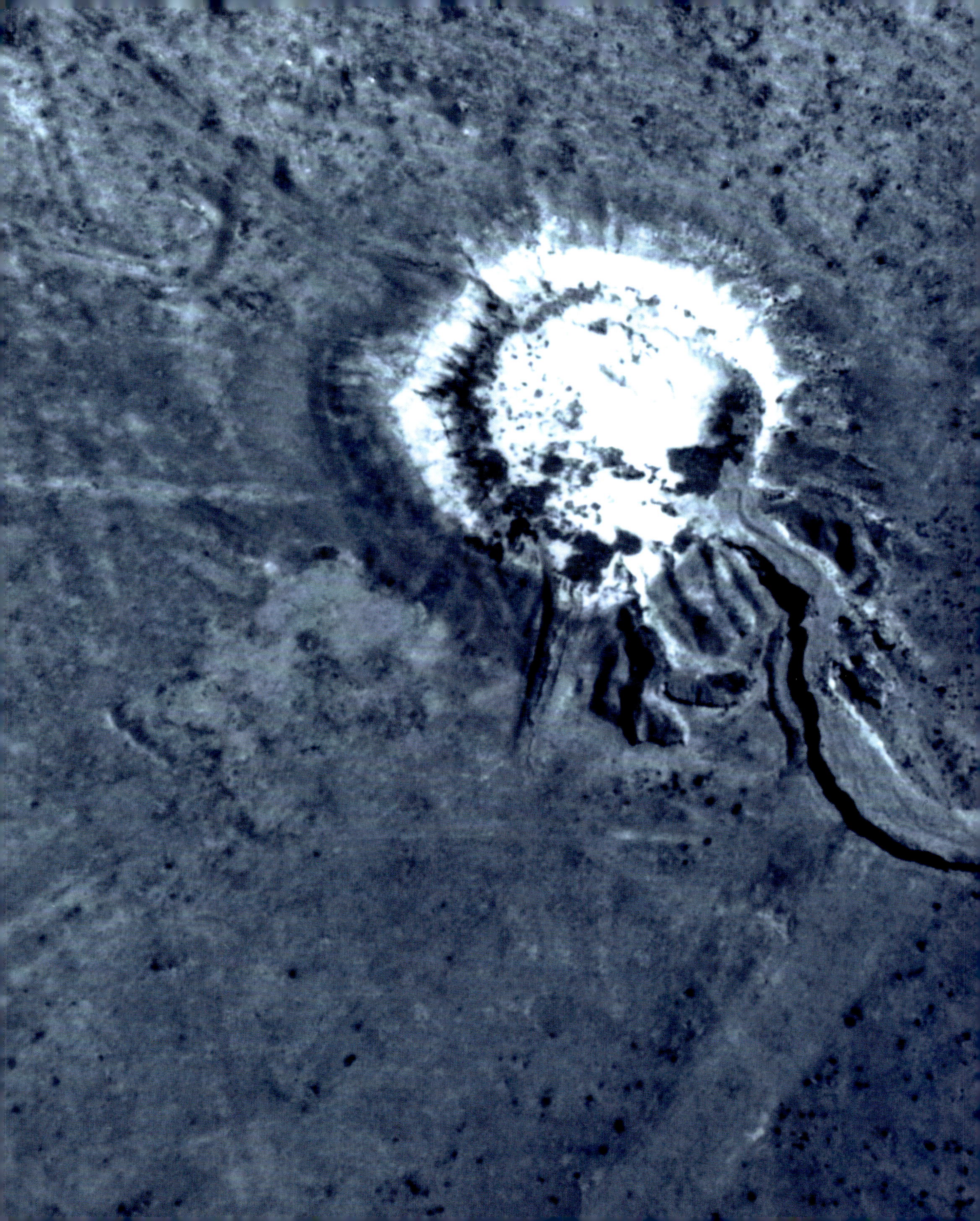

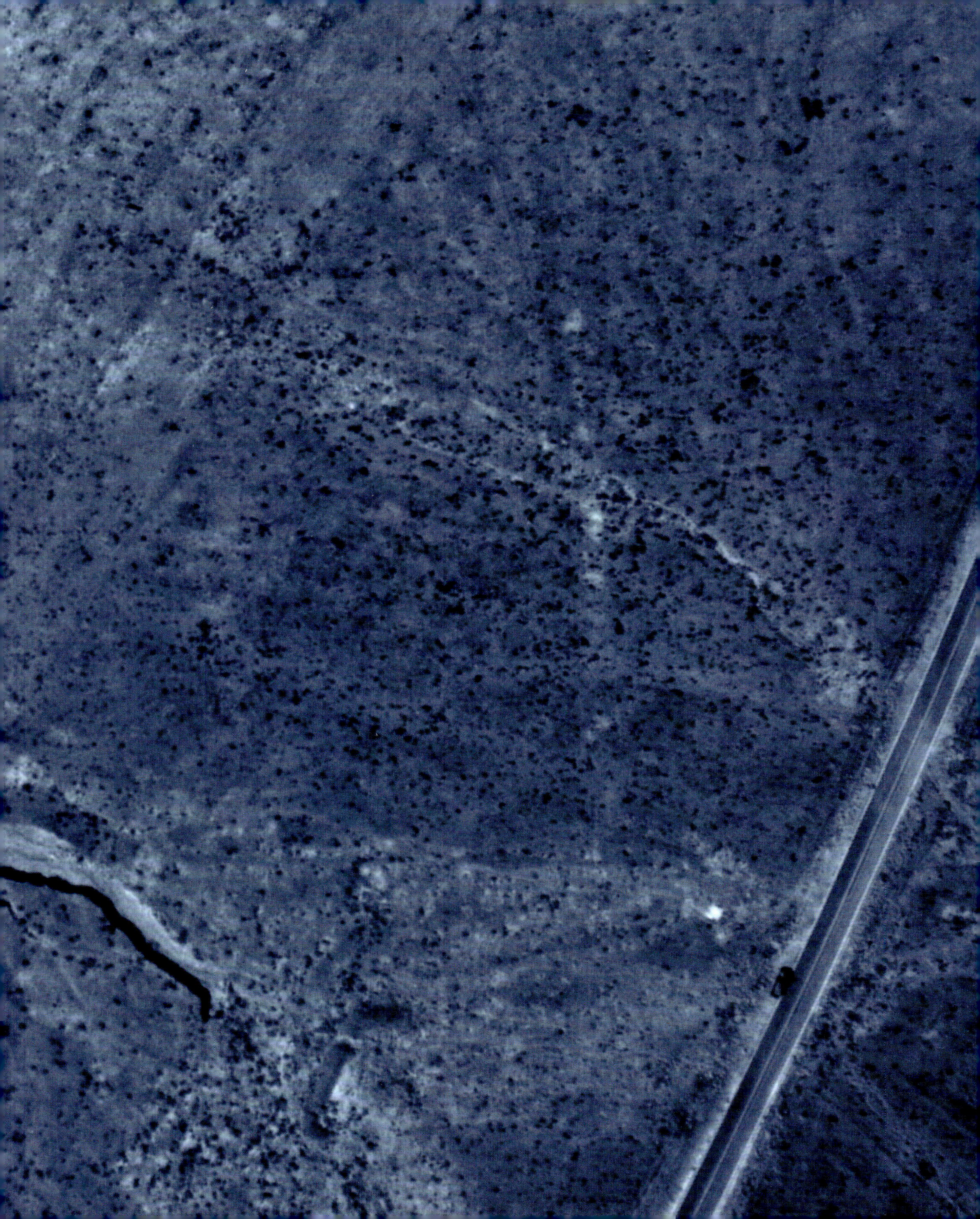

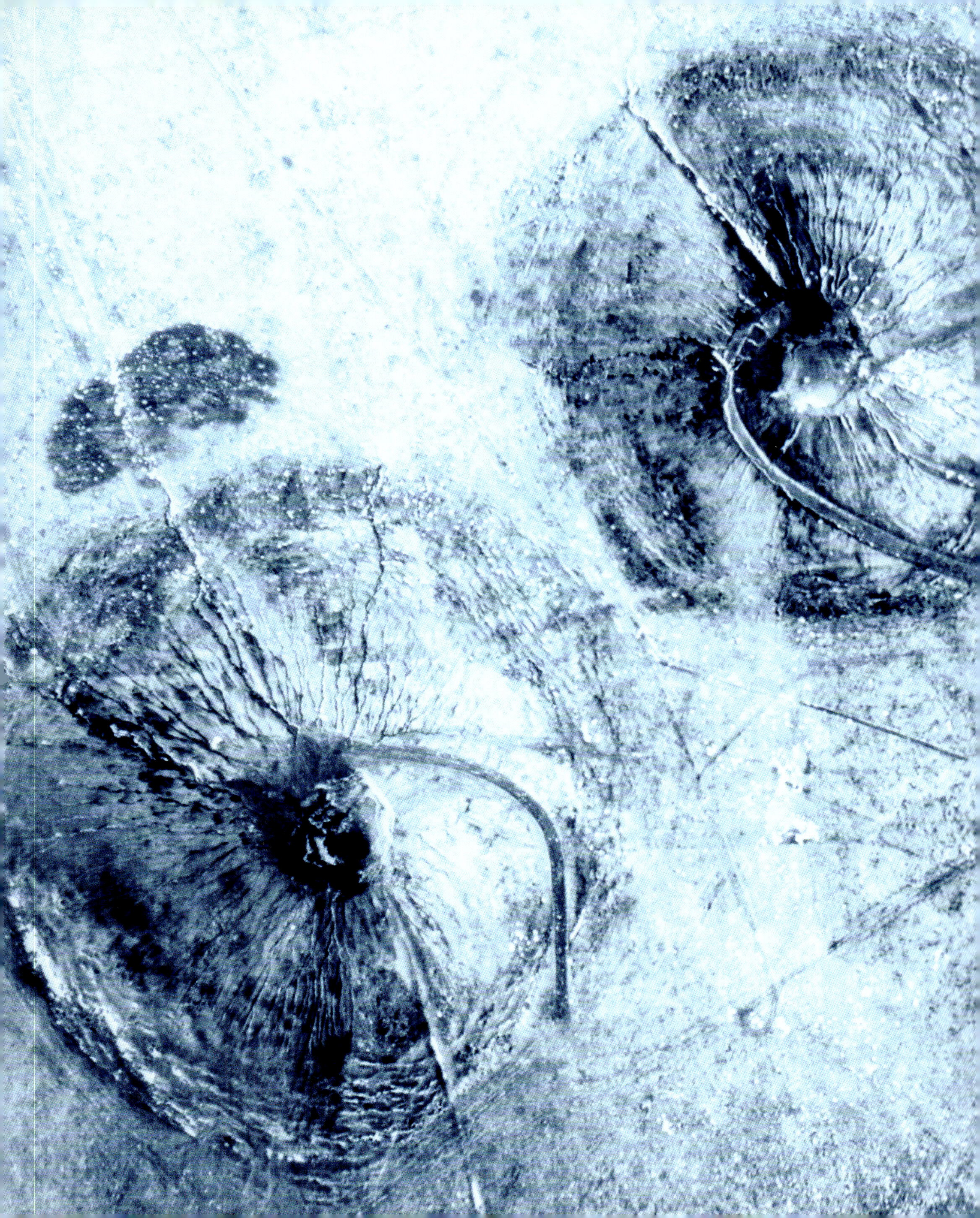

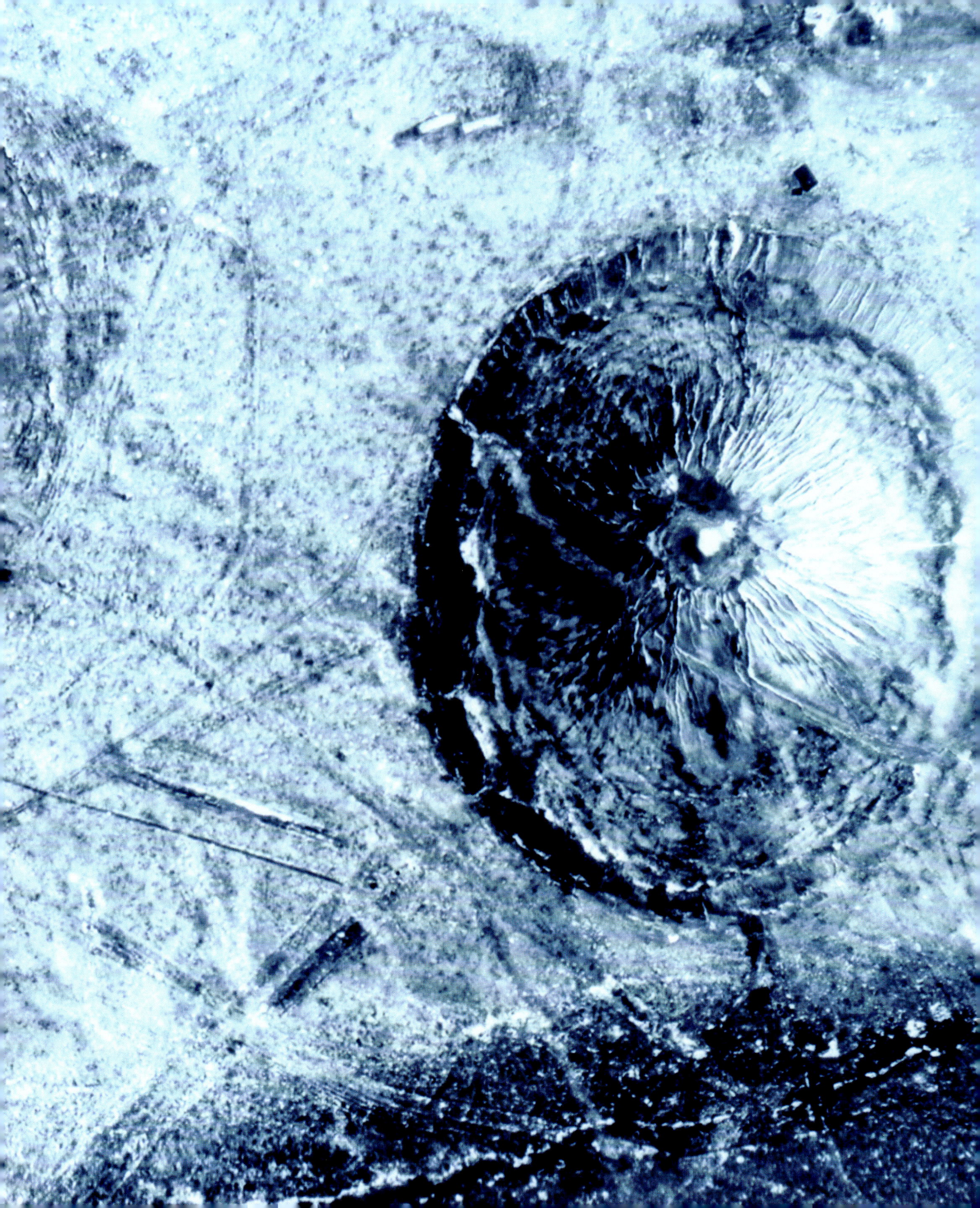

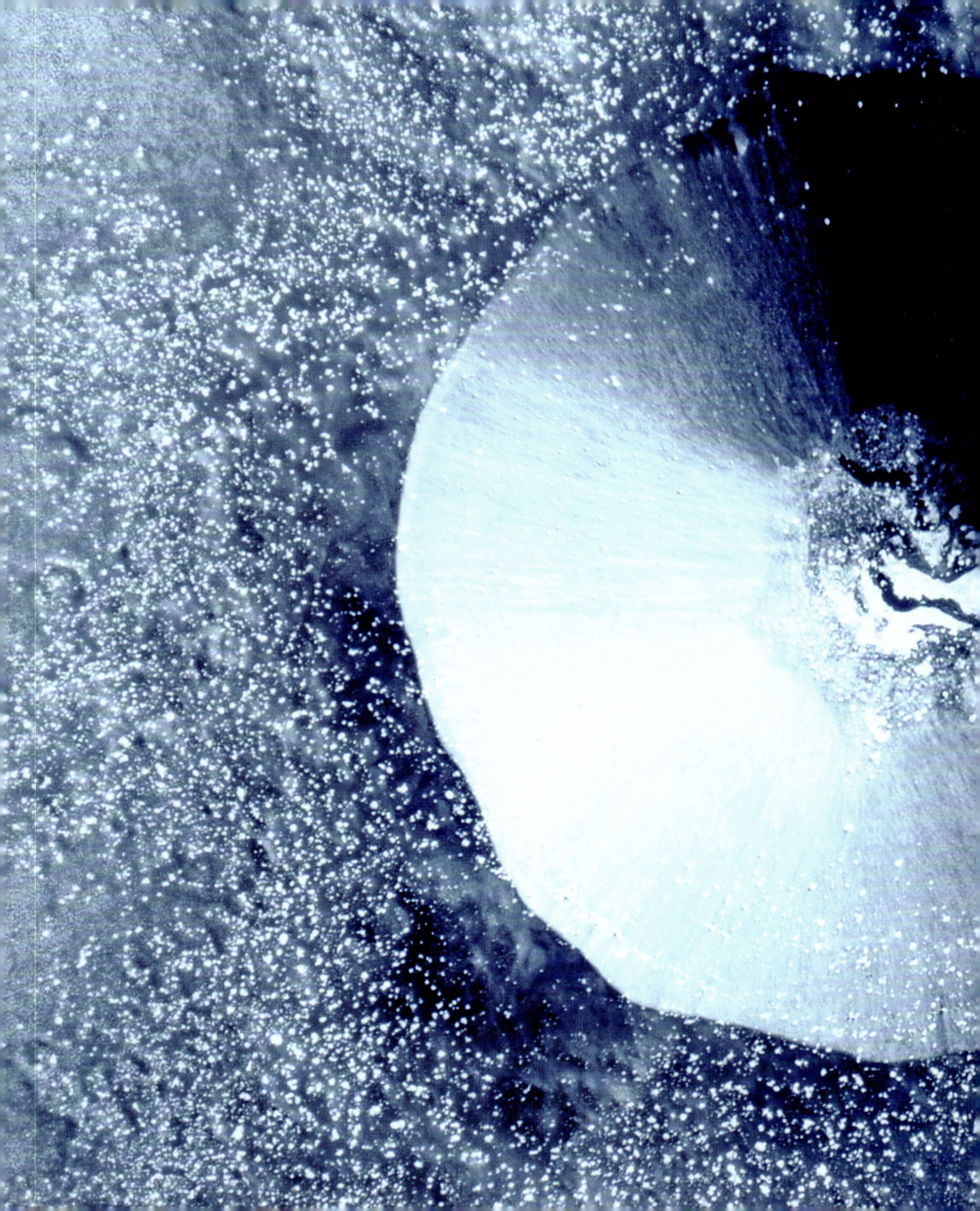

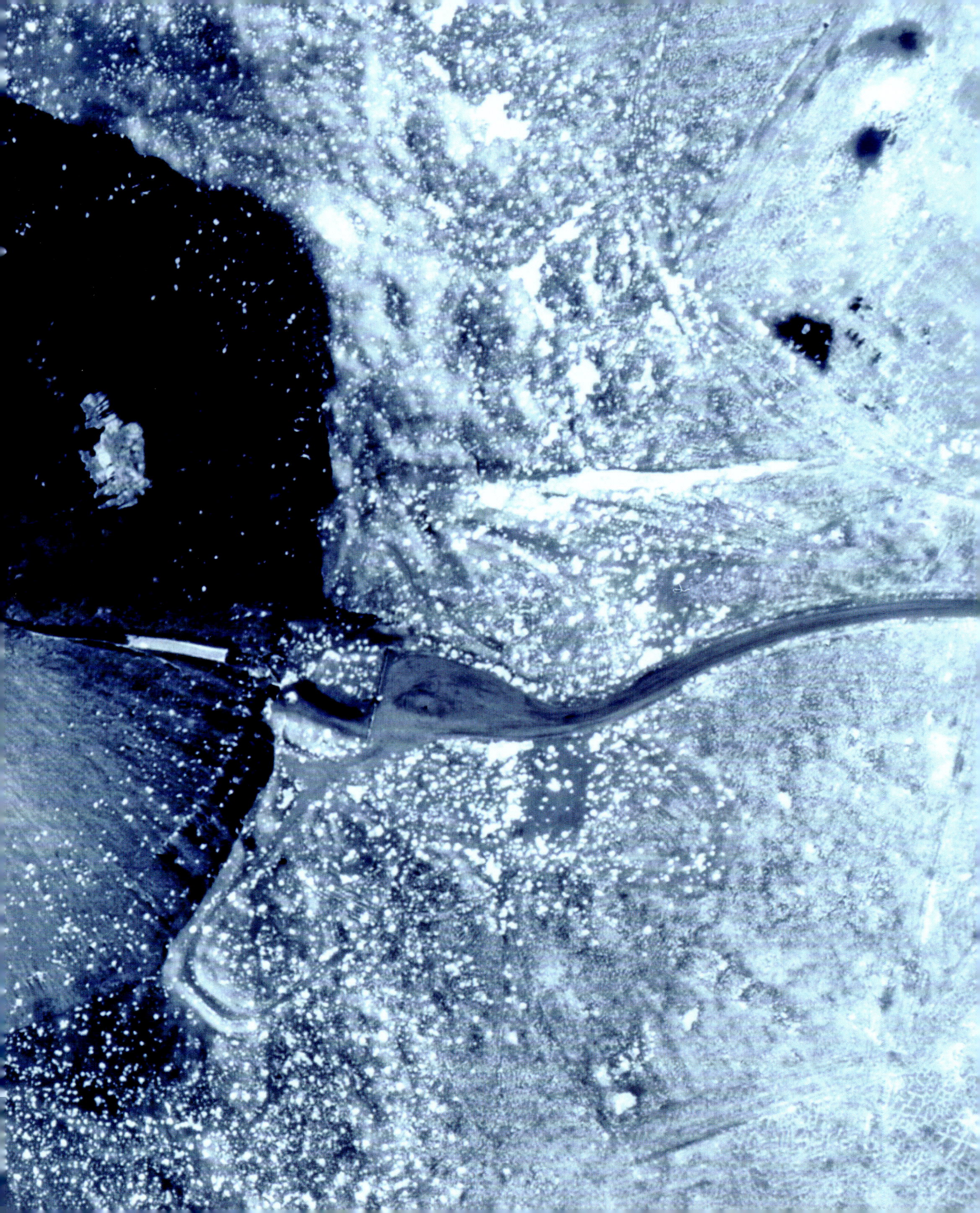

NAME AND DATE OF EVERY NUCLEAR TEST DETONATION IN THE US, 1945–1992*

* "United States Nuclear Tests: July 1945 through September 1992" (DOE/NV-209 REV15). Las Vegas, NV: Department of Energy, Nevada Operations Office. 2000-12-01. Retrieved July 2, 2020.

BOMB PULSE

cyanotype on animal bones, variable dimensions, 2020

BOMB PULSE

Carbon-14 (^{14}C) naturally exists in the air, plants, animals, and our bodies. Radiocarbon dating, a process of measuring how much ^{14}C is in organic material, allows researchers to gain an understanding of when those tissues were formed and how old they are. Radiocarbon dating is used in many fields, including archaeology and forensic science. Between 1955 and 1963, the use of atomic bombs doubled the amount of ^{14}C in our atmosphere; for example, a tree can reveal a spike in ^{14}C during the time of nuclear testing. Since the ban on atmospheric testing in 1963, ^{14}C has been decreasing.[1]

Tooth enamel, whether in humans or animals, doesn't regenerate once it is formed. Carbon-14 levels in enamel represent the levels in the atmosphere at the time of formation. Anyone born prior to 1955, when ^{14}C doubled, has very low levels of ^{14}C in their teeth. For those born in or after 1955, their teeth are marked from the bomb pulse. Isotopic analysis of carbon in enamel from a single tooth can provide an estimate of the year of birth and the general geographic origin of the individual.[2]

By accident, nuclear experiments provided a way for scientists to reveal the age of all living things on Earth. Radiocarbon chronicles the history of our bodies, marking our existence in both time and space.

All of us.
All living beings.
Nuclear testing ruptured the myth of isolation.

---

1 Carl Zimmer, "Nuclear Tests Marked Life on Earth with a Radioactive Spike," *The Atlantic*, March 20, 2020, https://www.theatlantic.com/science/archive/2020/03/how-nuclear-testing-transformed-science/607174/.

2 John D. Macdougall, *Nature's Clocks: How Scientists Measure the Age of Almost Everything* (Berkeley, California: University of California Press, 2009), pp. 228–229.

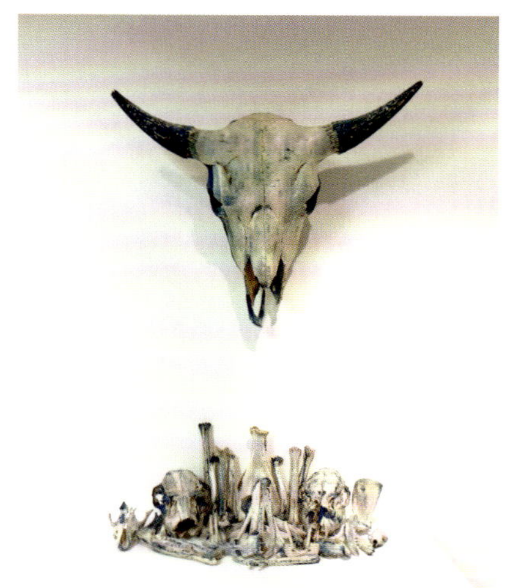

For *Bomb Pulse*, I took animal bones from my family's land in the southwestern United States and used the cyanotype process to imprint them with DNA sequencing data and the name and date of every nuclear bomb (1,040) detonated in the United States. Bones are of particular interest to me because two of my great uncles were first-generation downwinders who died of Myeloid leukemia at the ages of twenty-four and forty-two, respectively. Myeloid leukemia causes the body to make unhealthy blood-forming cells that grow in the bone marrow and is one of the illnesses with a known connection to atomic testing.[3] Subsequently, some members in the following generations of my family developed benign bone tumors.

Bomb Pulse installation

Platelist:

---

3   "The Radiation Exposure Compensation Act (RECA): Compensation Related to Exposure to Radiation from Atomic Weapons Testing and Uranium Mining," Congressional Research Service, January 31, 2020, accessed Sept. 18, 2020 https://crsreports.congress.gov/product/pdf/R/R43956.

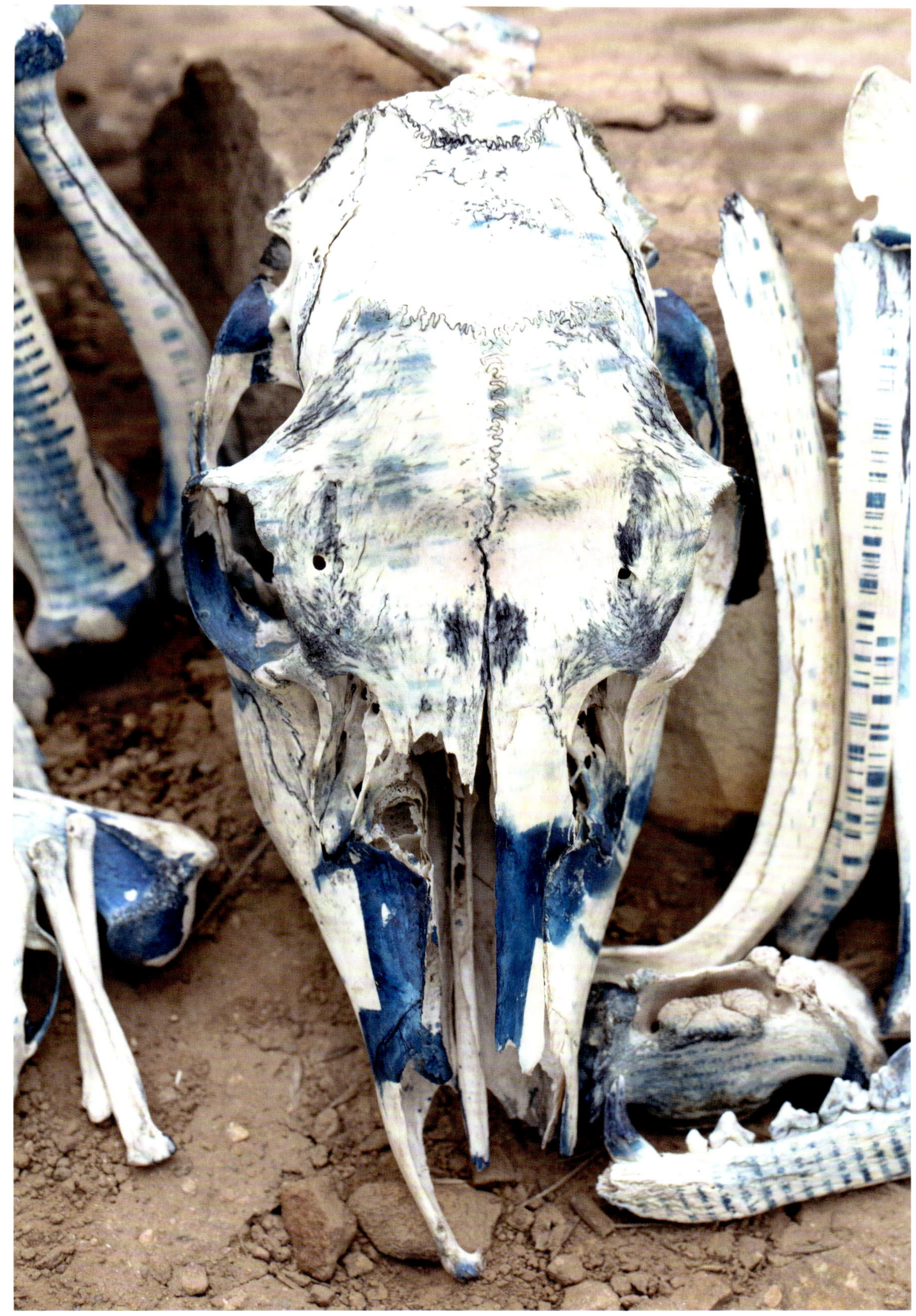

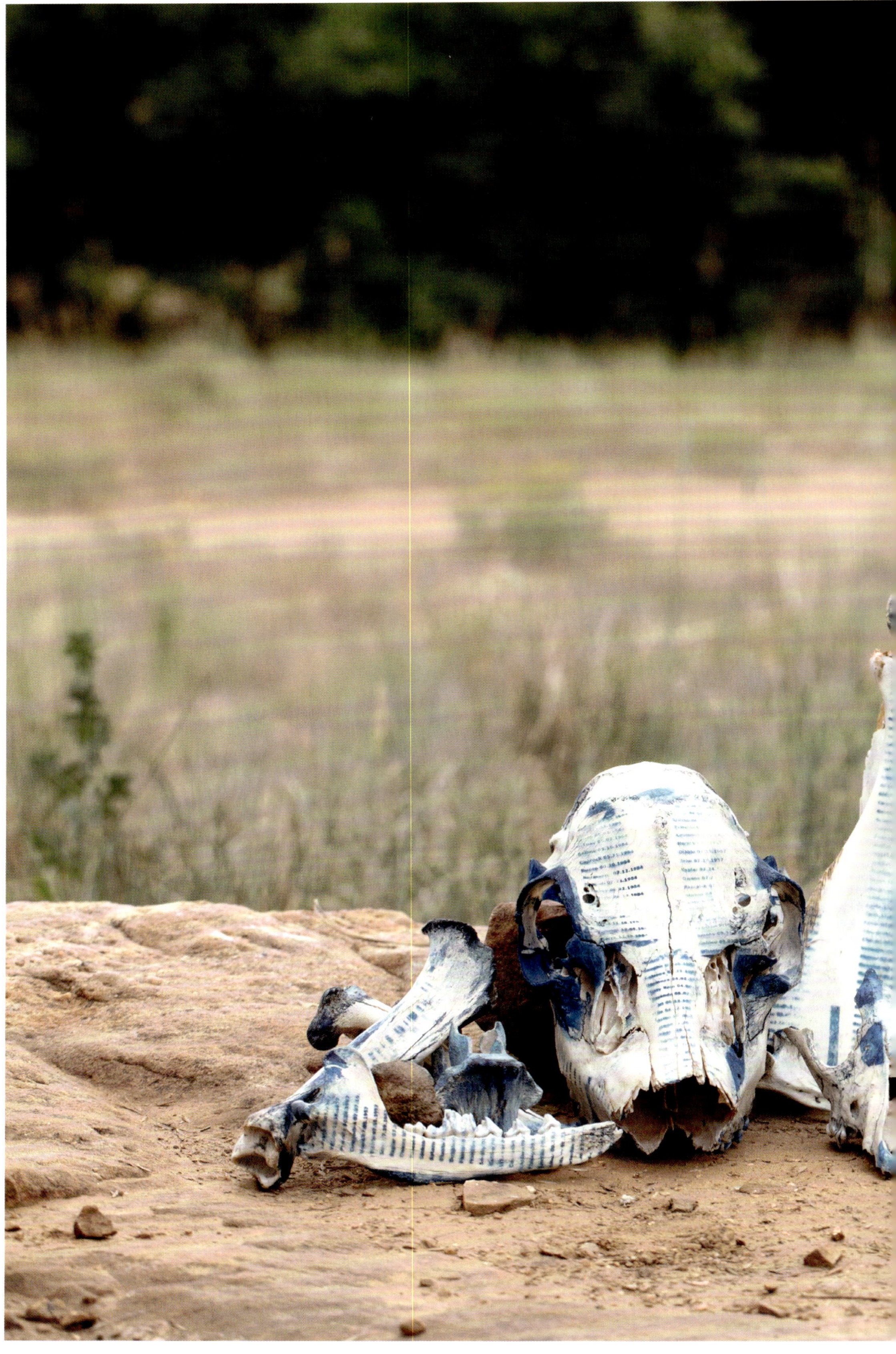

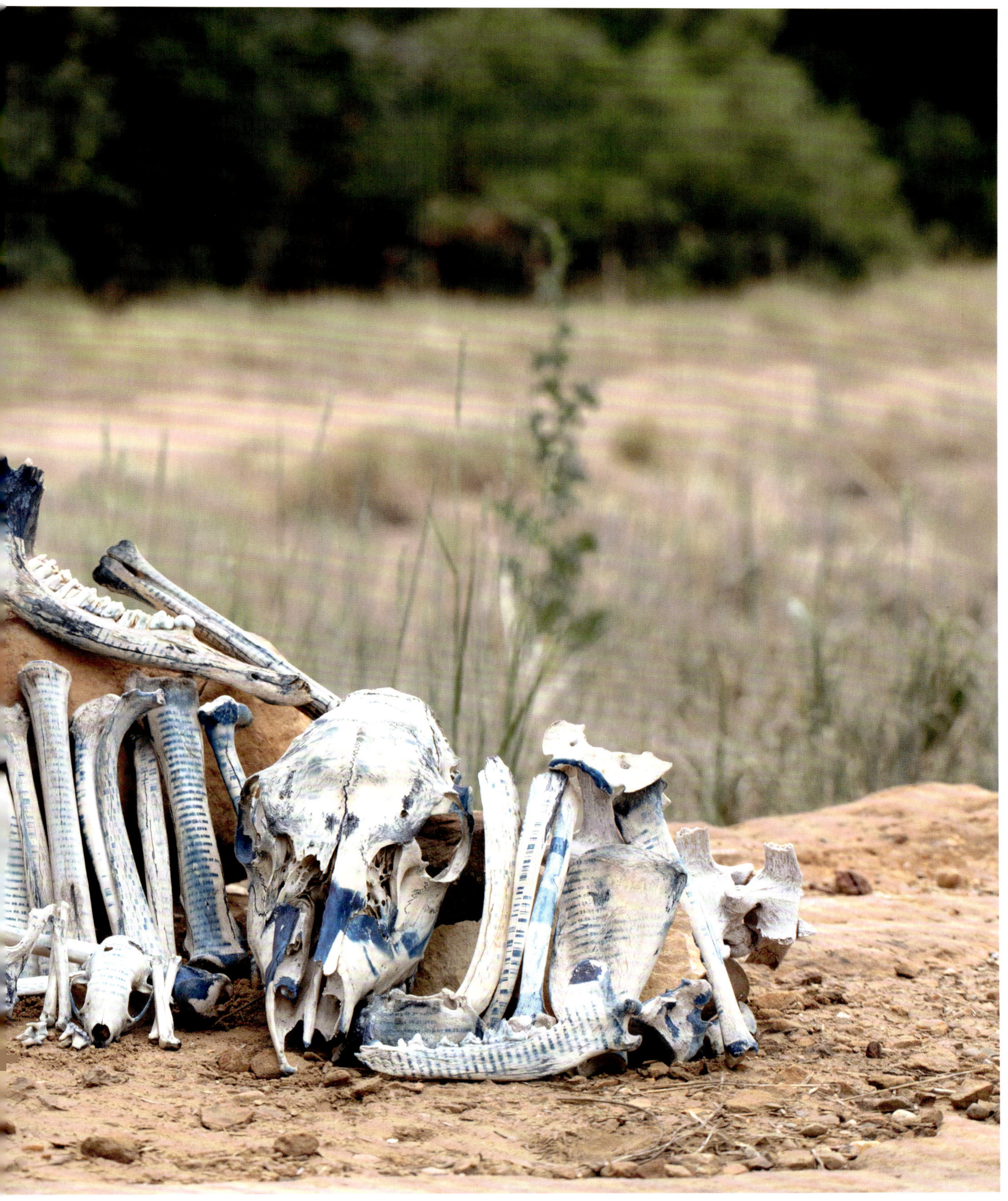

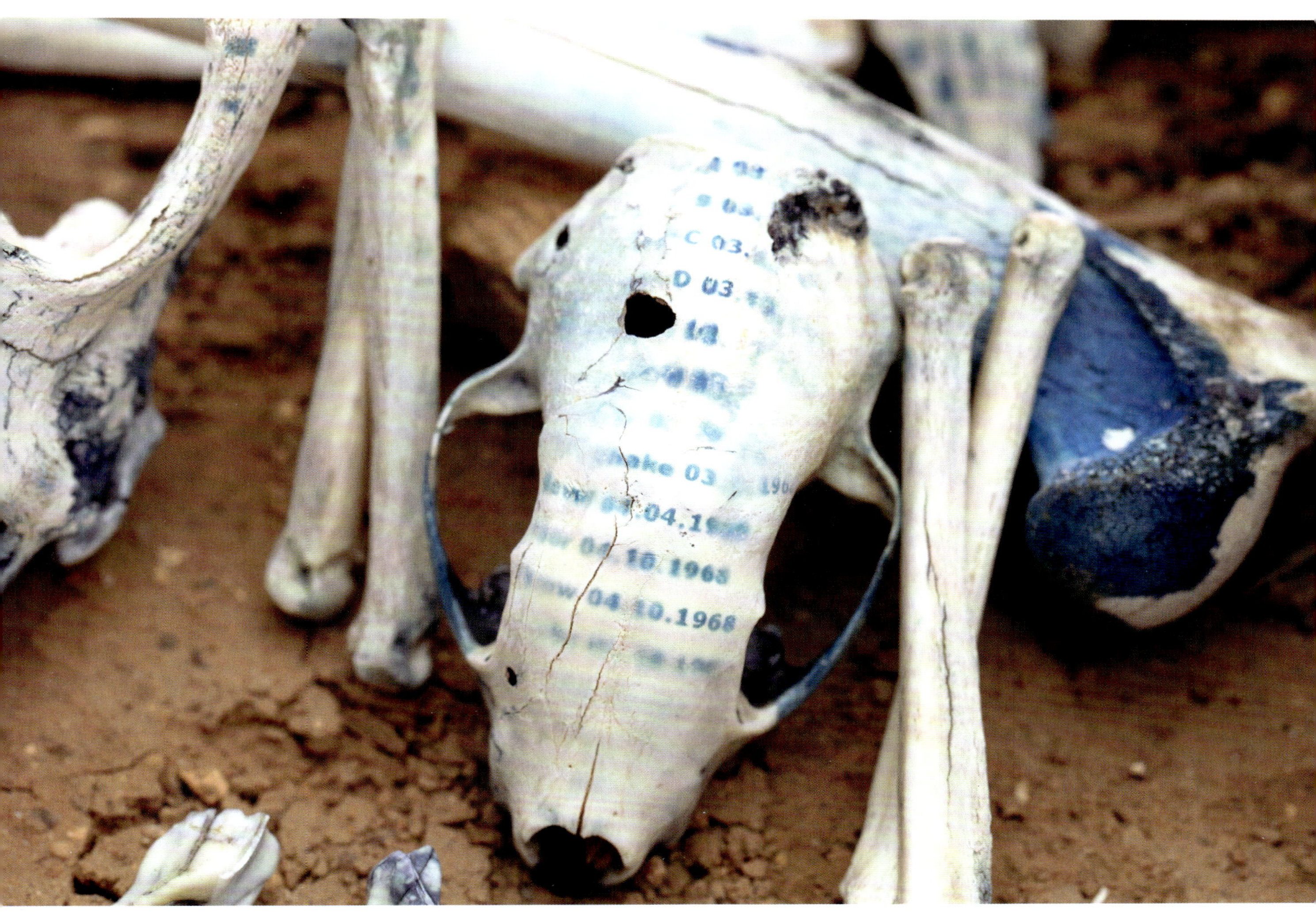

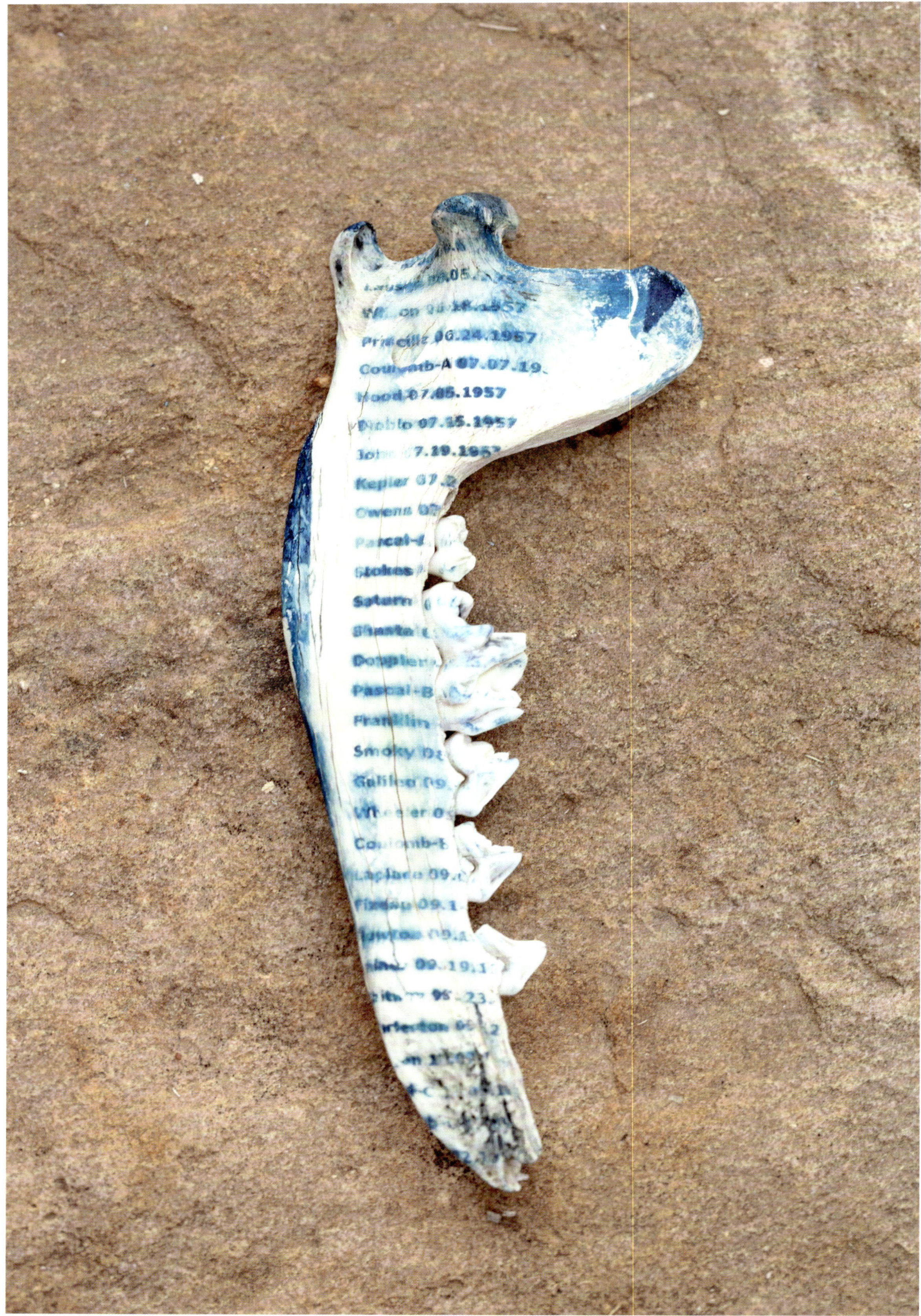

Lassen 06.05.1957
Wilson 06.18.1957
Priscilla 06.24.1957
Coulomb-A 07.07.19.
Hood 07.05.1957
Diablo 07.15.1957
John 07.19.1957
Kepler 07.2.
Owens 07.
Pascal-H.
Stokes
Saturn
Shasta
Doppler
Pascal-B
Franklin
Smoky 08.
Galileo 09.
Wheeler 09.
Coulomb-B
Laplace 09.
Fizeau 09.1.
Newton 09.
.na 09..19.1.
.ith.. 09..23.
.rleston 09.12.

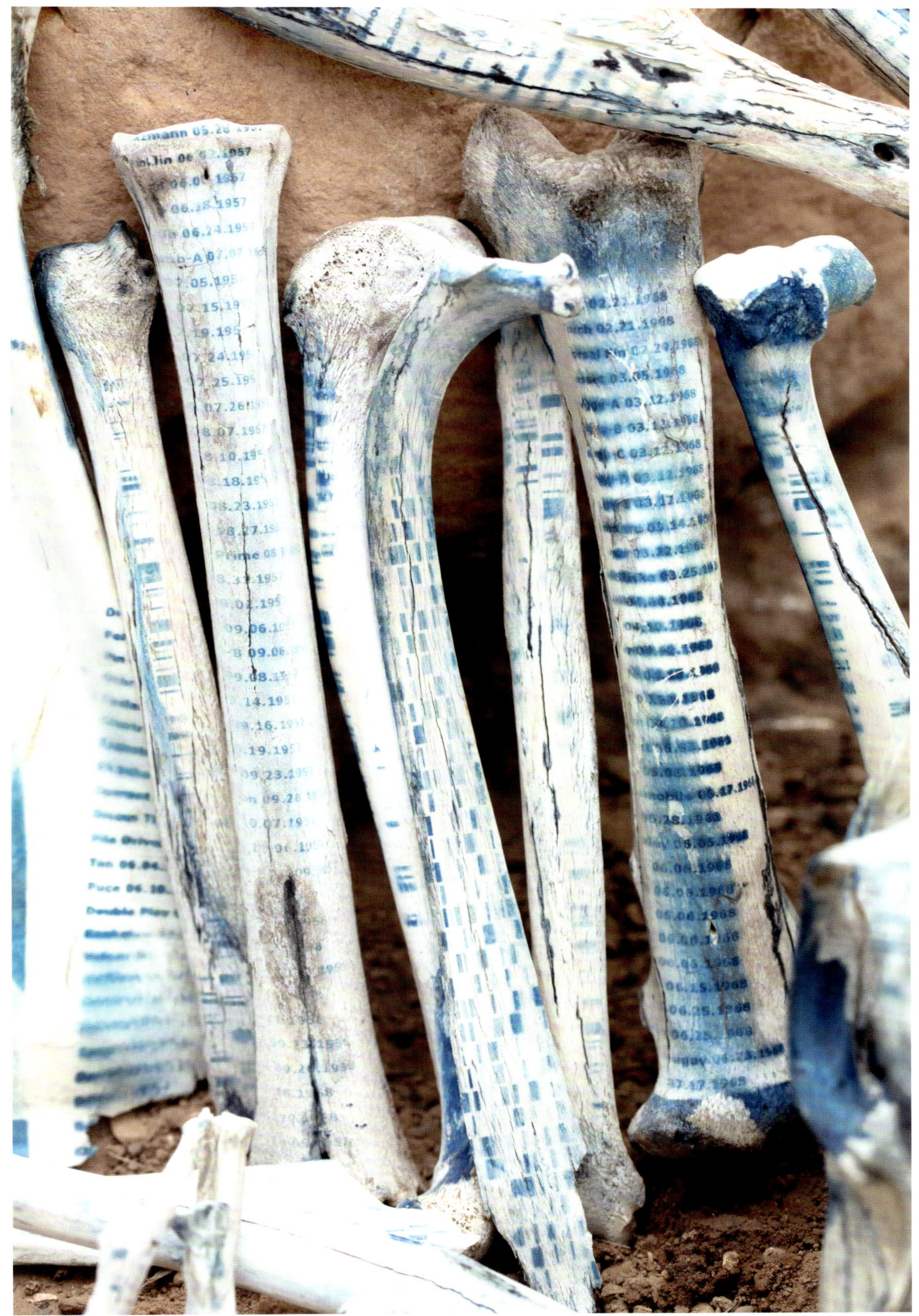

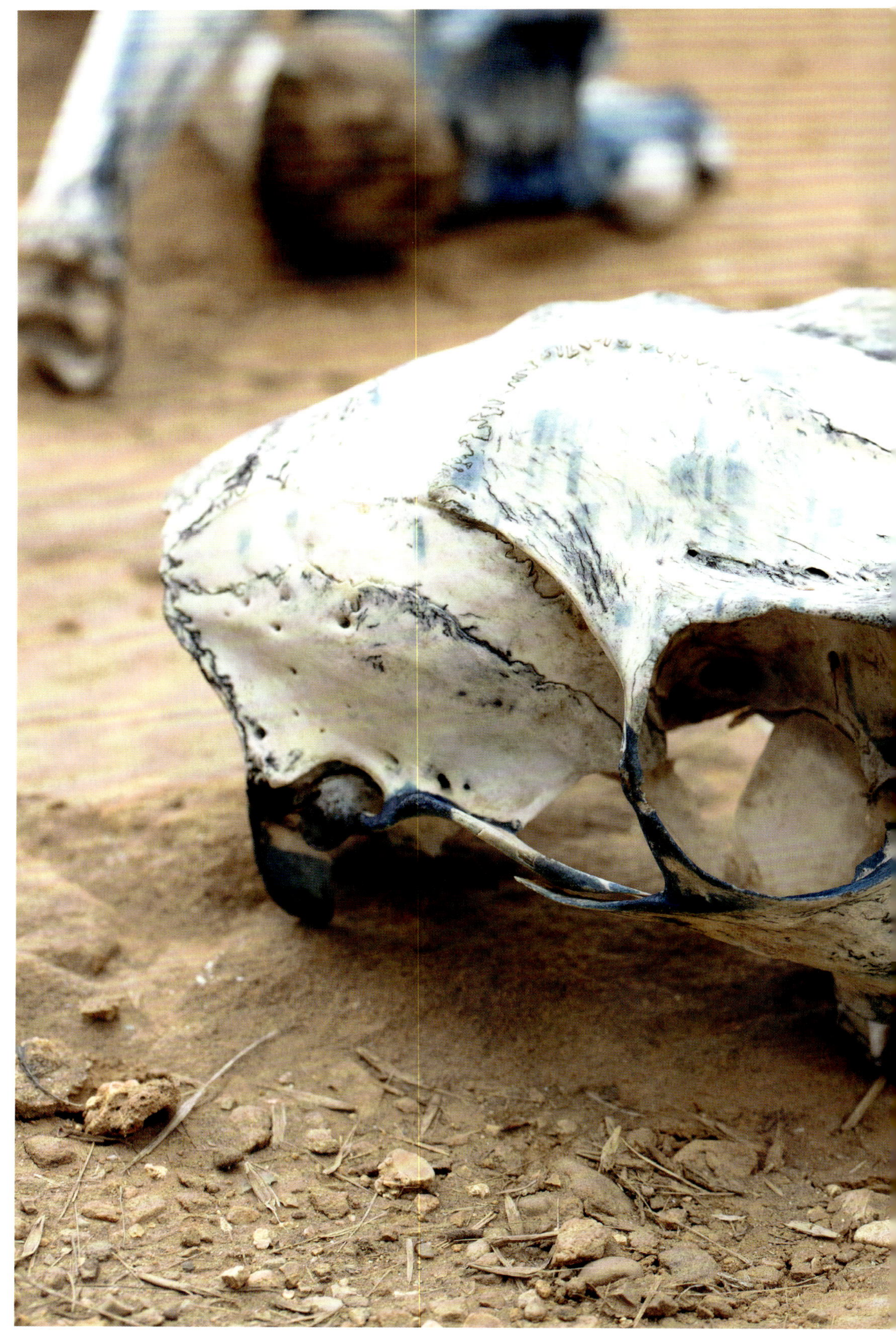

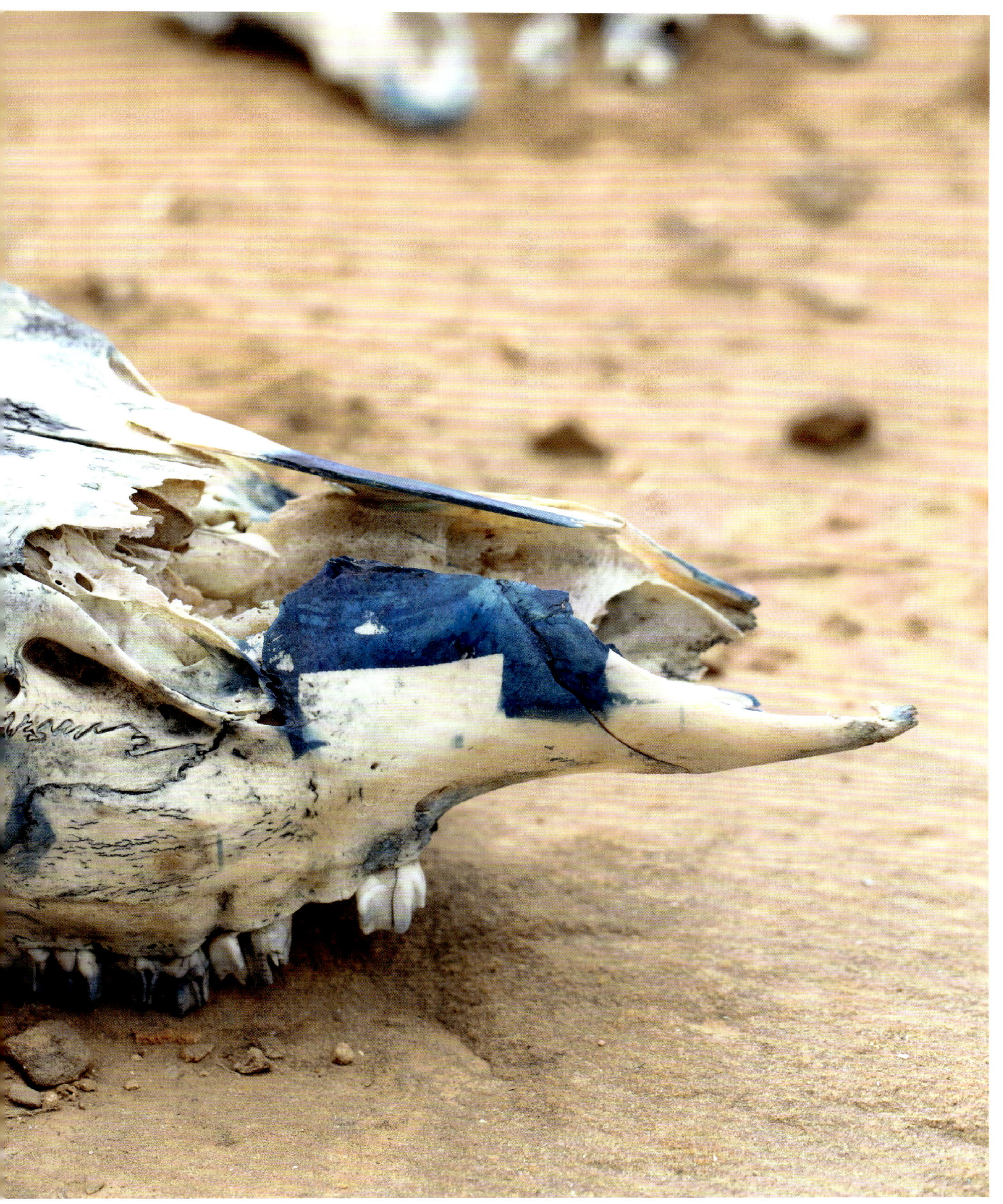

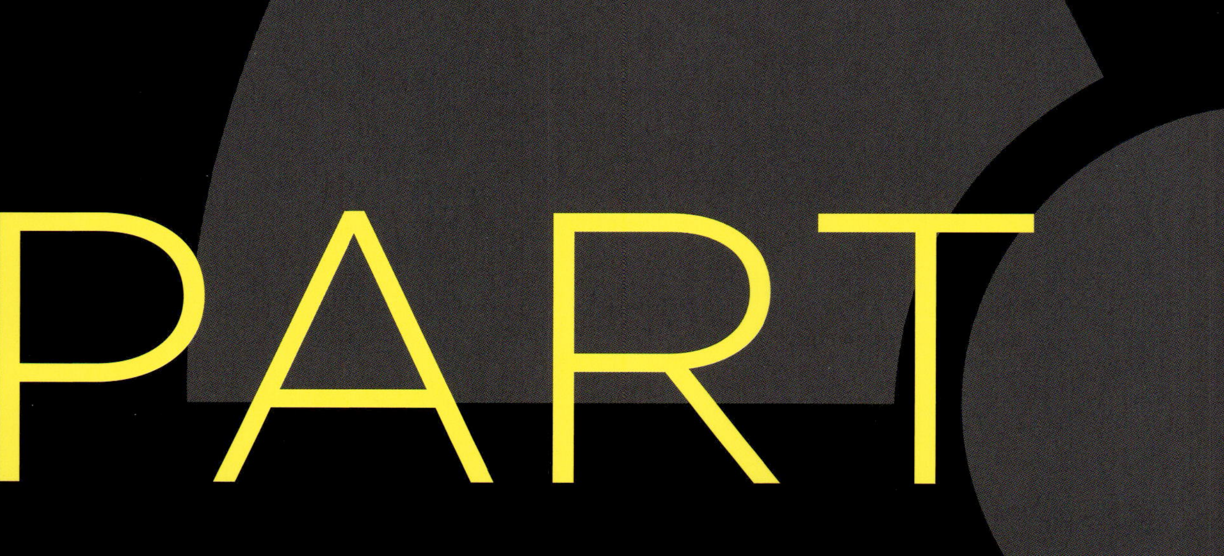
PART

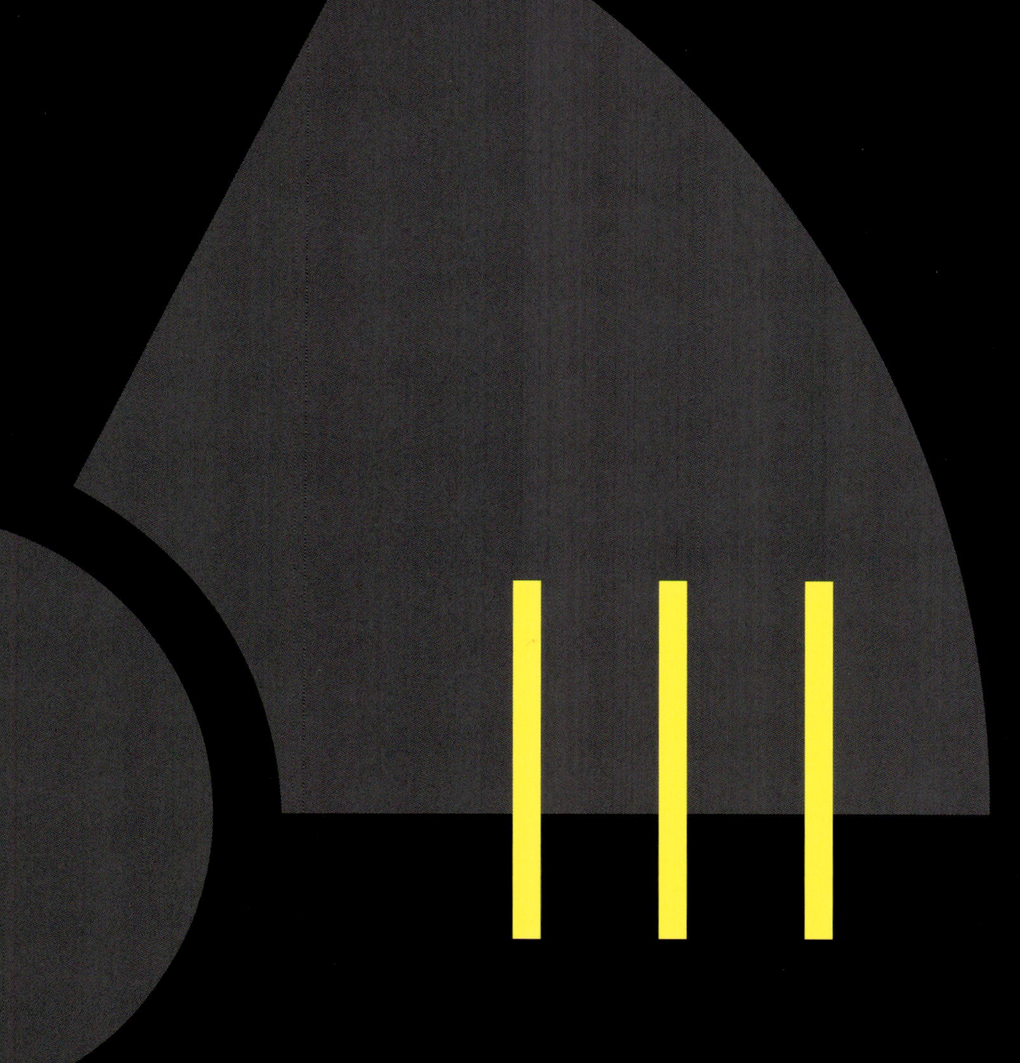

URAVAN

*laser-engraved archival pigment prints over clear
acrylic (backlit), 2020*

URAVAN

In western Montrose county, the town of Uravan, Colorado, can still be located on a map, however it isn't easy to find because it is buried under layers of clay, soil, and rock. Standard Chemical Company established the town of approximately 1,000 residents in 1912, naming it after uranium and vanadium, two minerals mined in the area. Activities at the local processing mill contaminated the soil and groundwater with radioactive chemicals so much so that by 1986 the Environmental Protection Agency (EPA) closed the town and relocated residents. Uravan was shredded, burned, and buried by the EPA, creating a 680-acre Superfund site.

Map of Uravan

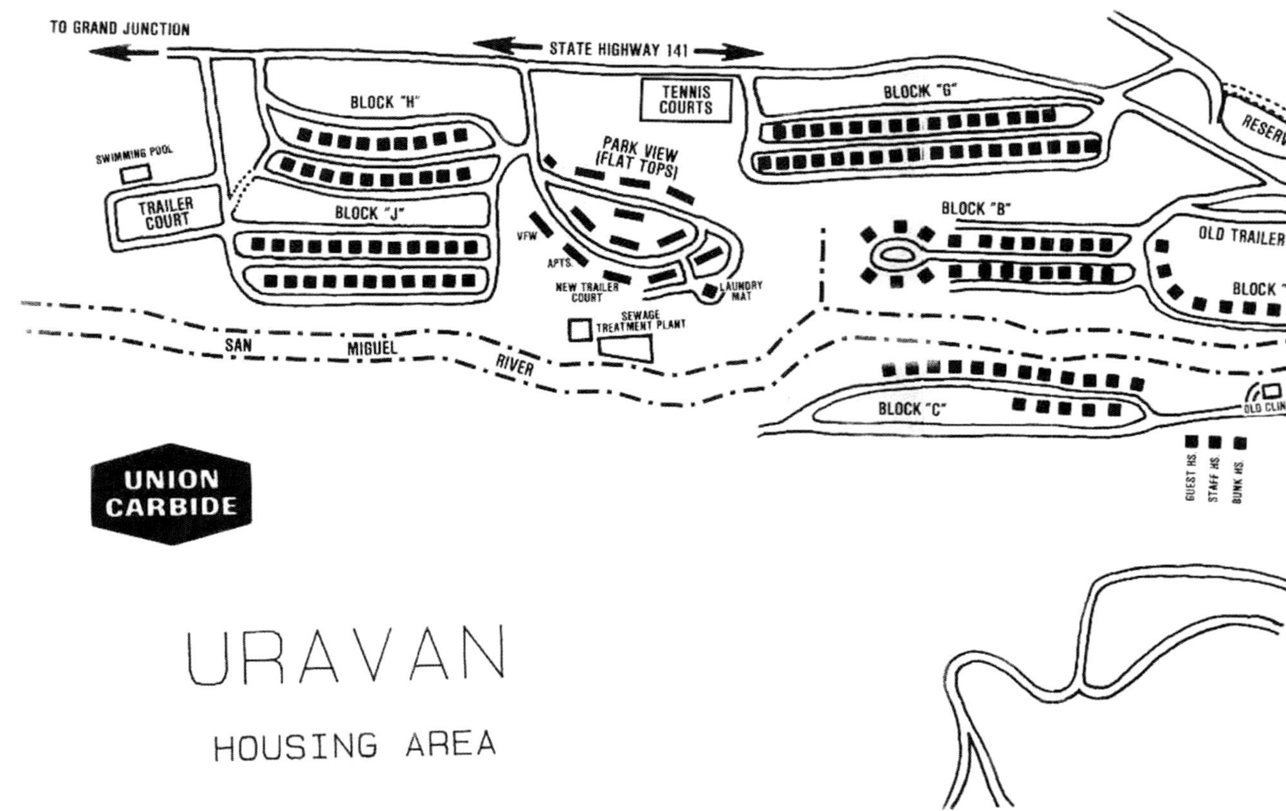

For *Uravan*, I created three-dimensional, laser-engraved pigment prints by photographing the exact locations as those in historical images of buildings that existed before the town was destroyed. Formed by the laser burning into layers of paper at various depths, the historic structures appear against bleak and empty contemporary landscapes.

Platelist:

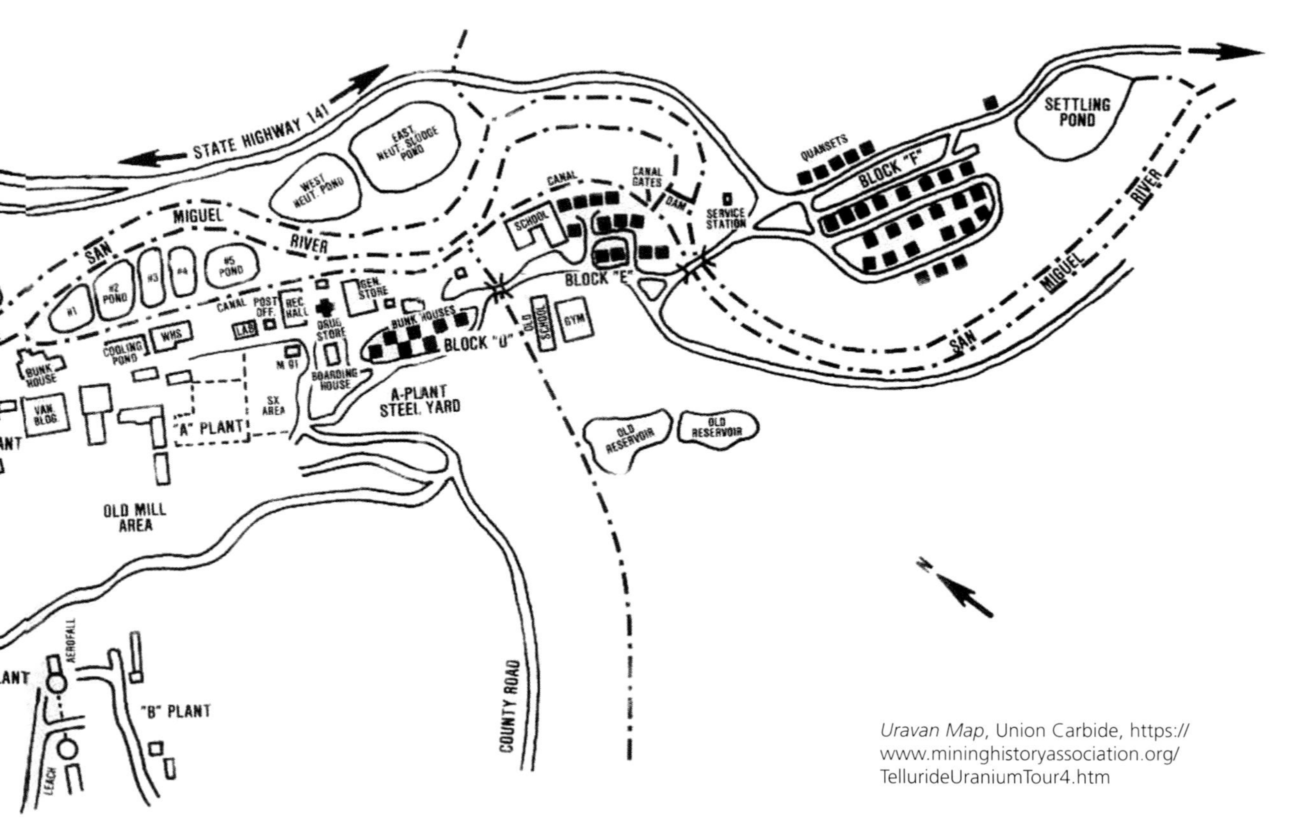

Uravan Map, Union Carbide, https://www.mininghistoryassociation.org/TellurideUraniumTour4.htm

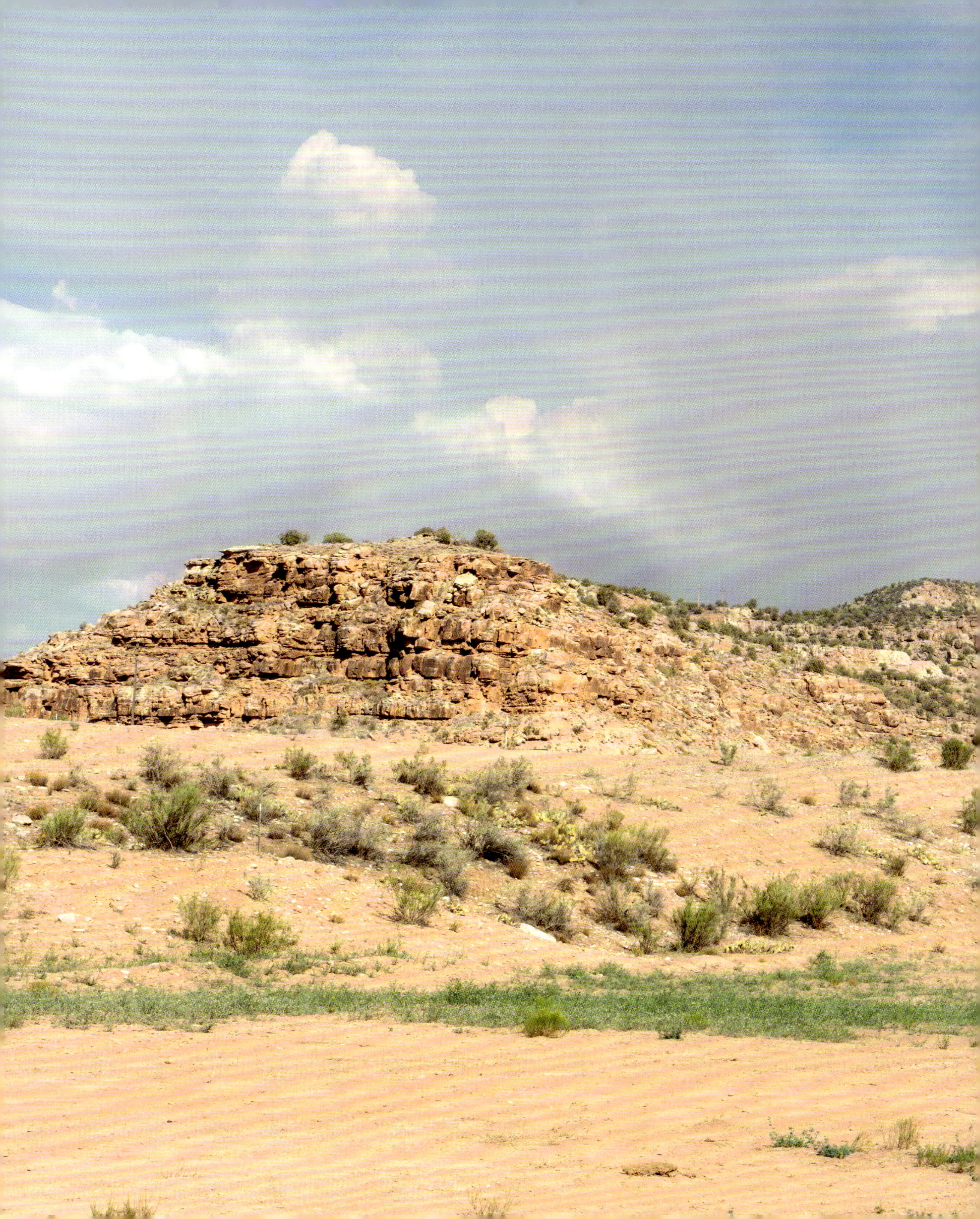

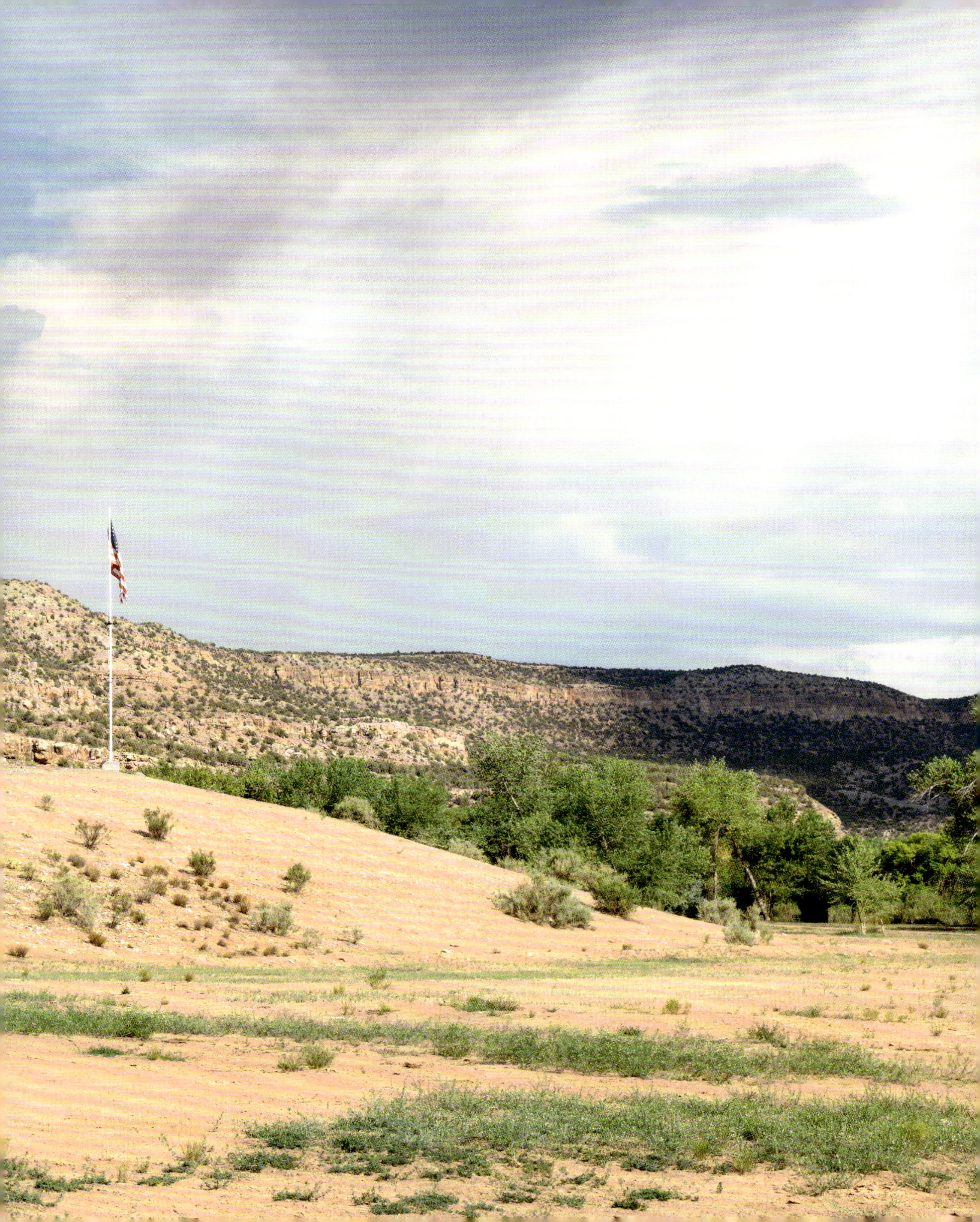

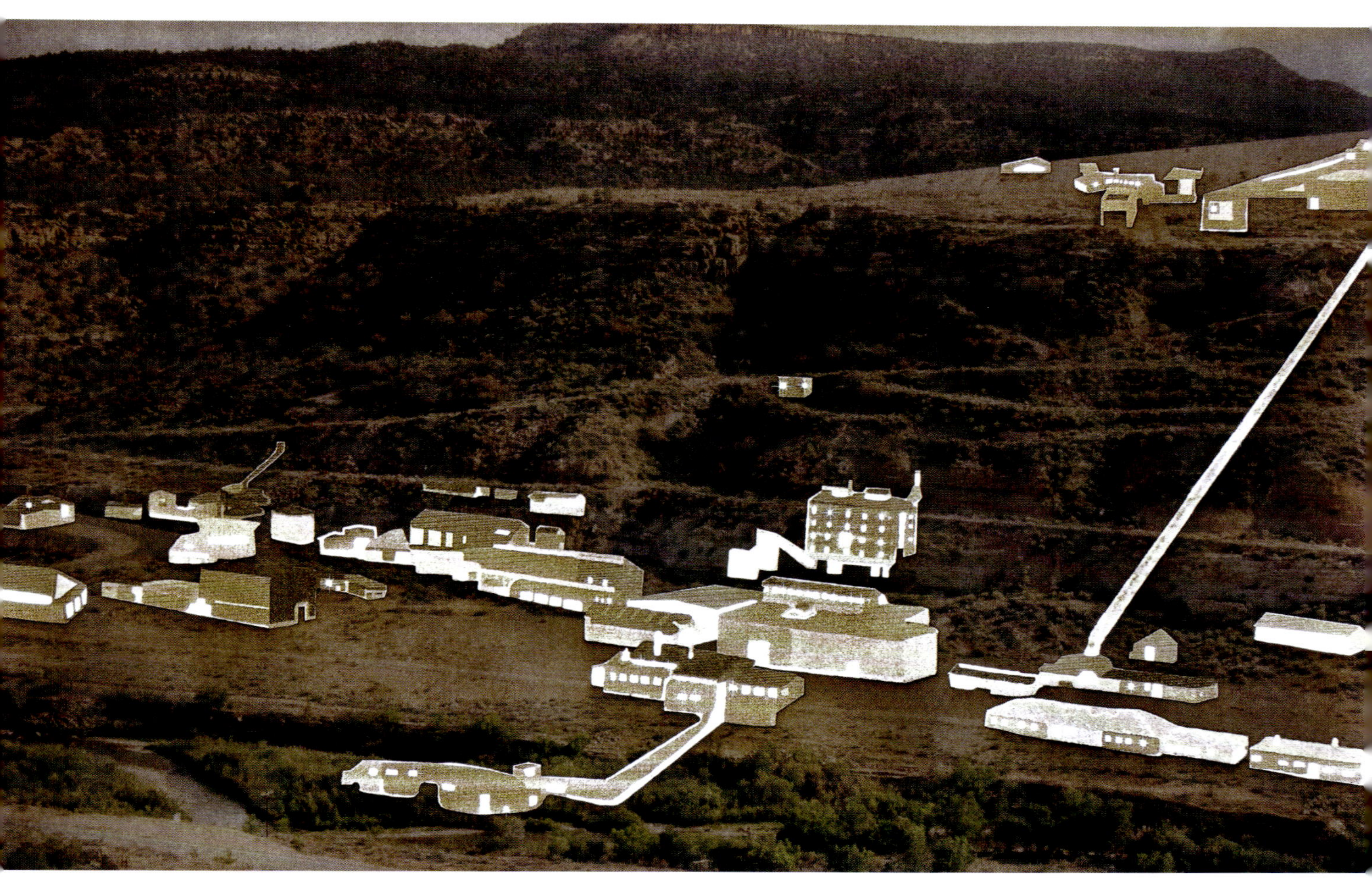

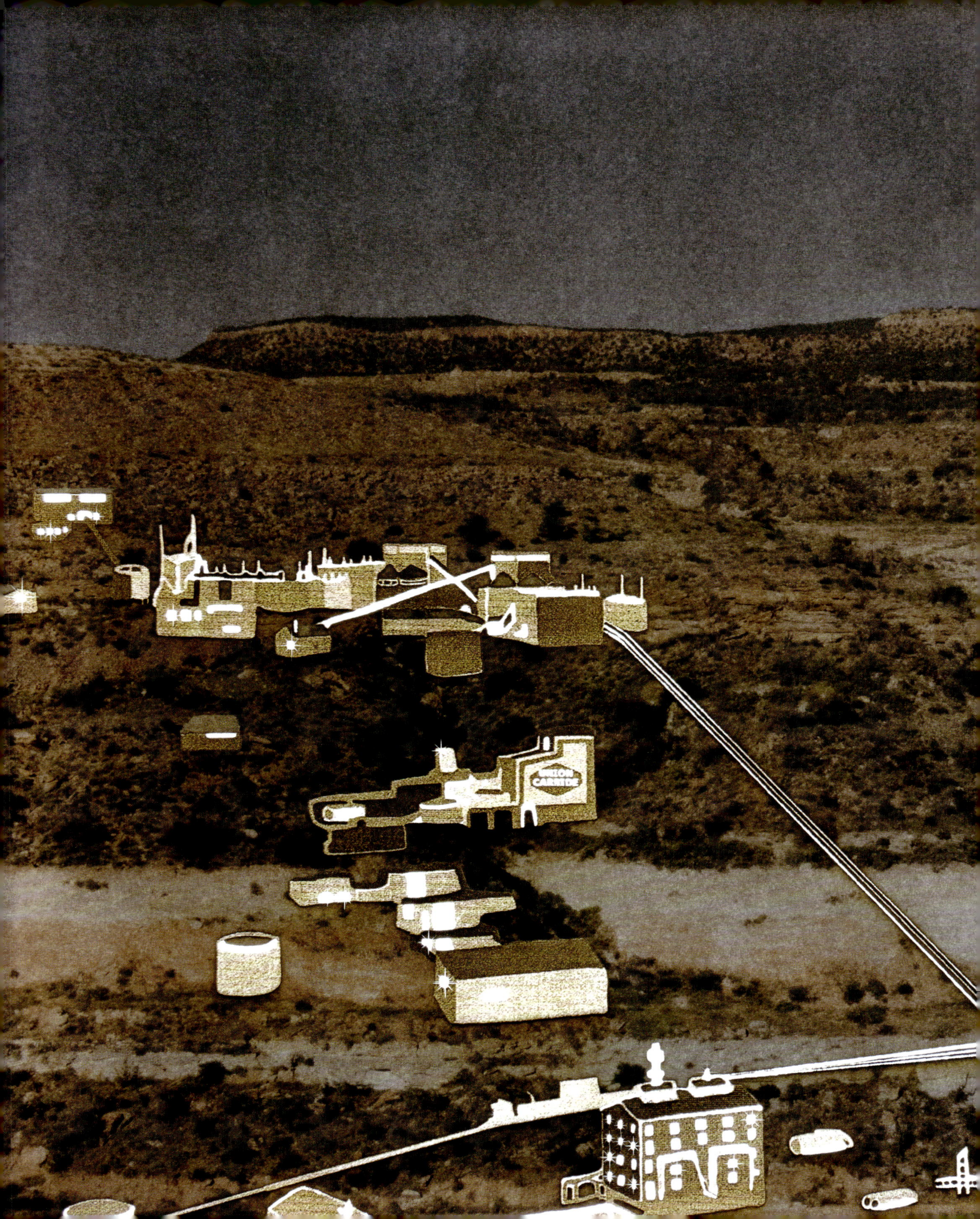

UNION CARBIDE

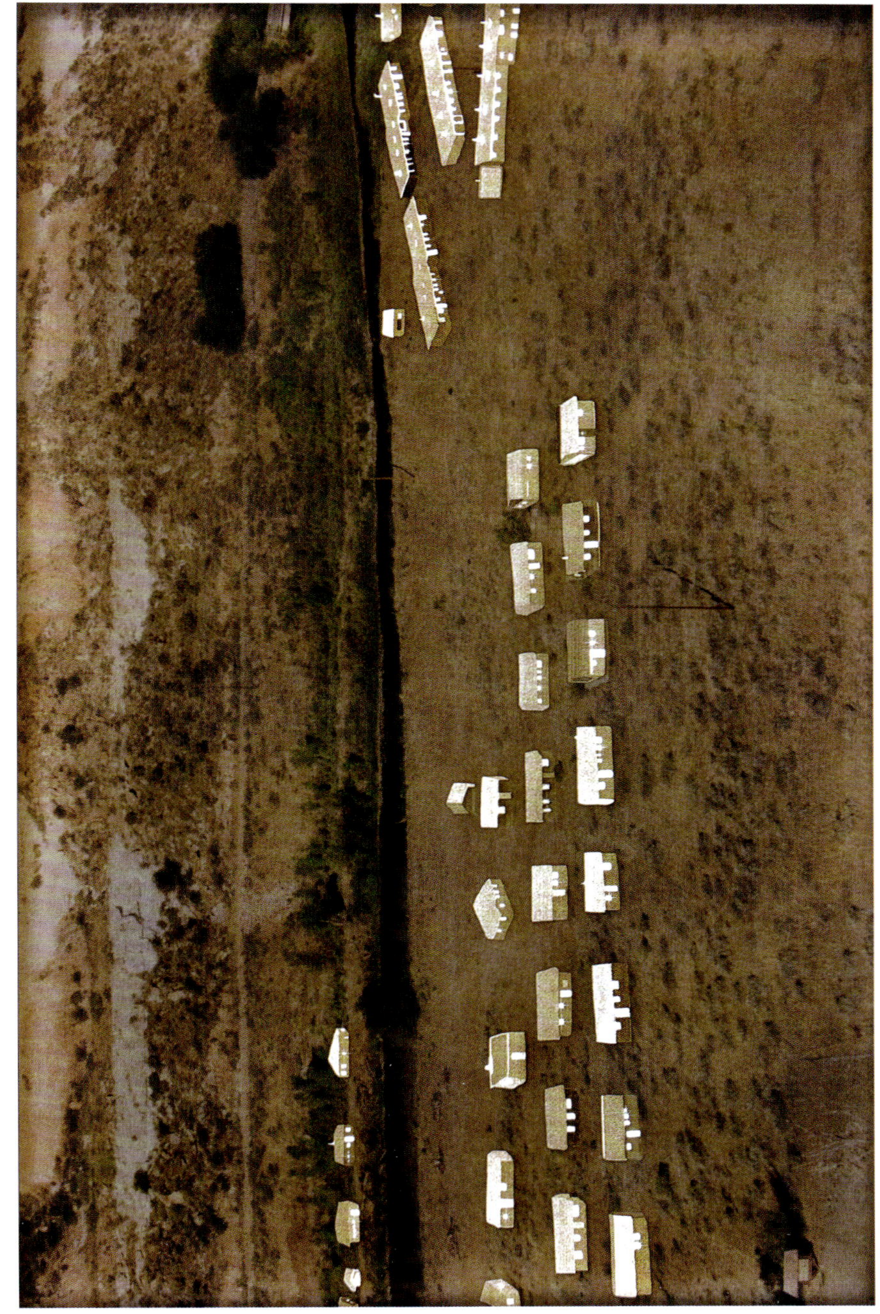

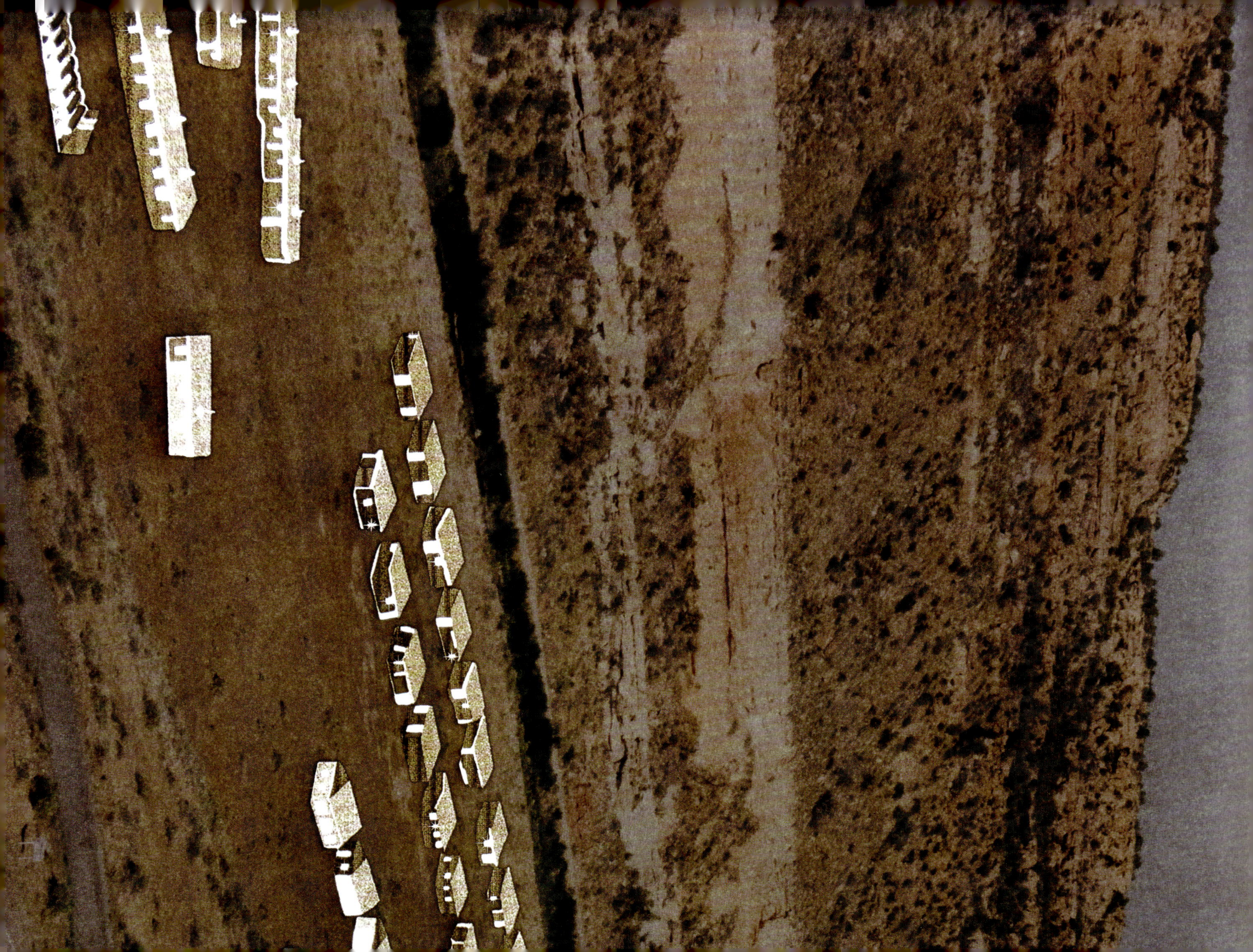

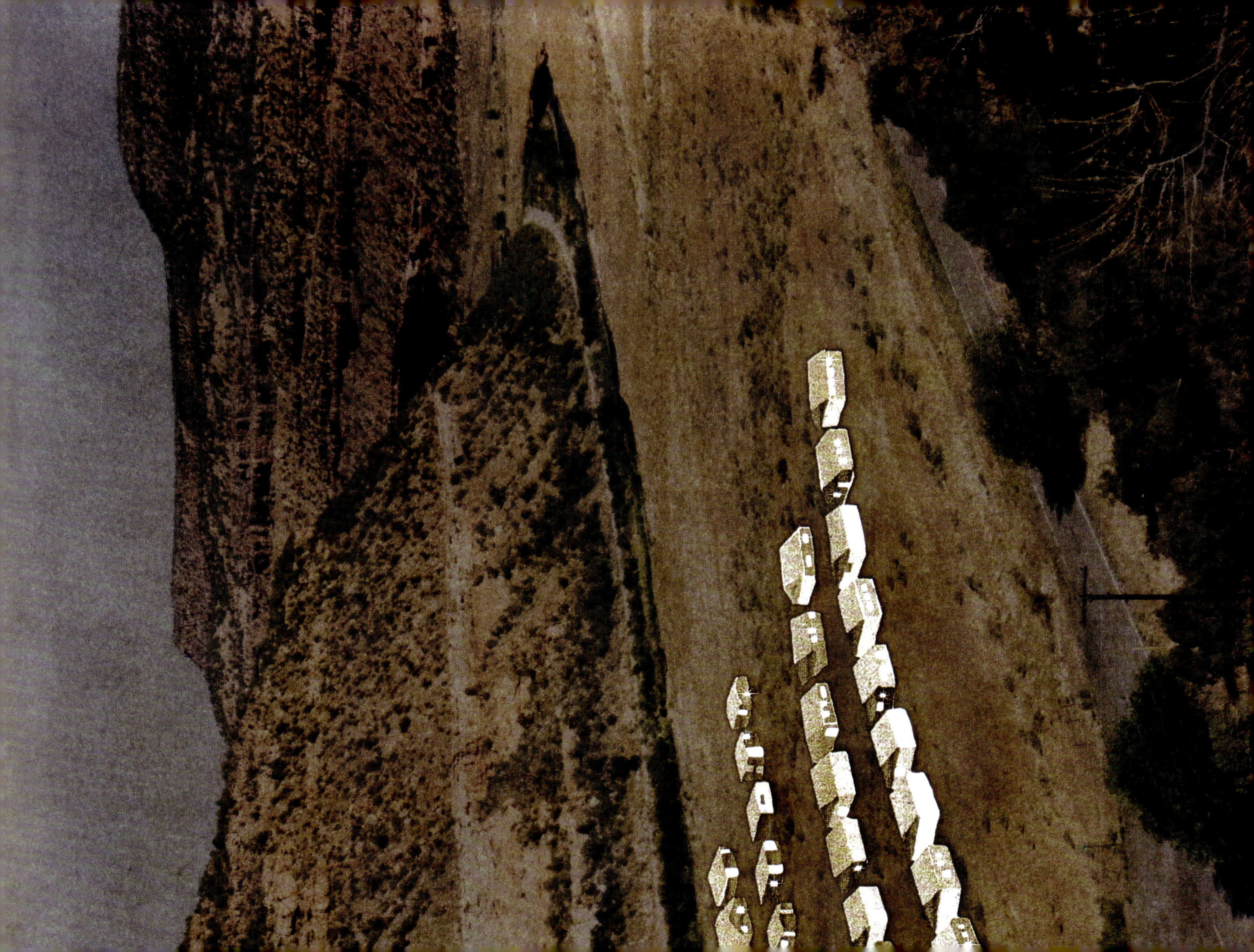

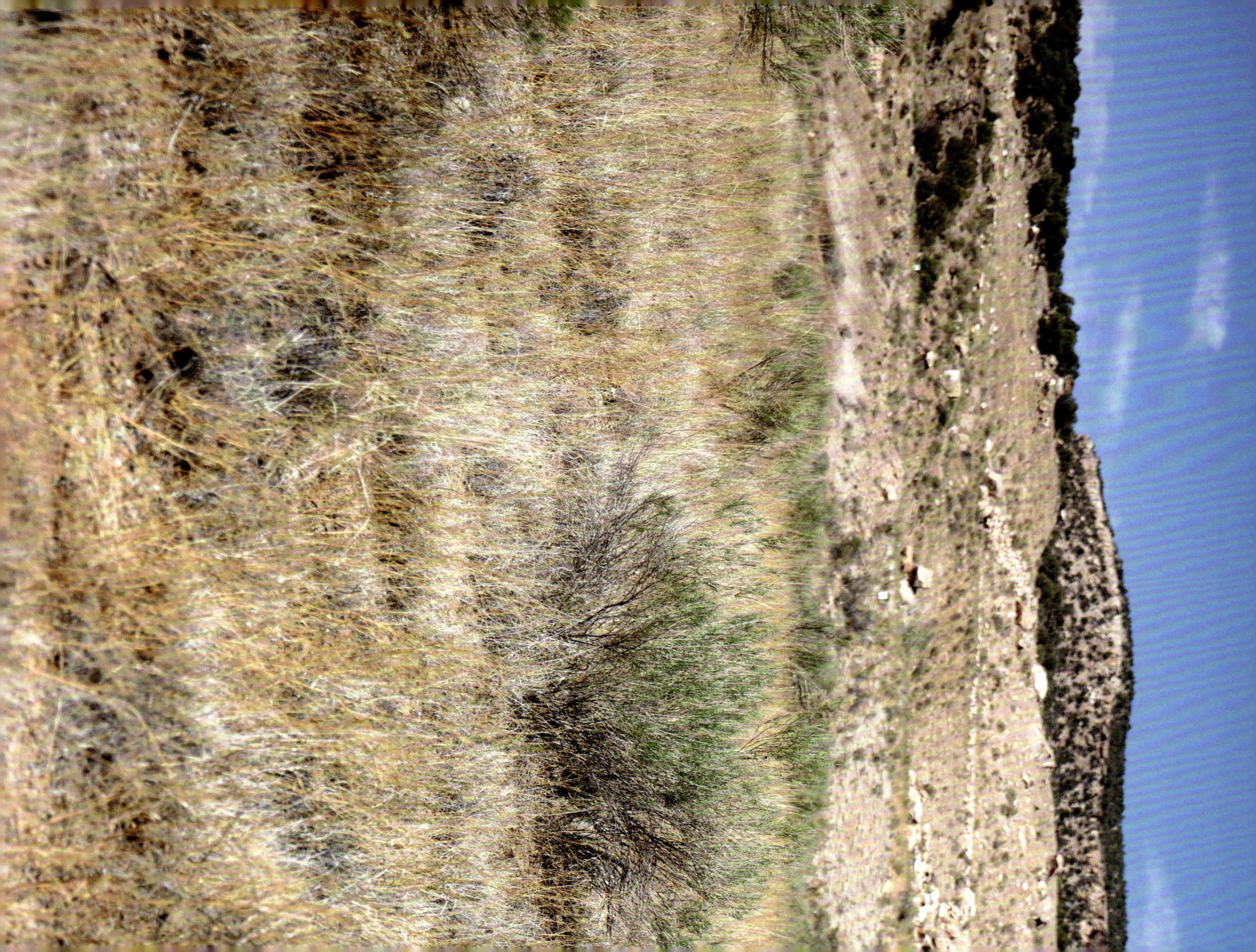

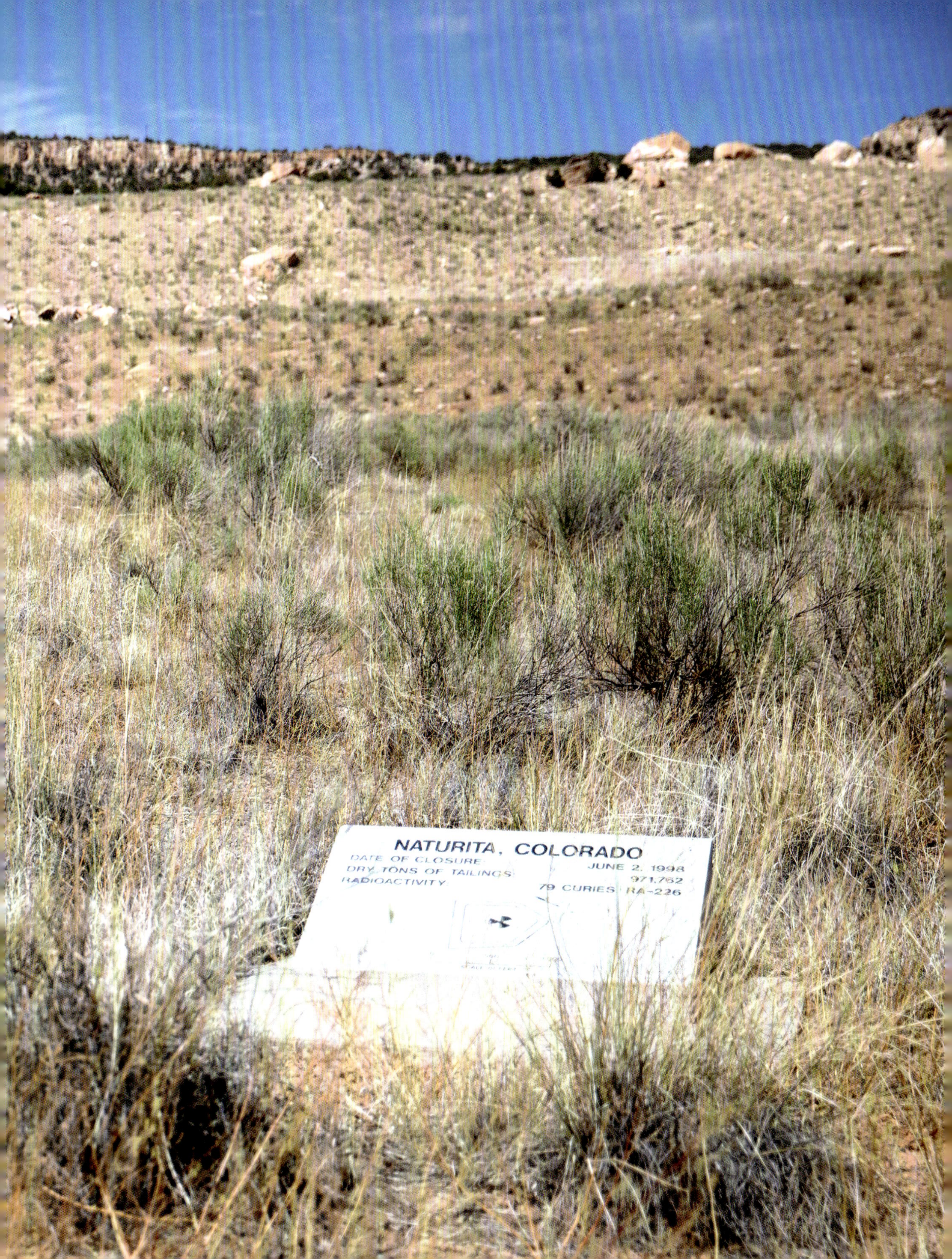

NATURITA, COLORADO
DATE OF CLOSURE   JUNE 2, 1998
DRY TONS OF TAILINGS   971,762
RADIOACTIVITY   79 CURIES RA-226

PART

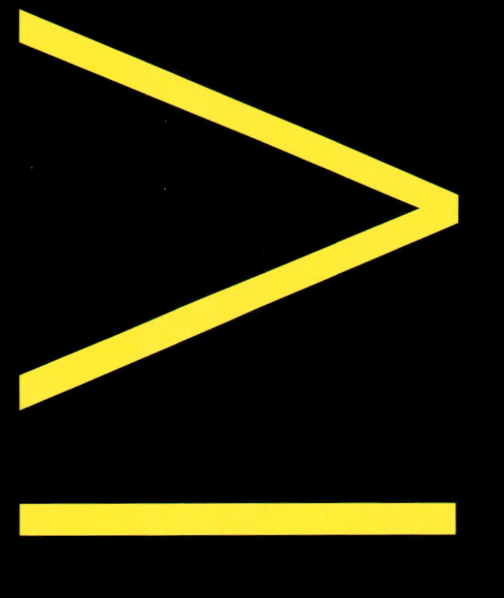

MONUMENT PLINTH

laser-engraved archival pigment prints over black acrylic, 20" x 12", 2020

MONUMENT PLINTH

Uranium disposal cells are geometric mounds engineered to isolate radioactive material from the surrounding environment. The mounds sit above the ground and cover surfaces from a few acres to half a mile and consist of an outer shell of riprap rock and a clay soil layer that covers the radioactive material. They are designed to allow for rain runoff and to prevent plant growth from forming on top and penetrating the clay layer. Typically, the cells in the Southwest are made from demolished buildings at uranium mines, and the cells in the Midwest and East are most commonly from uranium metal engineering and processing sites.[1]

Some sites that produced the waste contained in the cells date back to the Manhattan Project and were created to mine and construct nuclear weapons; some of the sites continue to operate today for the nuclear energy industry. The amount of radioactivity in the cells varies, but most radiation comes from Uranium-238 with a half-life as old as the earth, or 4.47 billion years. There are over one hundred sites like these that exist in the United States and the number is growing.[2]

Disposal cells are architecturally fascinating sites. They are often designed to blend in with the landscape, but their shapes form mounds on the earth, and their suture materials seldom remain as invisible as intended. They are otherworldly to see up close, but even more fascinating to see from an aerial view where their odd geometry takes shape. While some sites are constructed away from populated cities, others such as those in Weldon Spring, just outside St. Louis, Missouri, are difficult to ignore and function as recreational destinations.

1   "Perpetual Architecture: Uranium Disposal Cells of America," The Center for Land Use Interpretation, accessed June 5, 2020, http://www.clui.org/newsletter/winter-2013/perpetual-architecture.
2   "Perpetual Architecture," The Center for Land Use Interpretation.

Monument Plinth features aerial images from forty uranium disposal cells across the United States. The images were collected with the assistance of Dr. Mark Finco and acquired by the National Agriculture Imagery Program. I printed and mounted each image on black acrylic and laser engraved the cell detail into the surface, reflecting an internal space or void.

Platelist:

Uranium Disposal Cells and Spent Nuclear Fuel Storage Sites Map

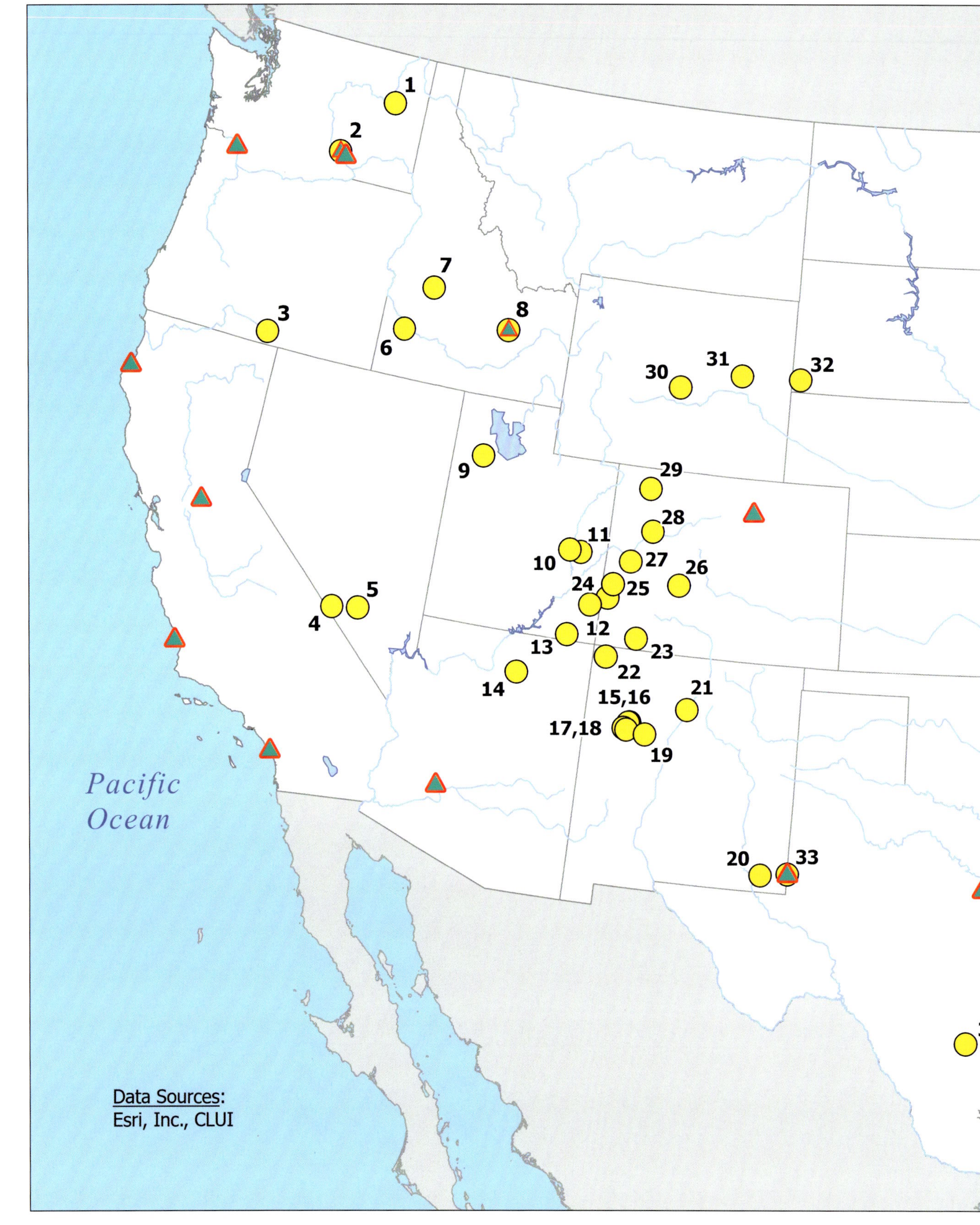

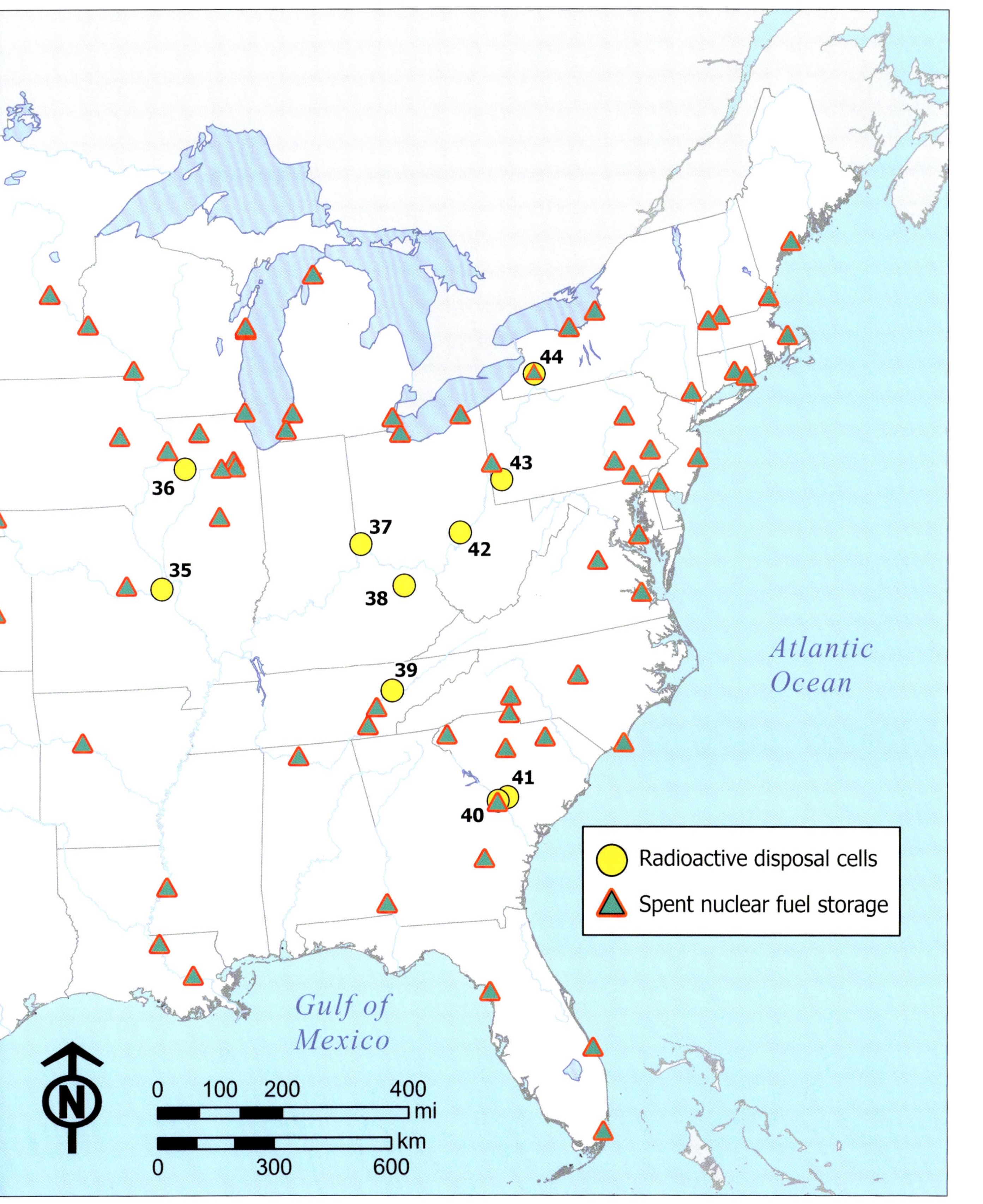

Atlantic Ocean
Gulf of Mexico
44
43
36
37
42
35
38
39
41
40
Radioactive disposal cells
Spent nuclear fuel storage
N
0 100 200 400
mi
0 300 600
km

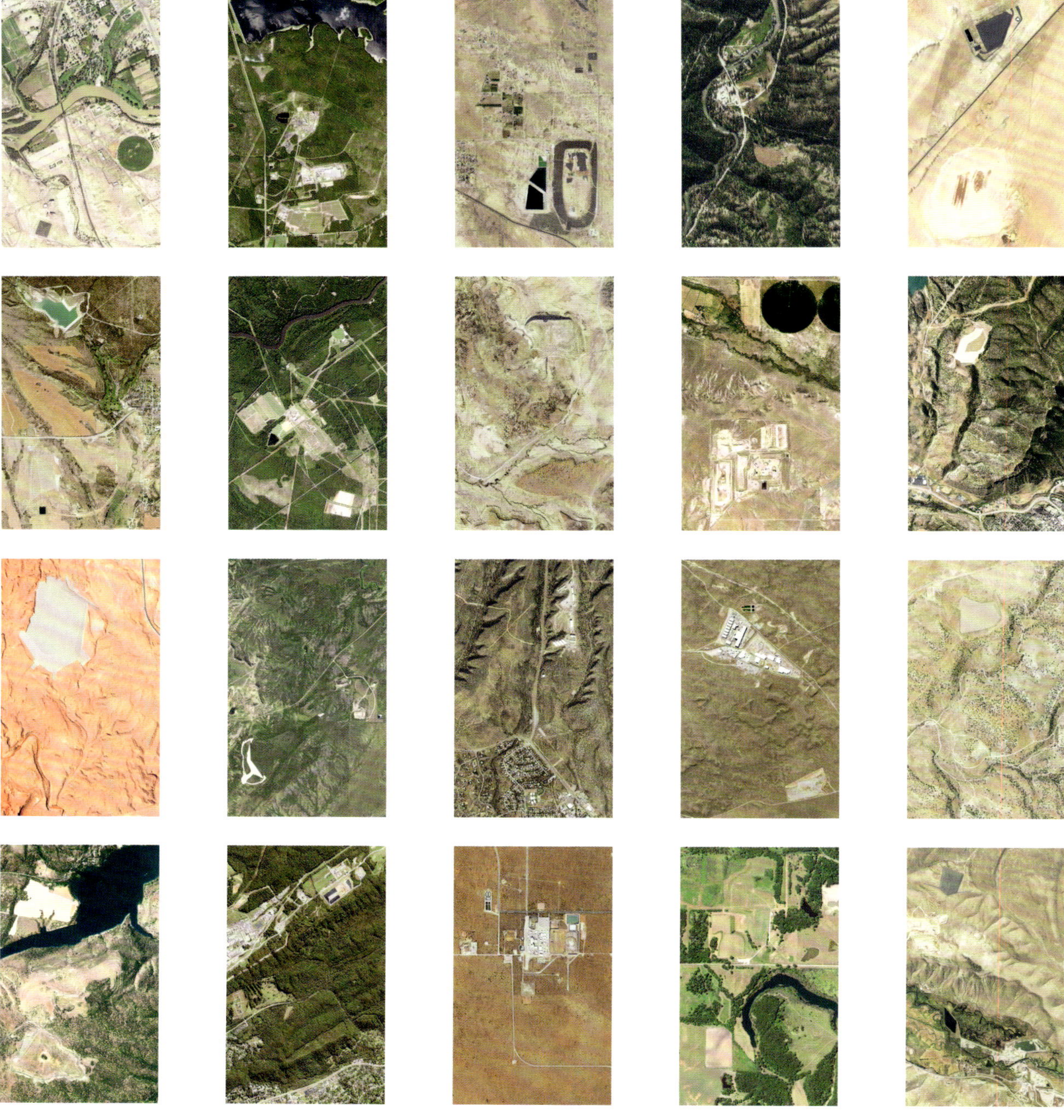

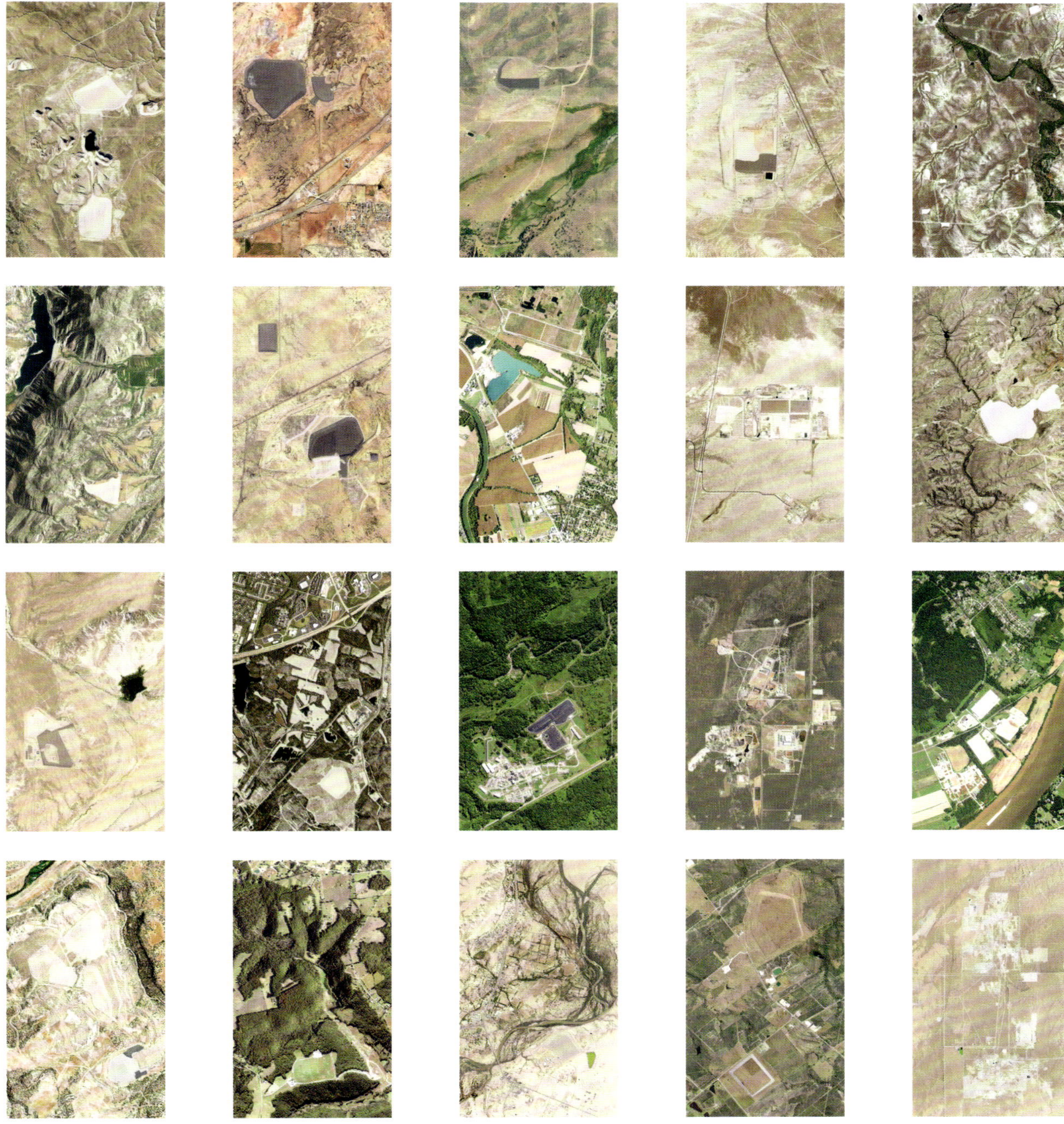

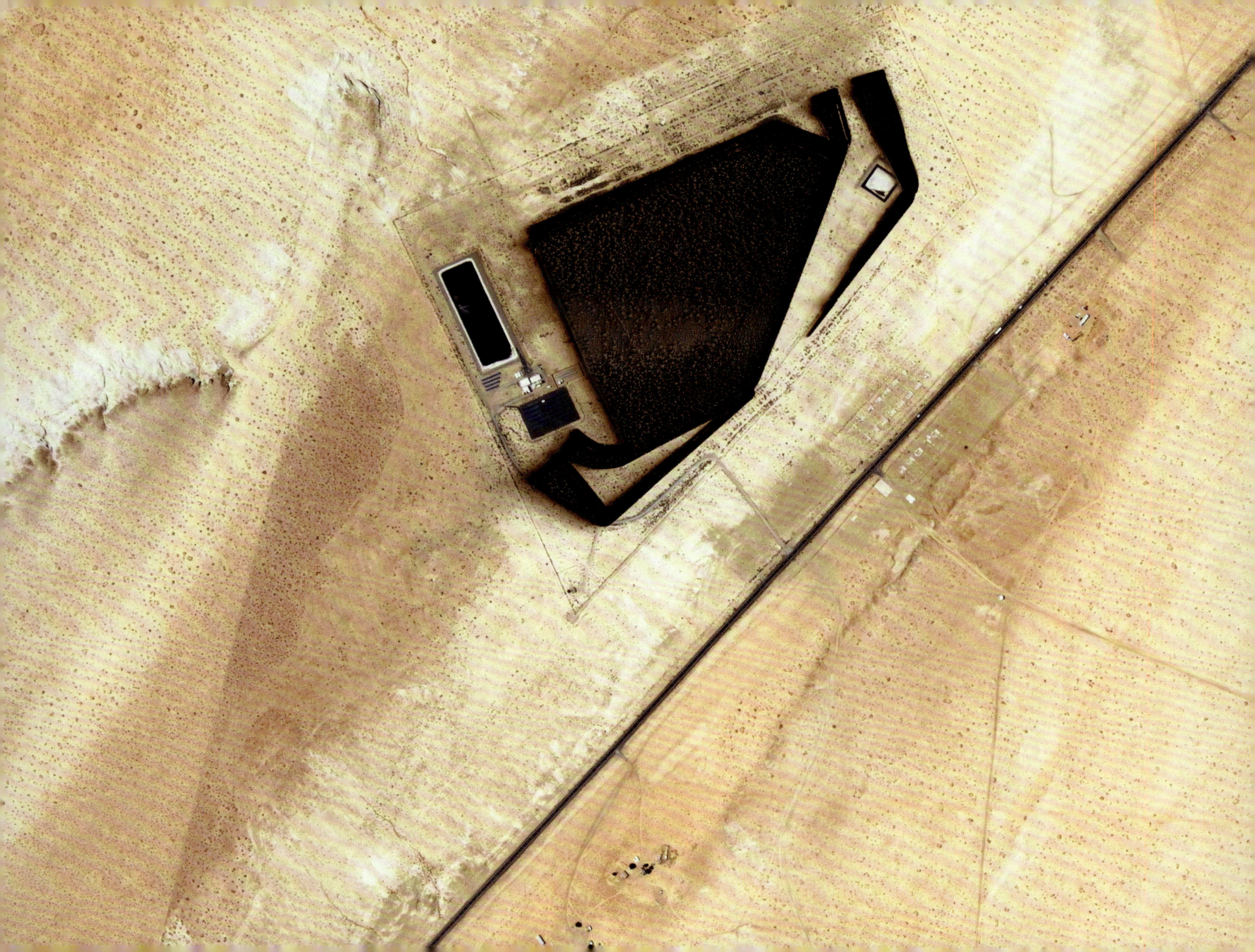

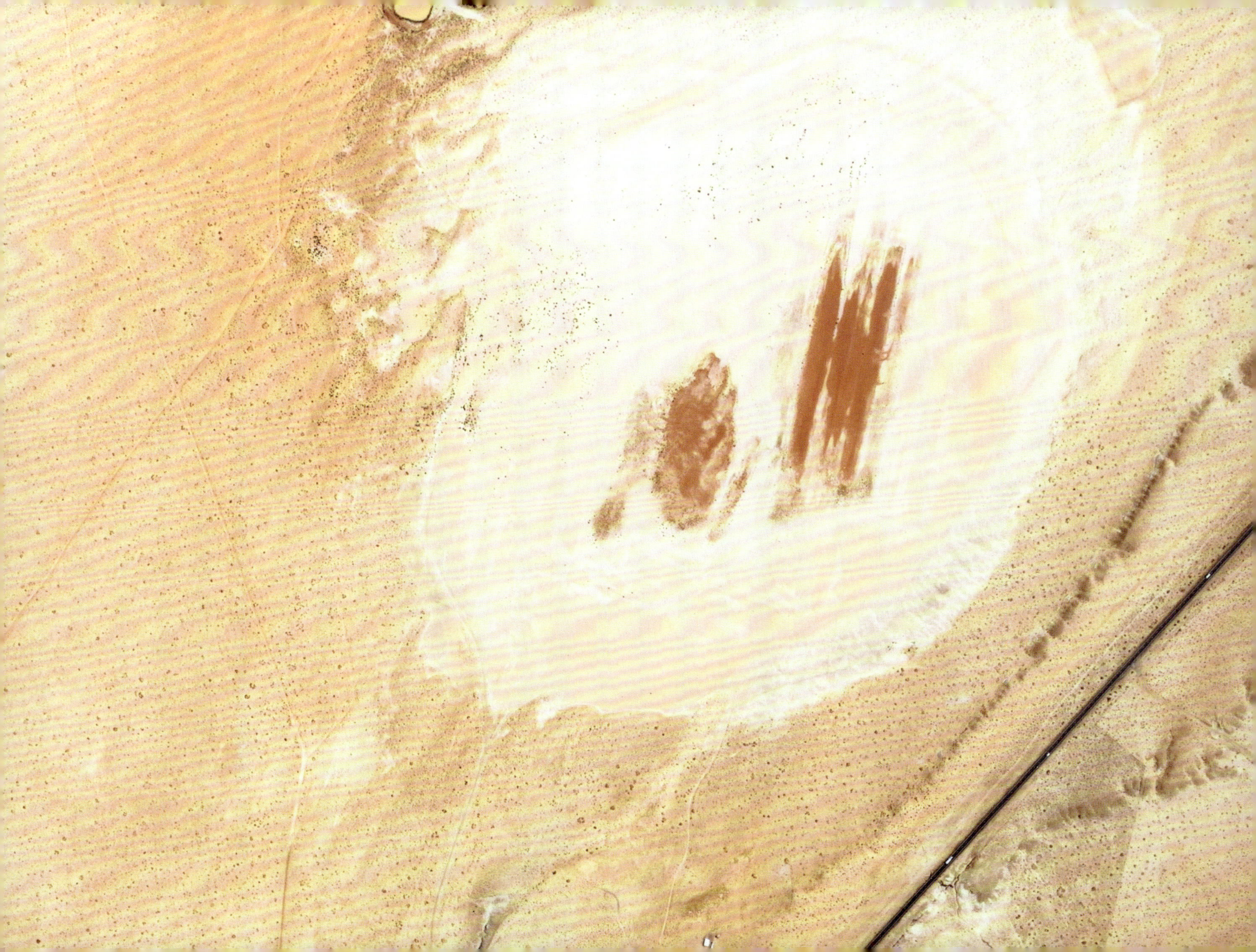

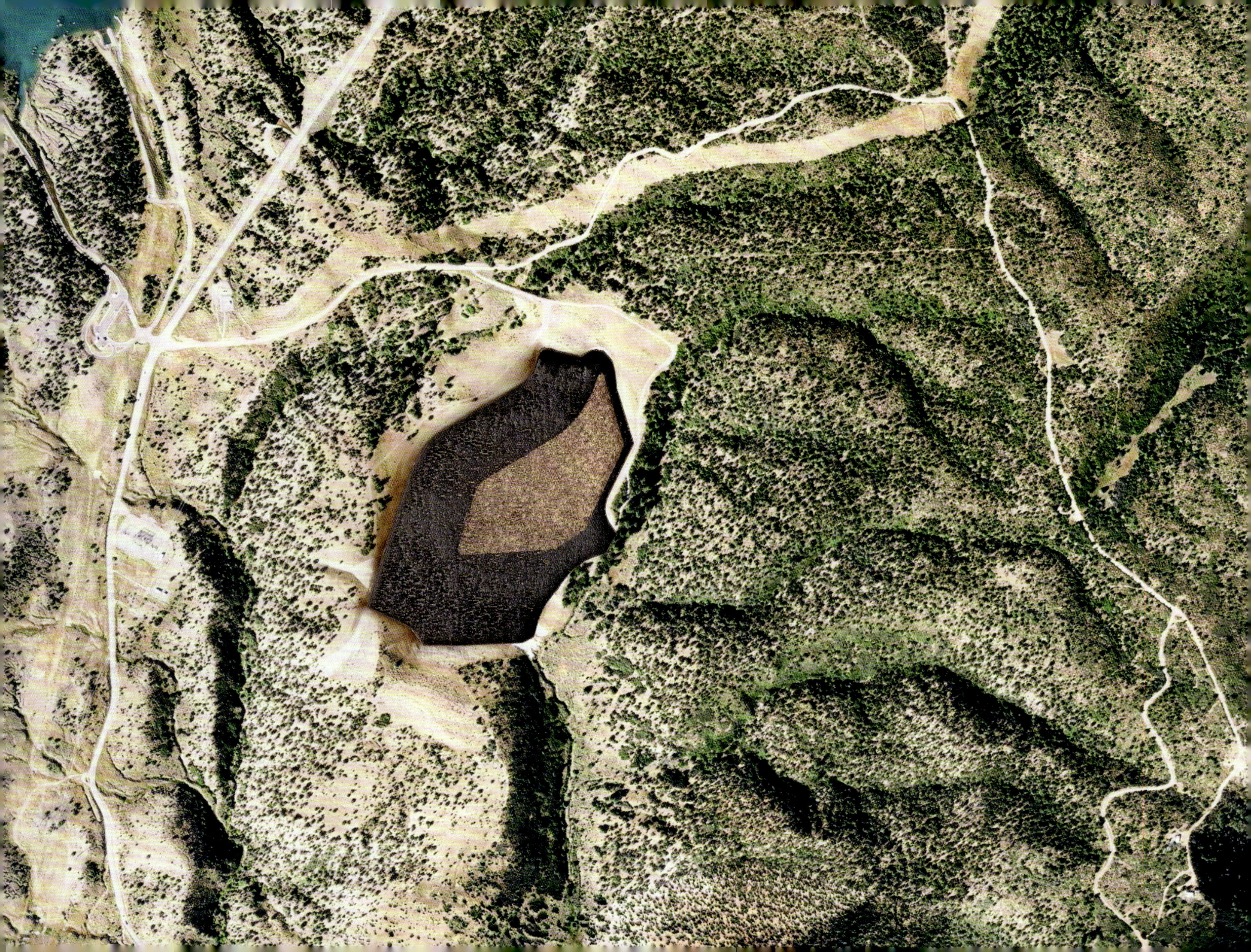

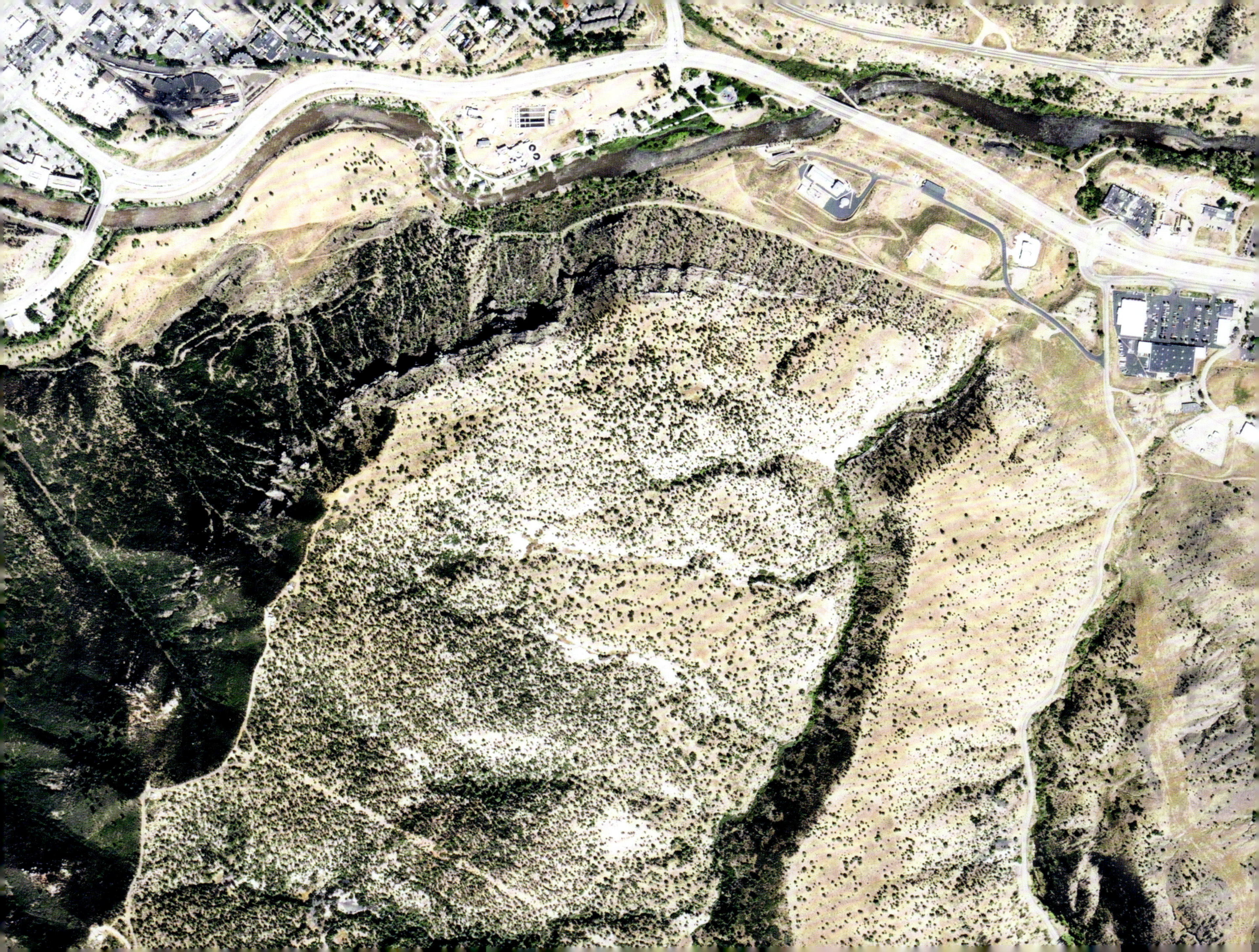

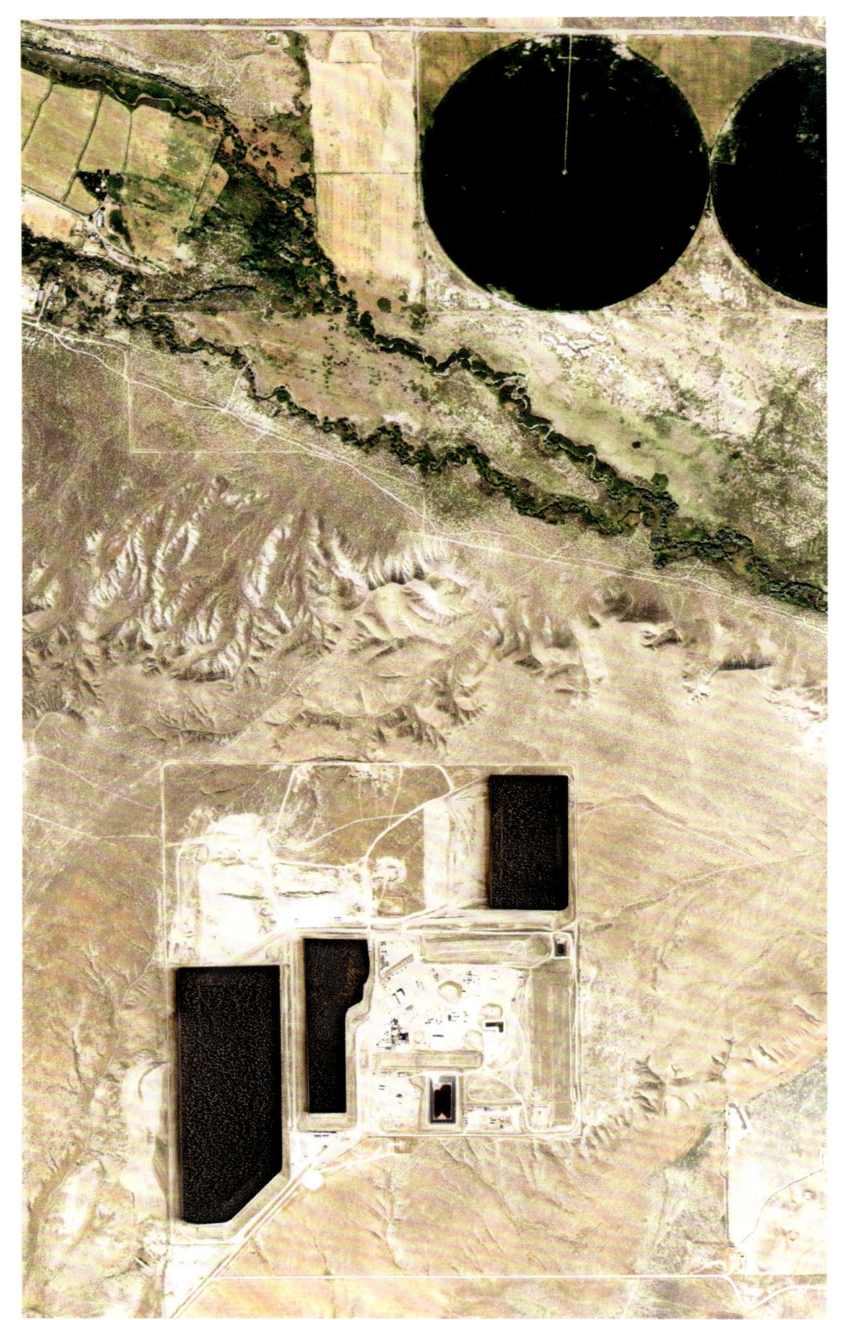

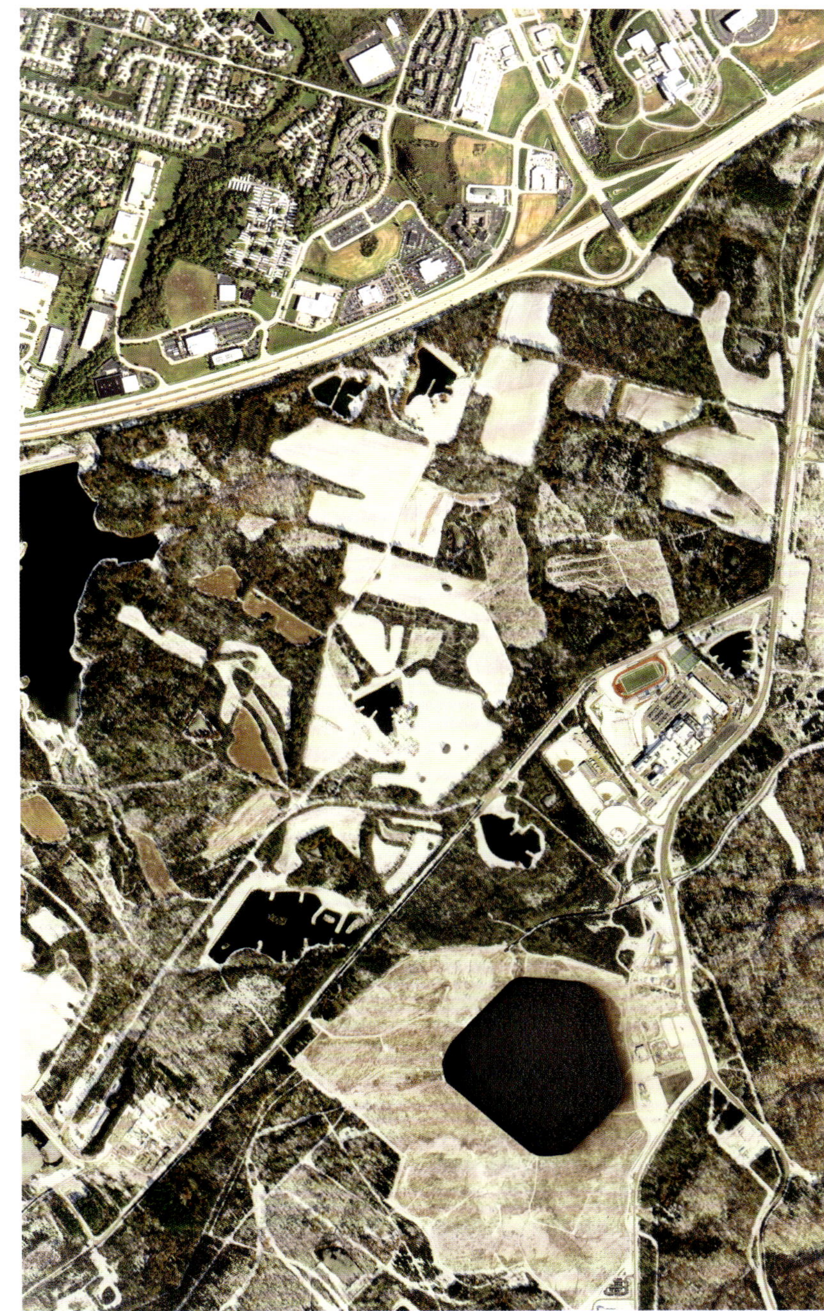

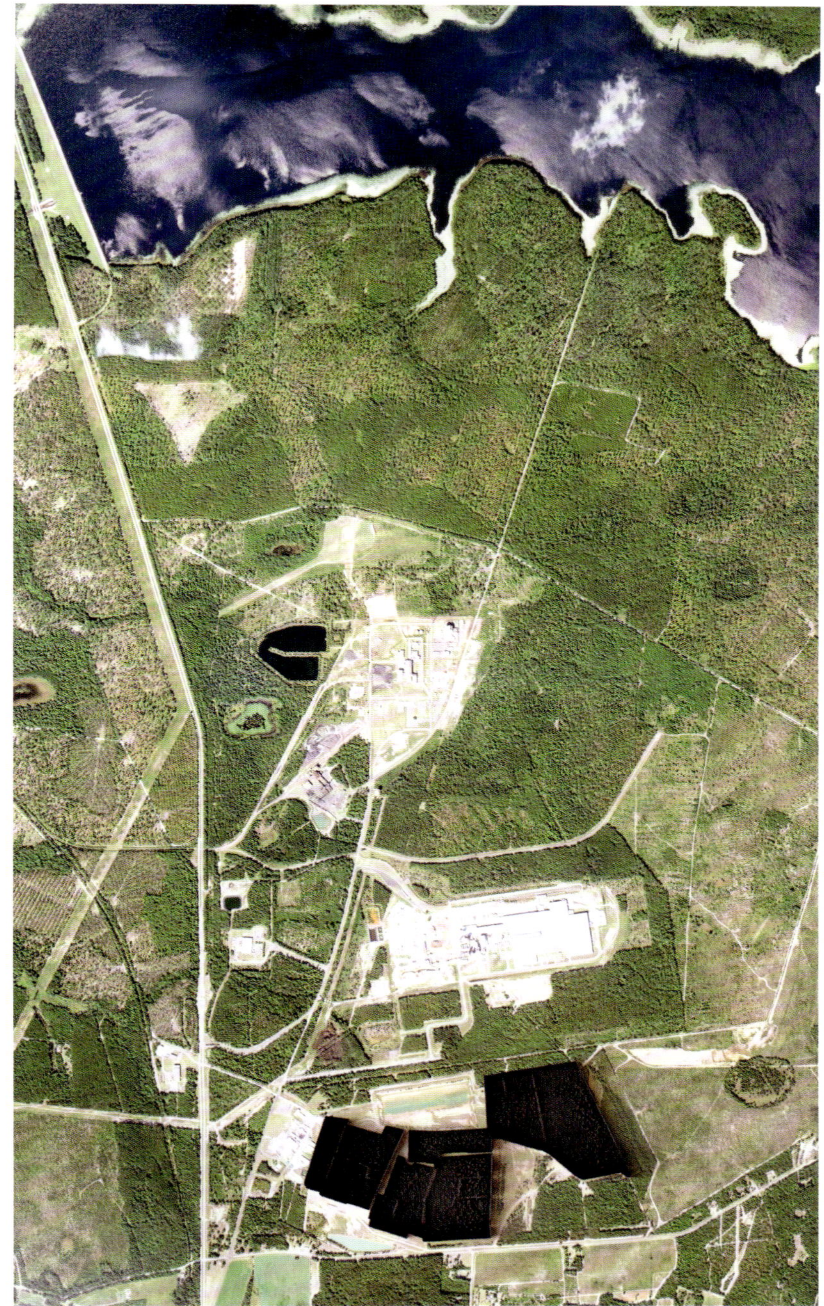

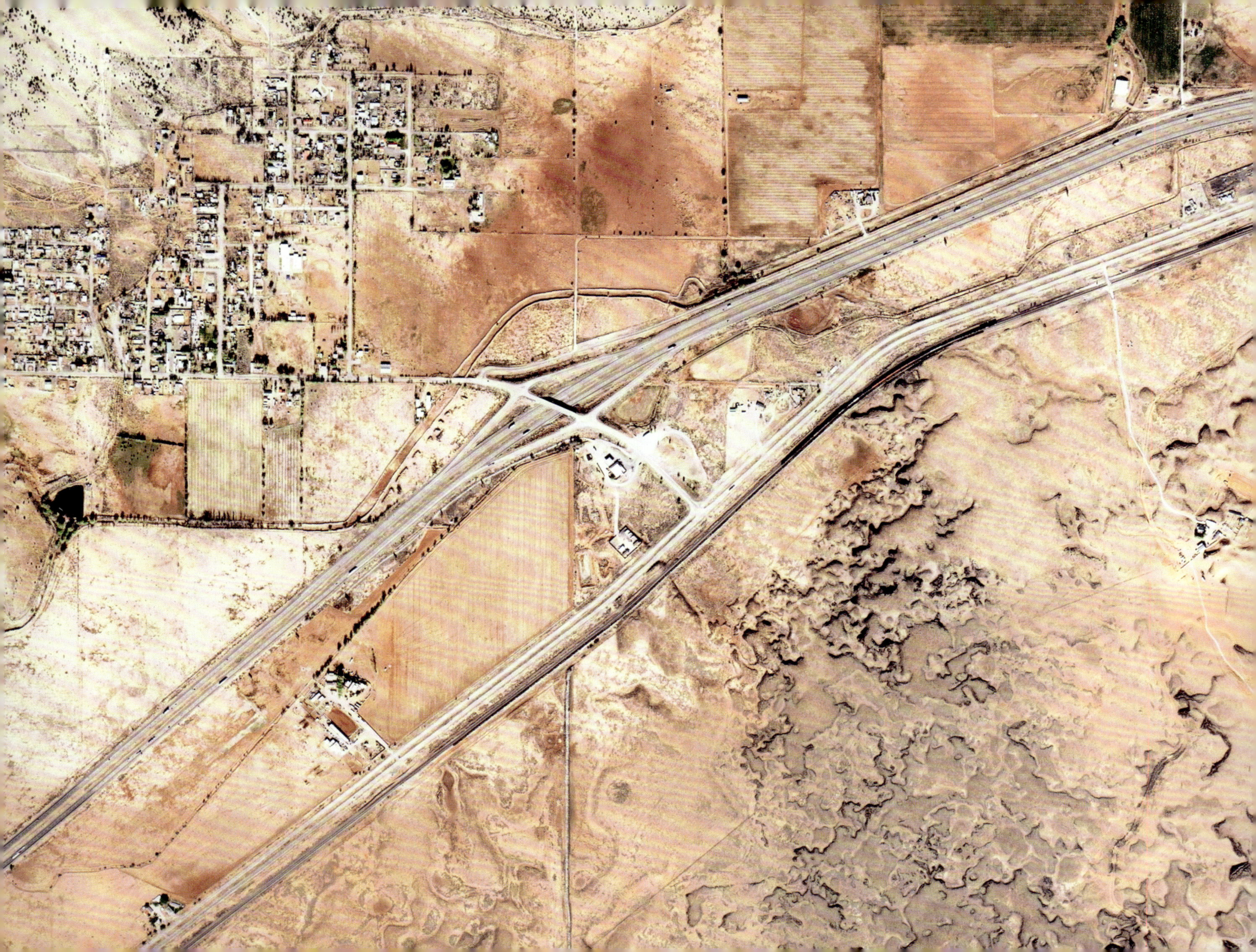

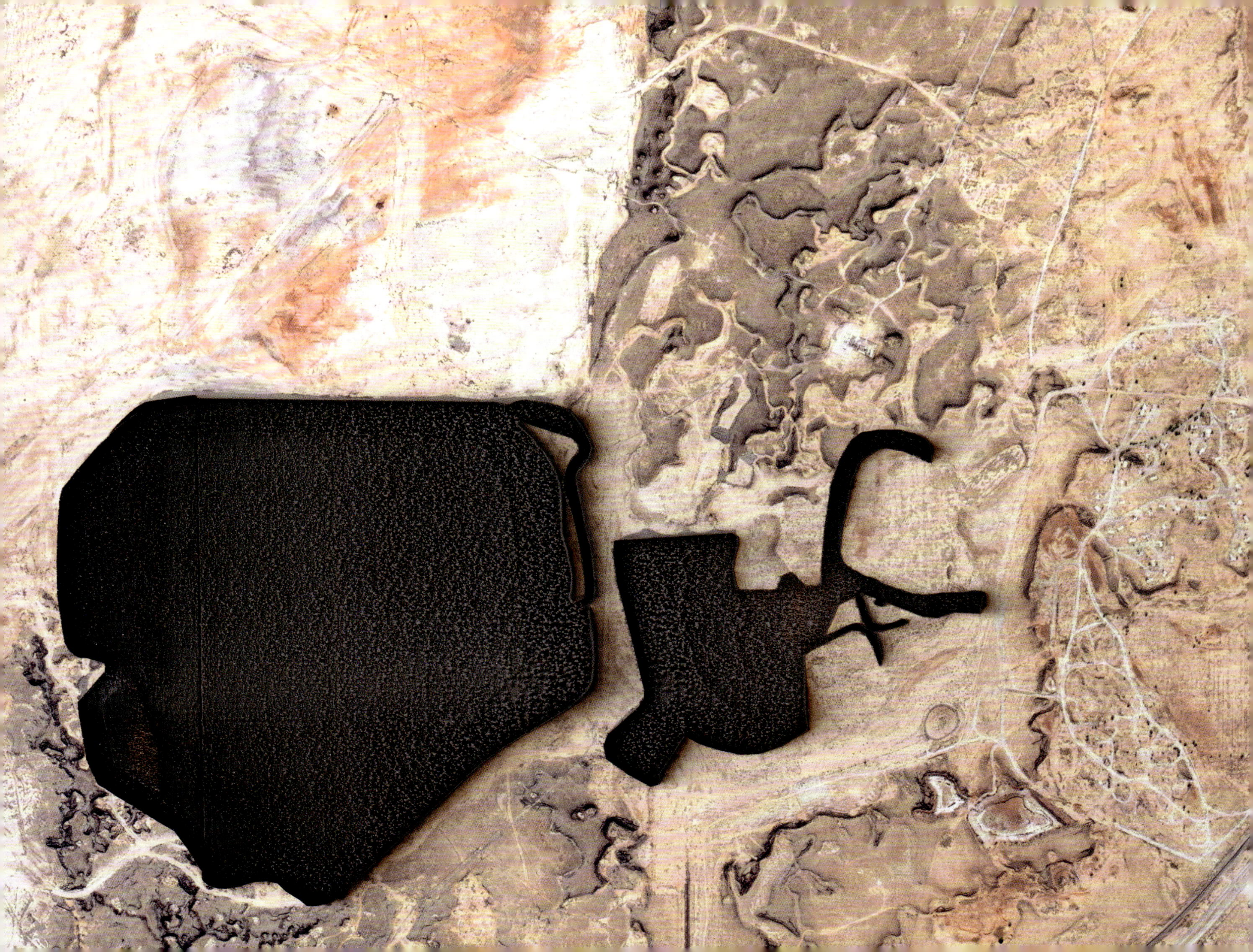

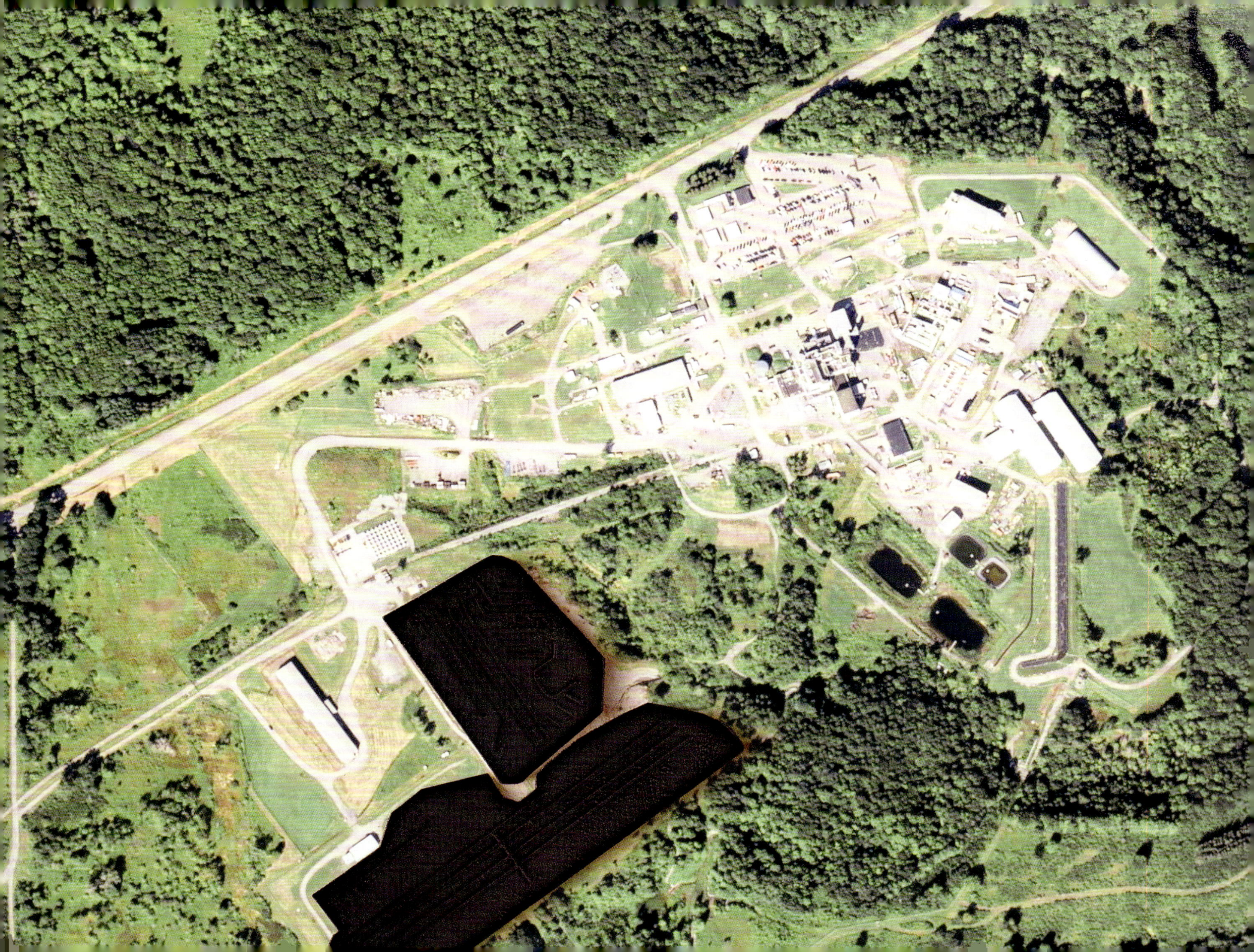

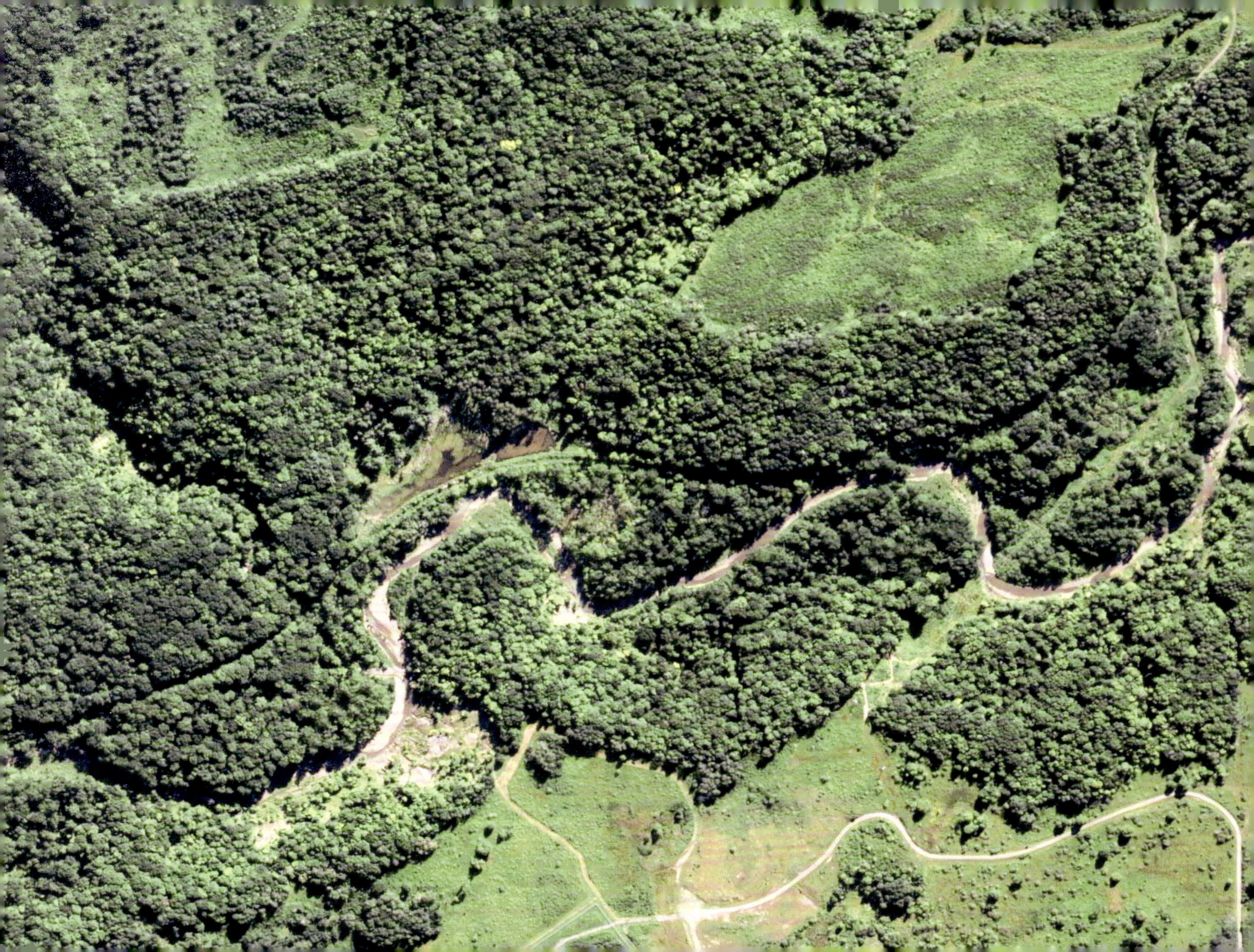

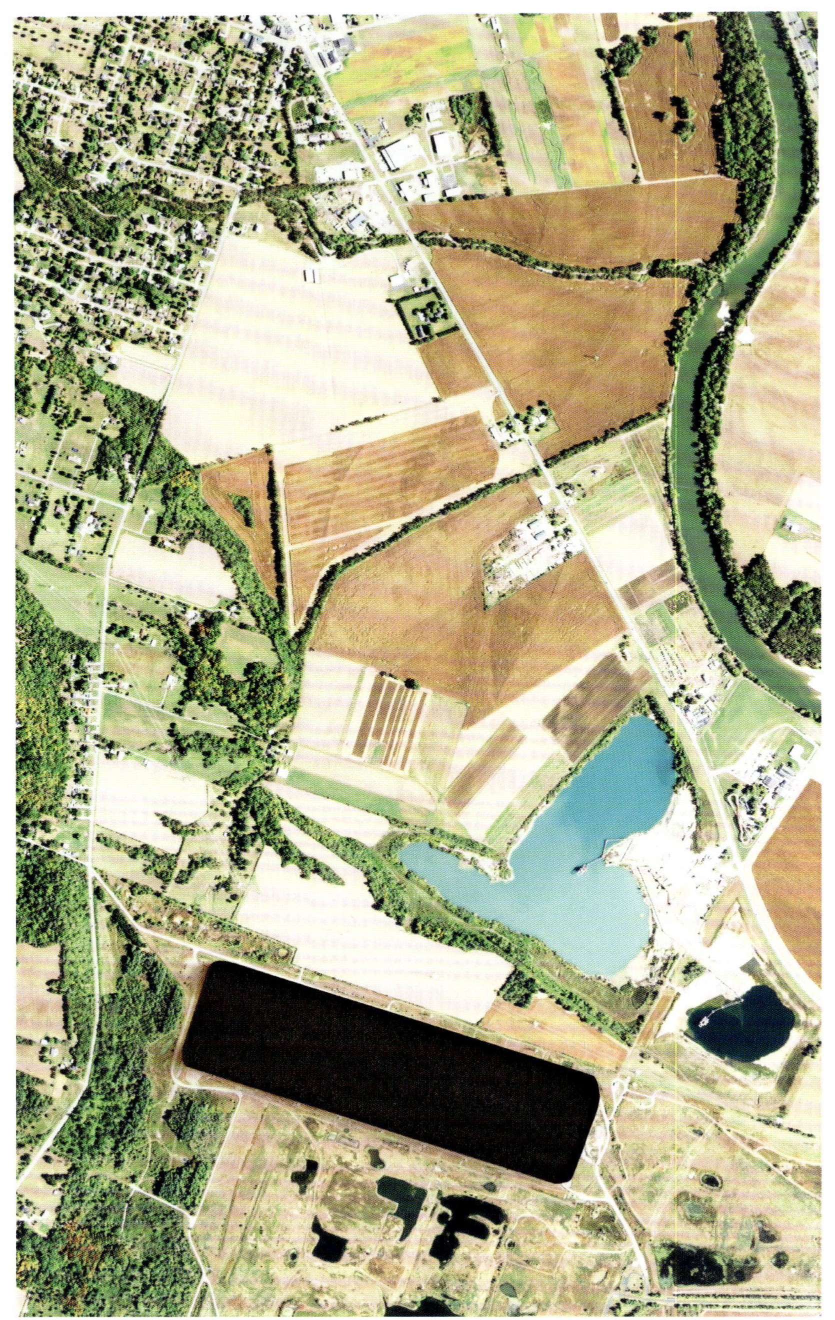

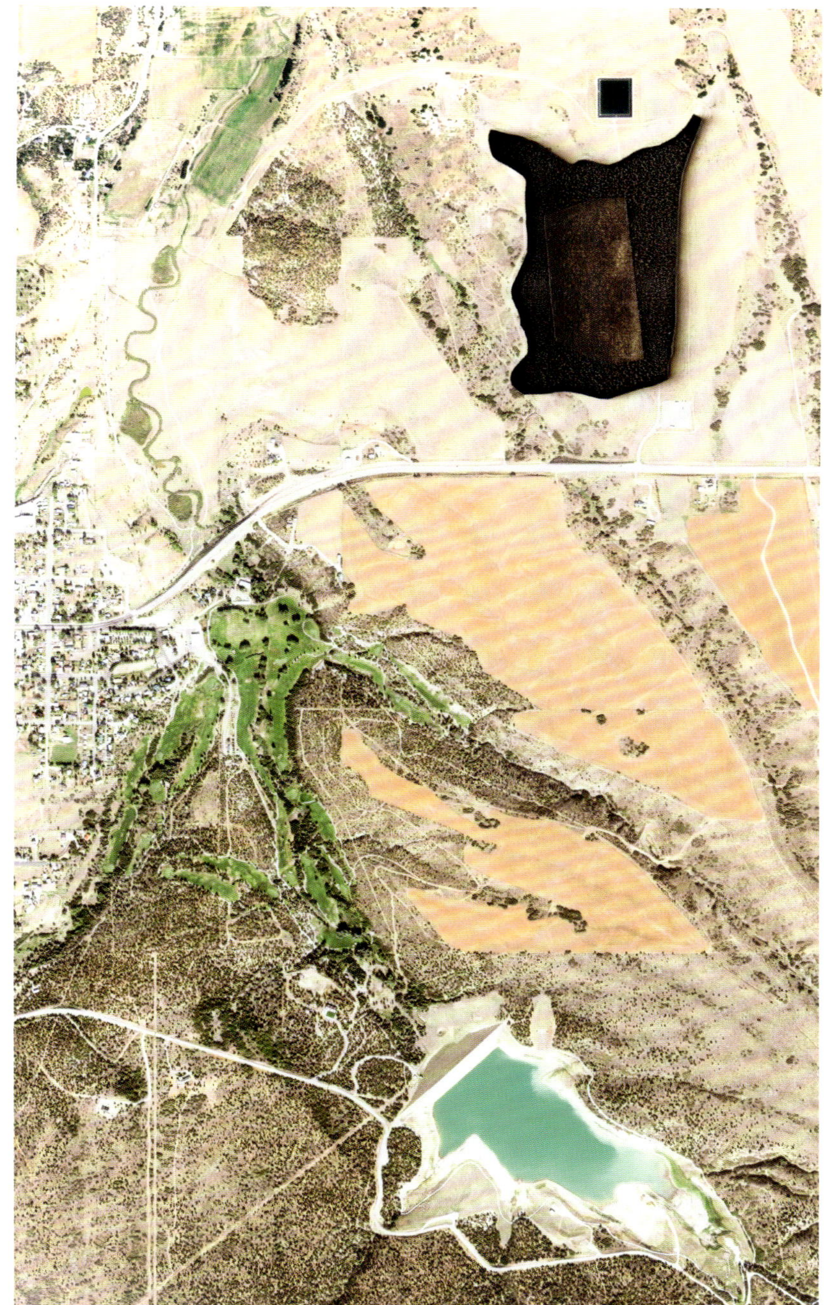

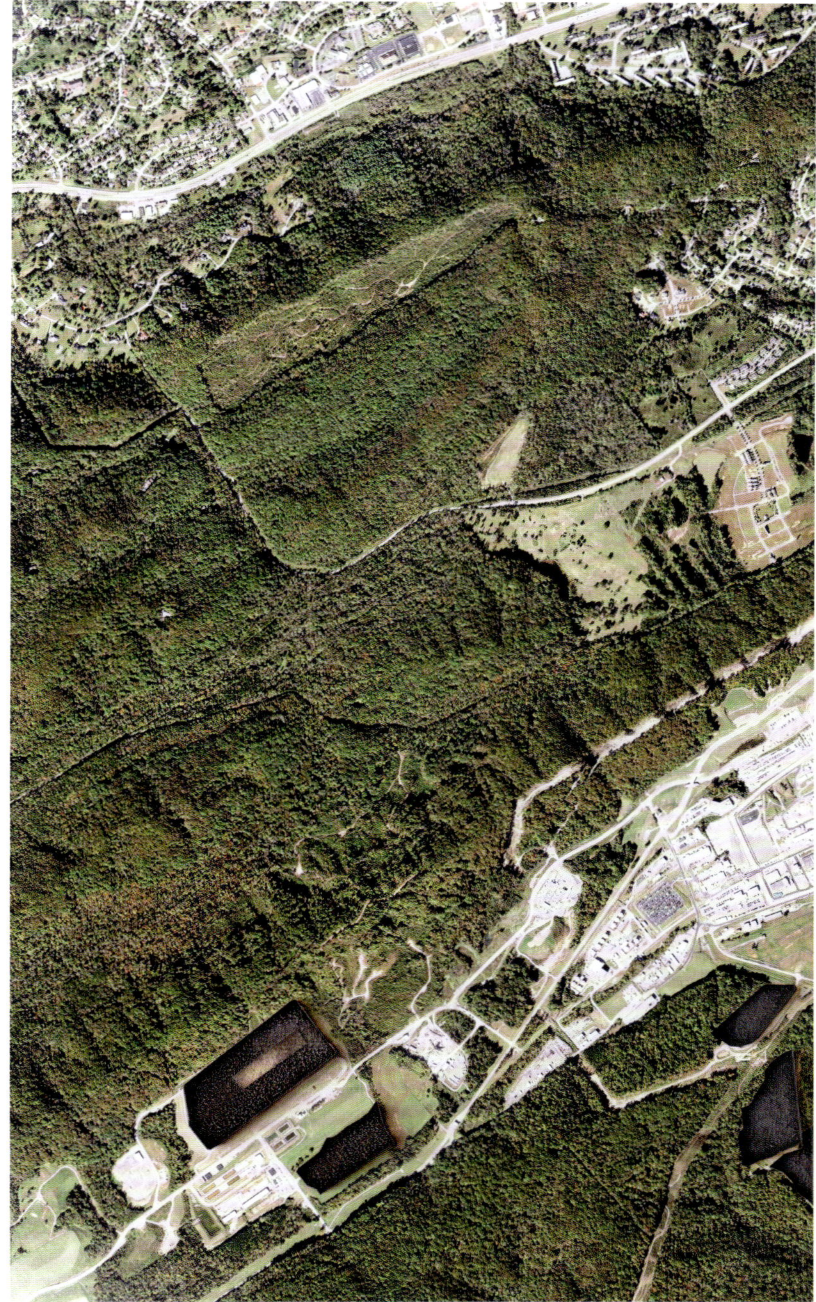

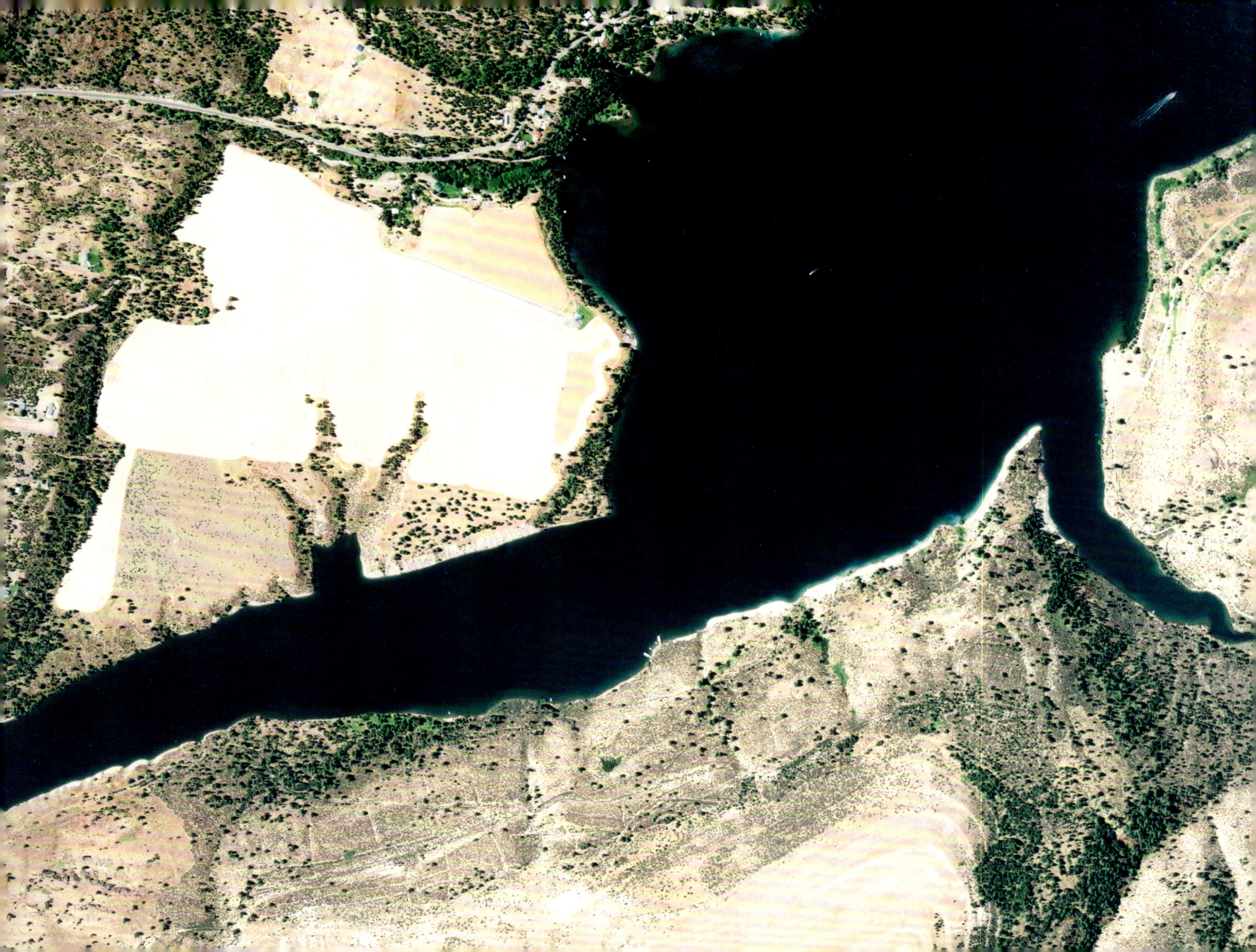

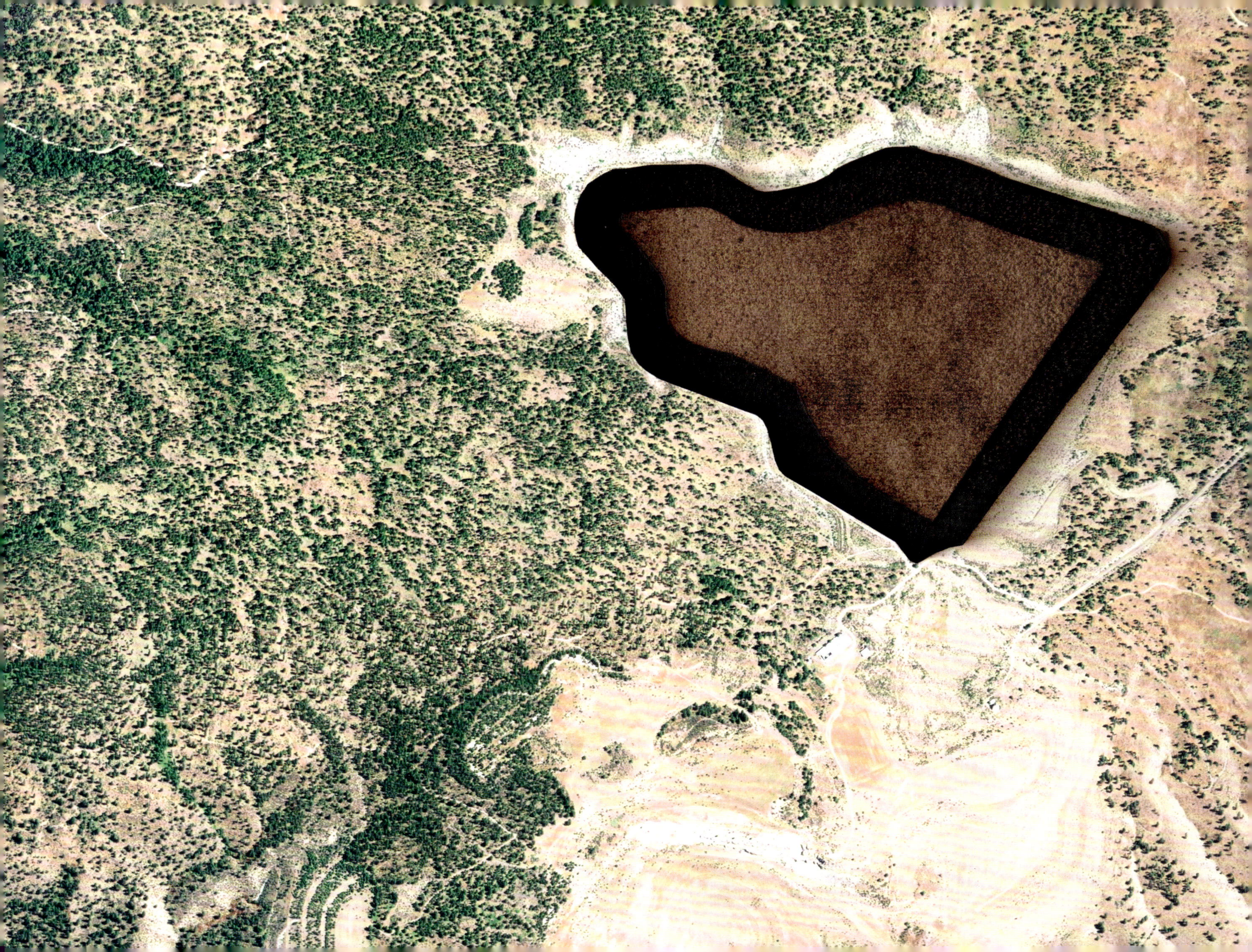

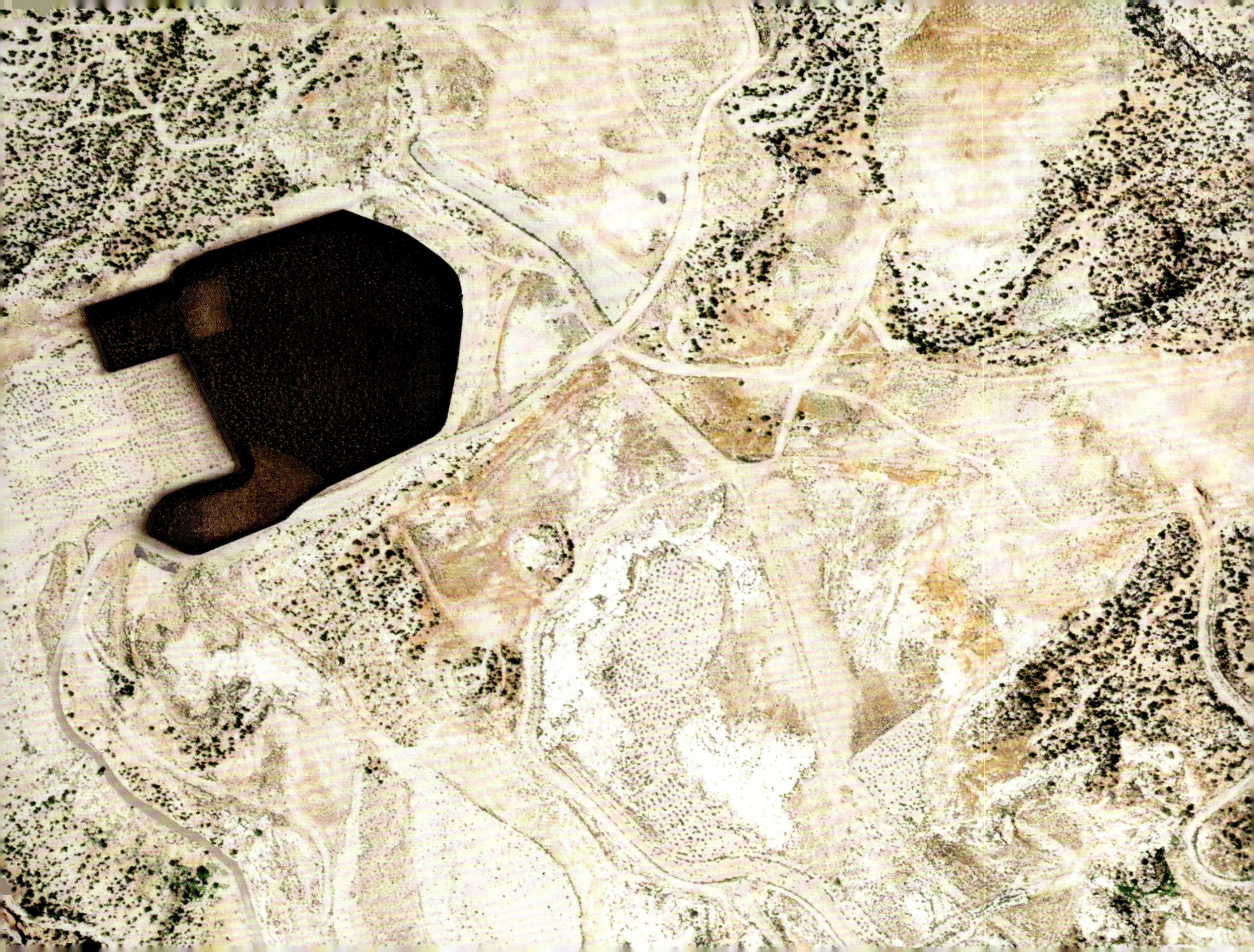

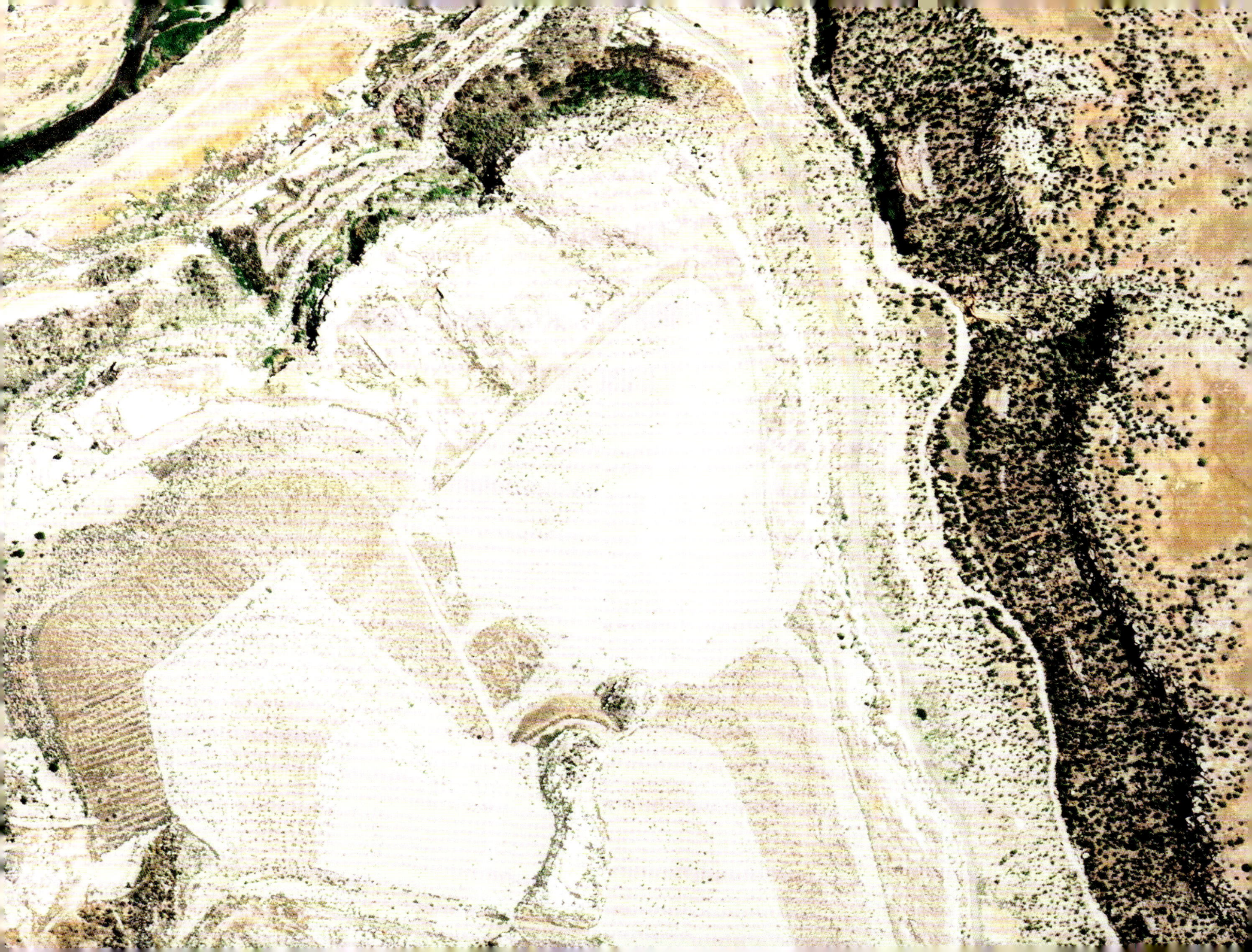

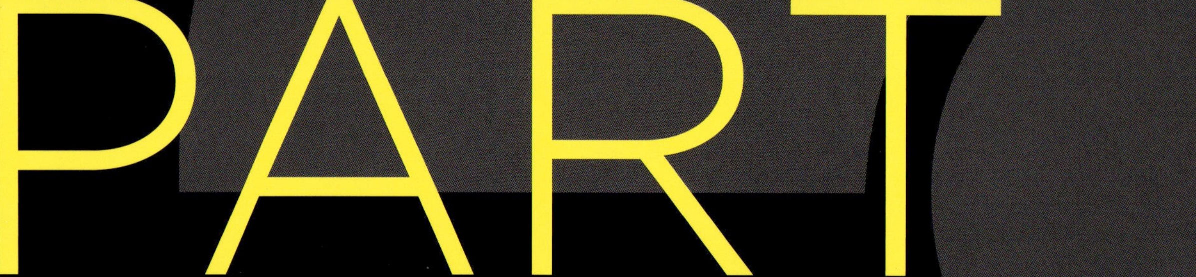
PART

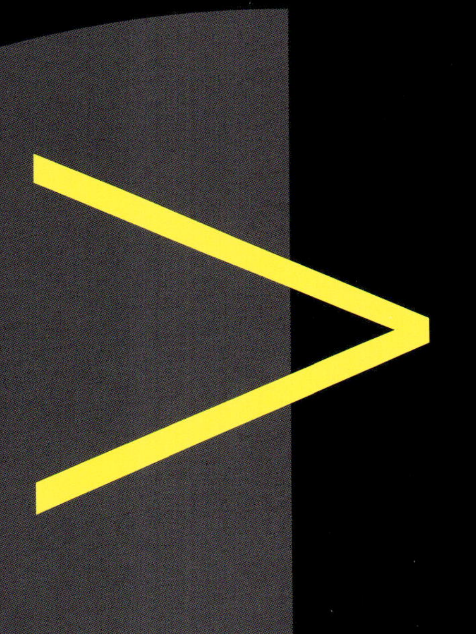

TRANSURANIC
uranotypes (uranium prints), 13" x 9", 2014

Transuranic Waste Project Sites in the Western US and County Populations
Hanford Site
Idaho National Engineering Laboratory
Rocky Flats
Lawrence Livermore National Laboratory
Nevada Test Site
Los Alamos National Laboratory
WIPP
Pacific Ocean
County population (2016 estimate)
1,000,000
500,000
100,000
50,000
10,000
N
0 100 200 400 mi
0 150 300 600 km
Transuranic waste project sites
Site locations and extents
Counties with sites
Data Source: Esri, Inc.

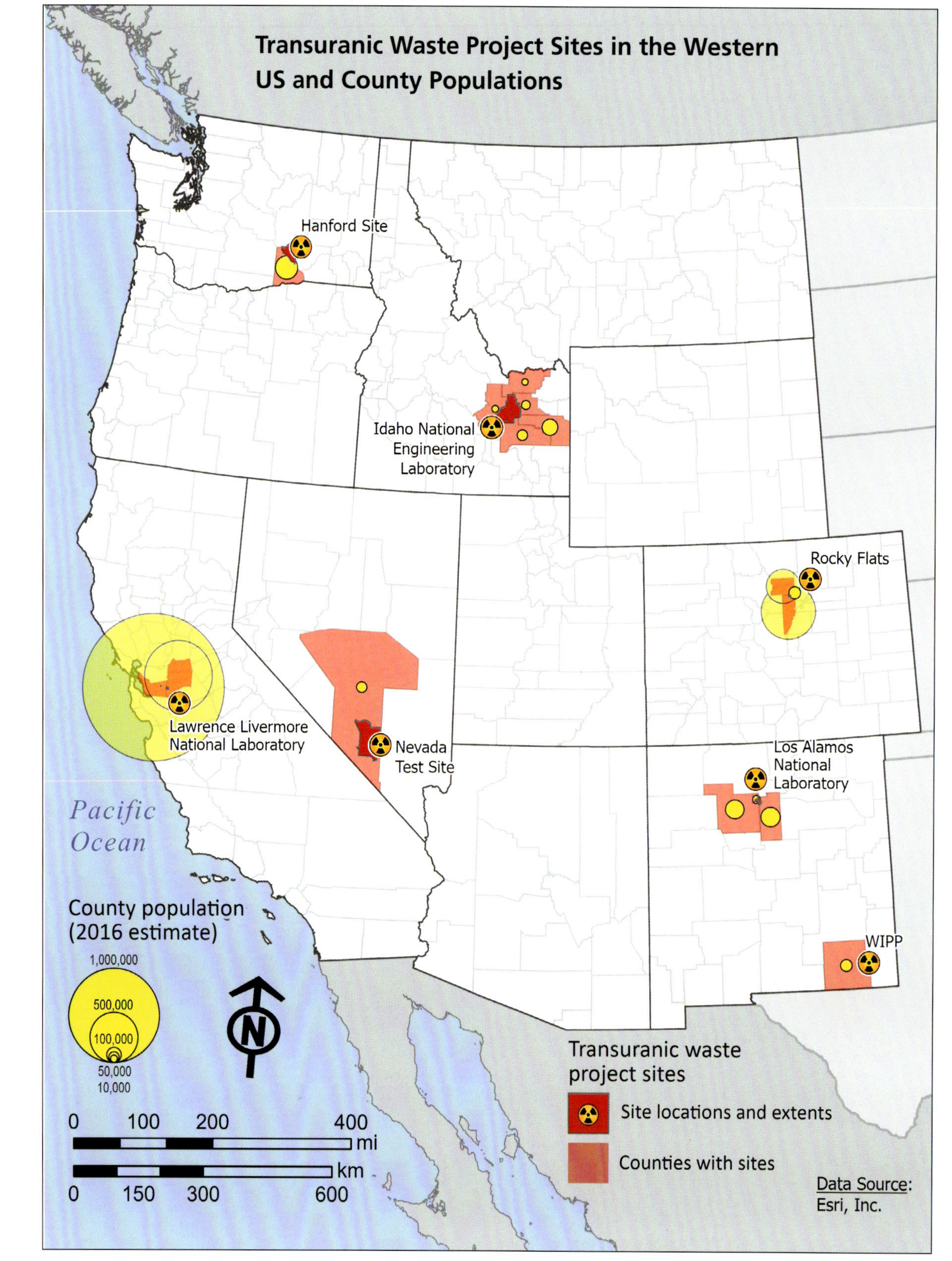

80

TRANSURANIC

Upon moving to New Mexico from Japan, where I participated in disaster relief work following the 2011 tsunami and nuclear meltdown, I set out to understand the impact of the nuclear industry on my immediate surroundings. I photographed every site in the western United States that transports radioactive waste to the Waste Isolation Pilot Plant (WIPP) in New Mexico. Places like WIPP, seemingly transparent in their operations, as indicated by signage, still rest amongst us like scars on the landscape.

Transuranic Waste Route Map from the Department of Energy

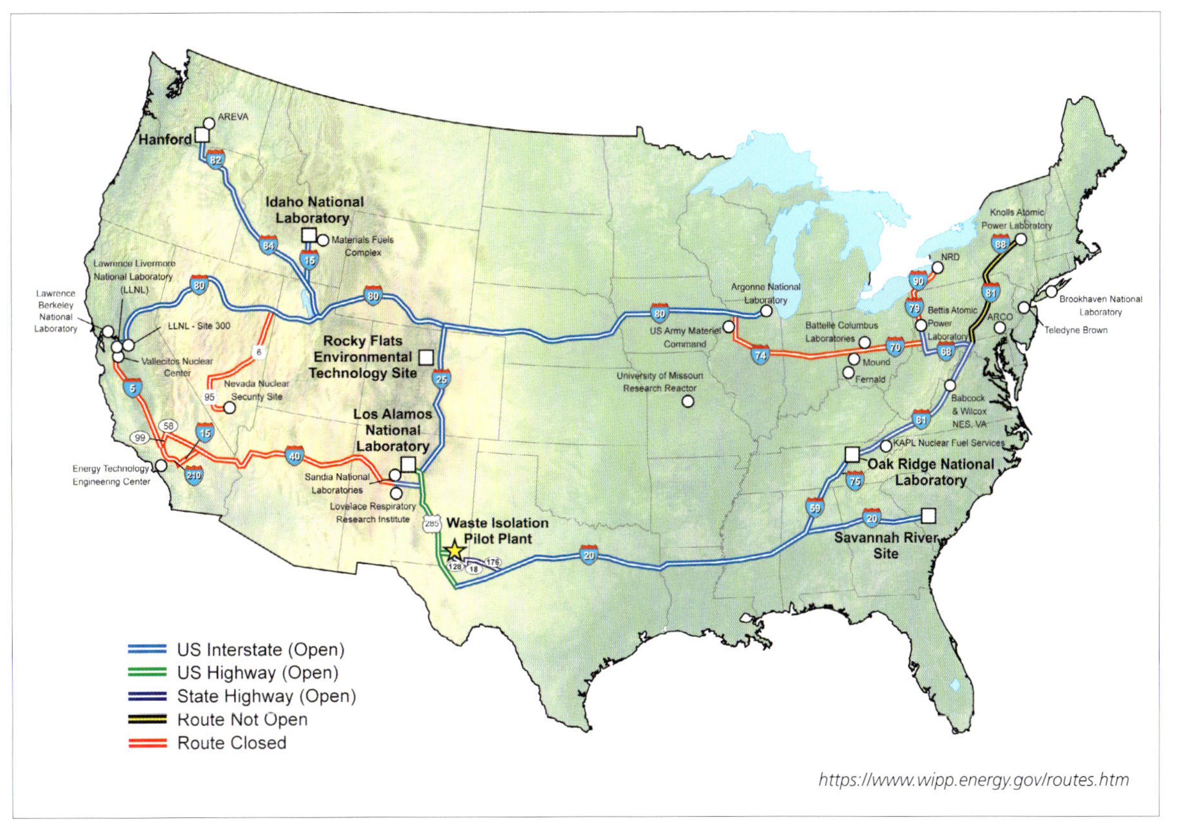

Transuranic is a series of uranotypes, an obsolete nineteenth-century photographic process that uses uranium instead of silver to form the image; uranium is an element used to make nuclear bombs and is the basic fuel for nuclear power reactors. The series documents nuclear facilities from an outsider's perspective. The red and yellow hue of the uranotypes is likened to the color of the sky after the bomb was dropped on Hiroshima, and the material presence negates the unassuming and banal nature of these sites, reminding us of the reality ever present in the images and in the places we inhabit.

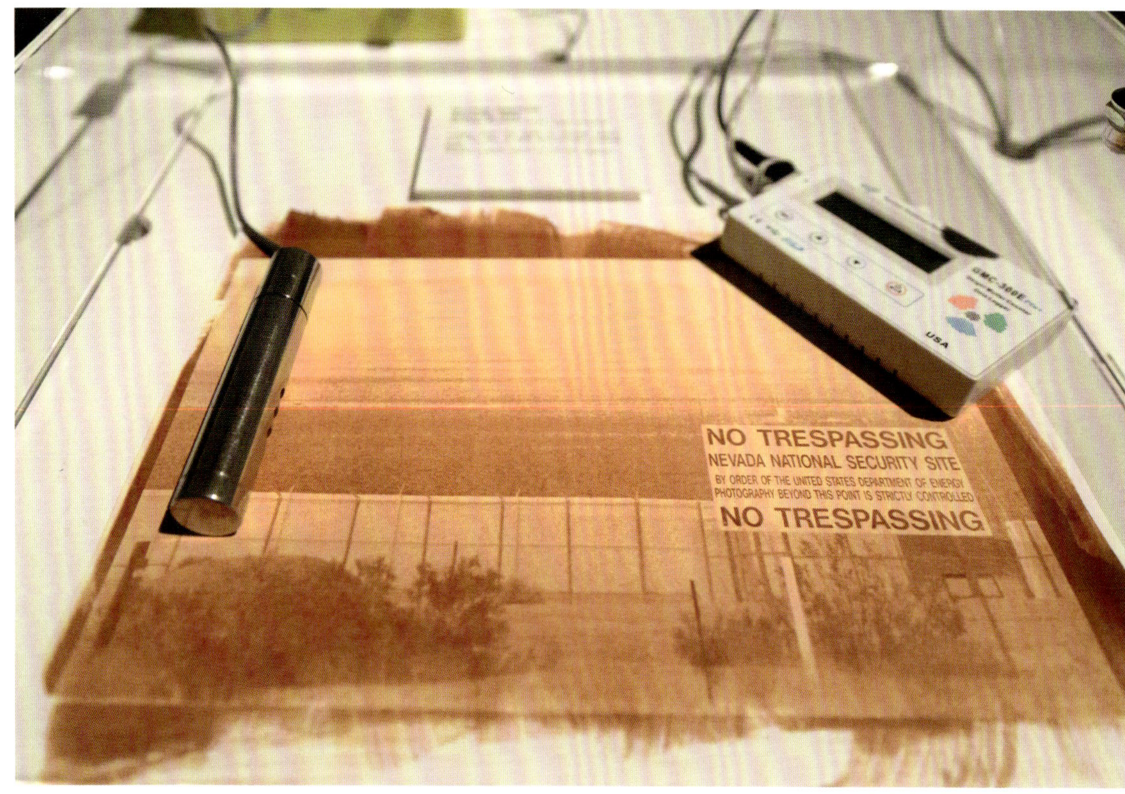

Transuranic installation view: Geiger counters on uranotype. Nevada National Security Site, outside Las Vegas, Nevada. Radioactive Waste Shipped to WIPP: 107,087 gallons.

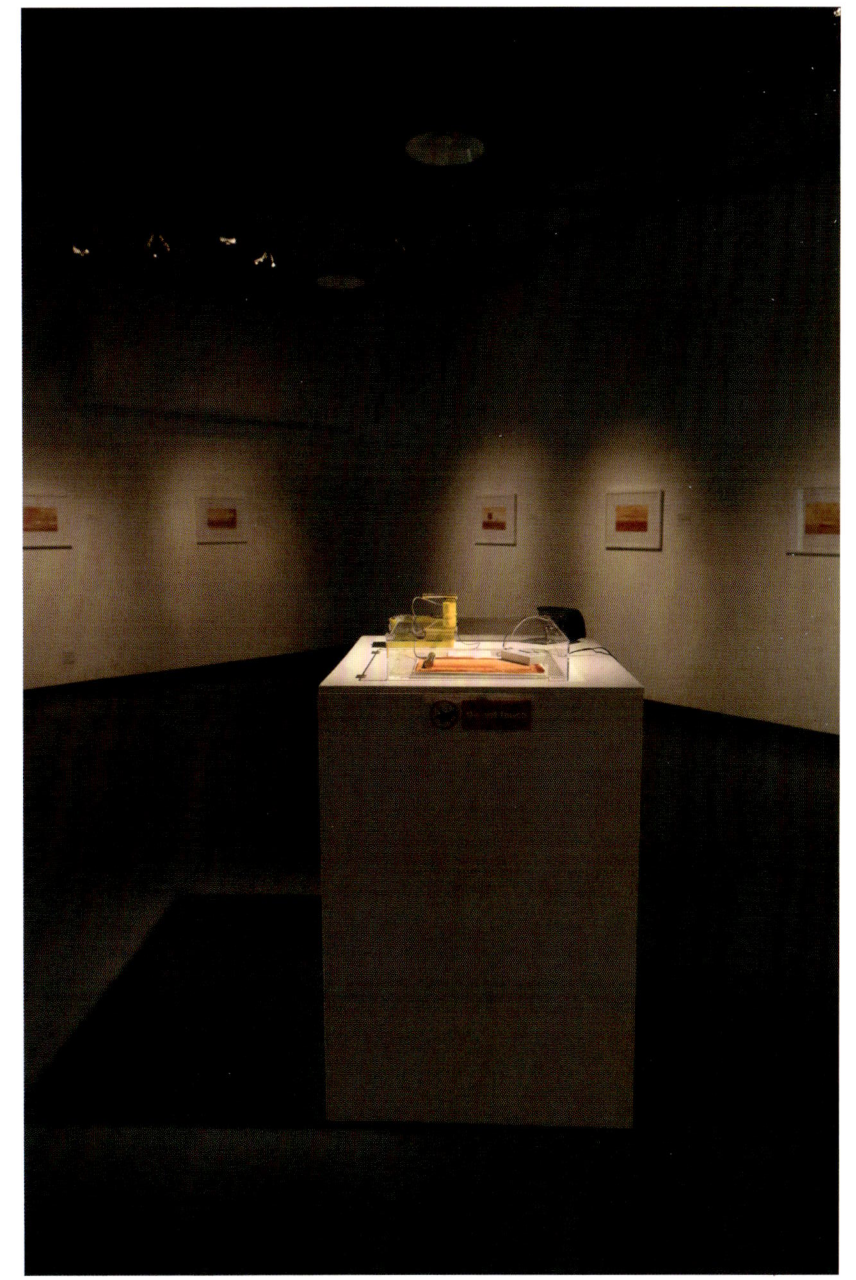

Transuranic installation view: Thirteen framed uranotypes, pedestal with Geiger counters and a uranotype in a locked box, speaker. The Geiger counters are a Cold War-era model and a post-Fukushima digital consumer model, commenting on the repetition of history. The Geiger counters read the radioactivity in the print and emit a warning sound, in clicks, based on counts per minute above background.

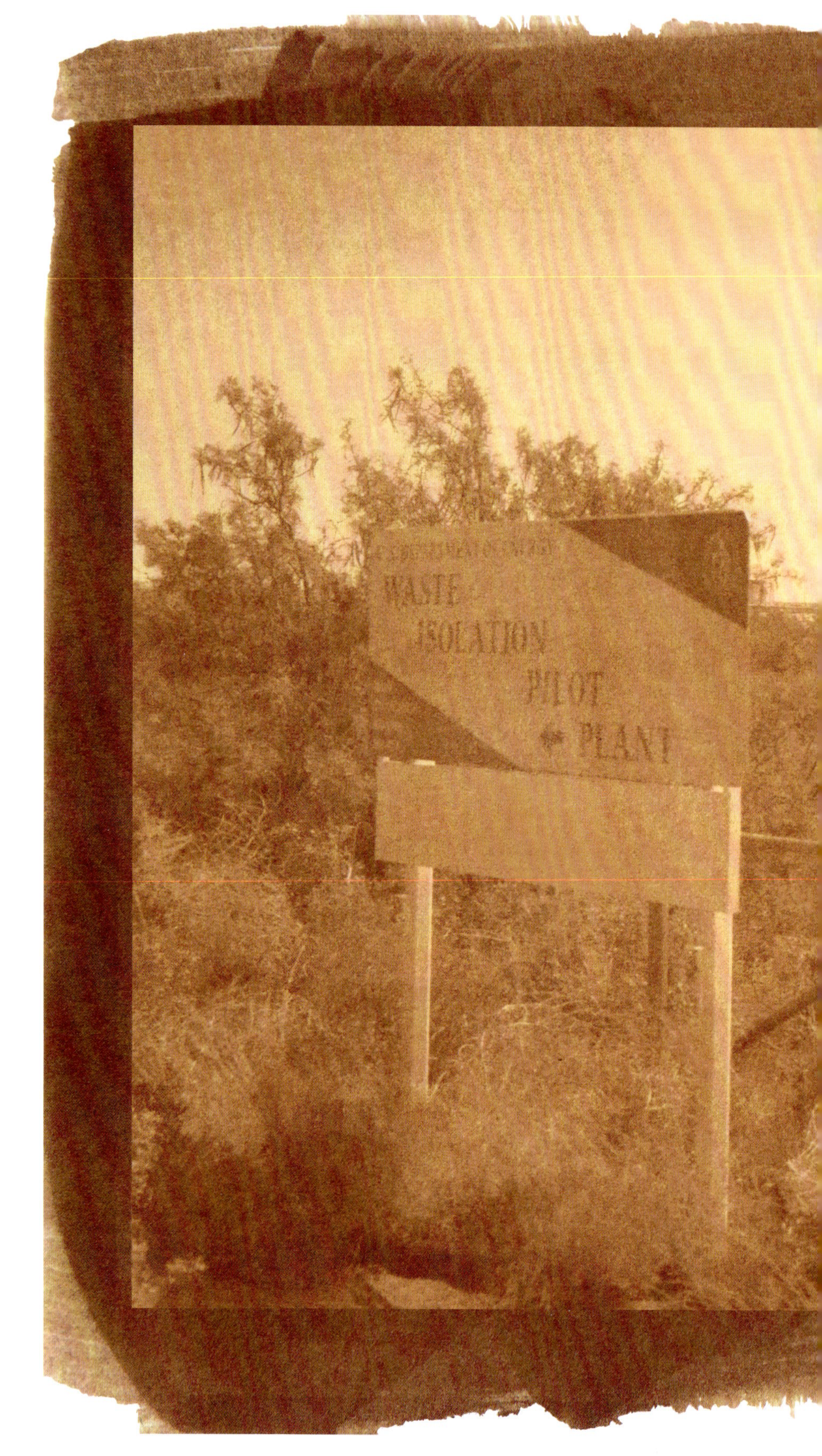

**Waste Isolation
Pilot Plant 2,**
Carlsbad, New Mexico.

Amount of waste
emplaced to date:
25,857,295 gallons.

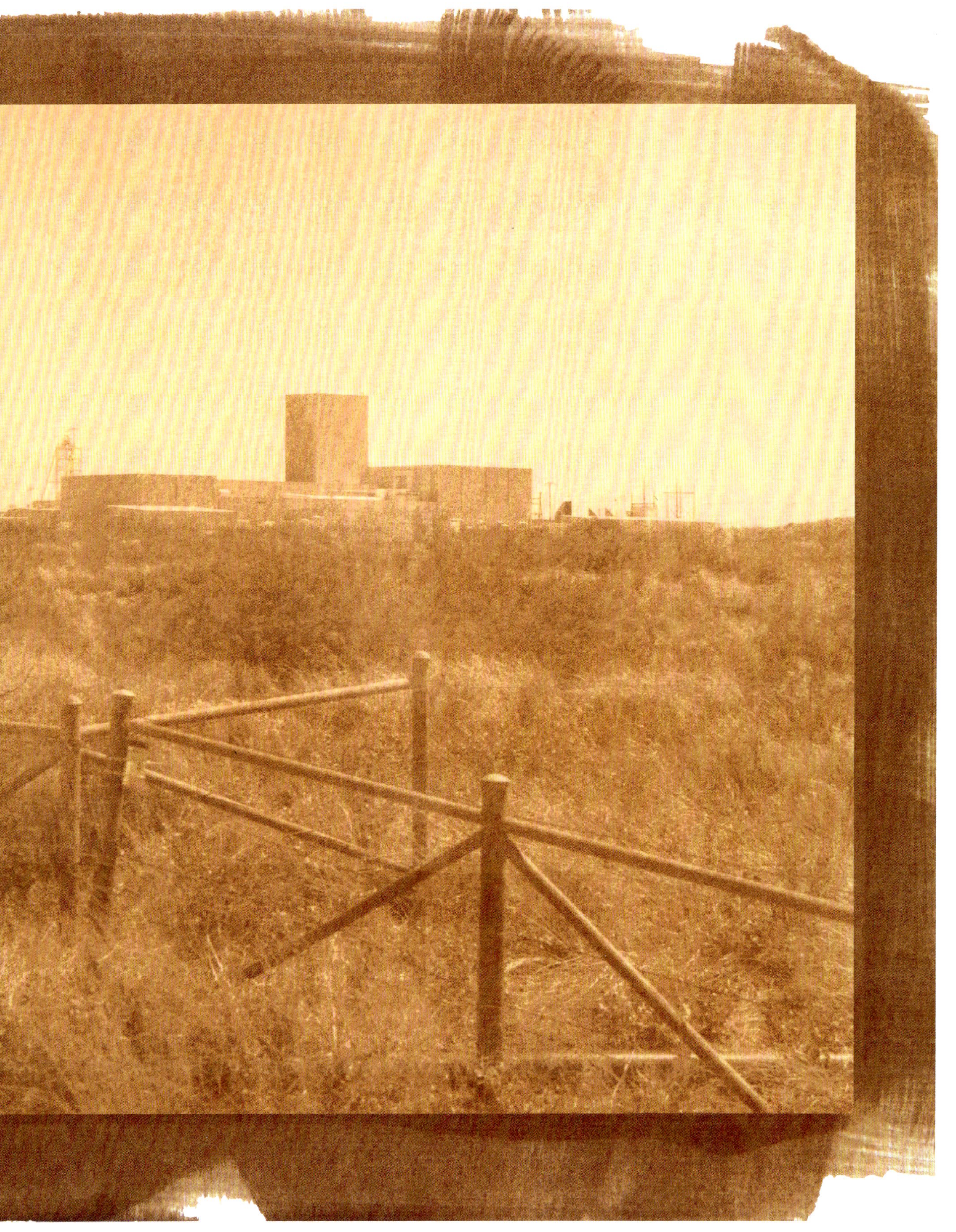

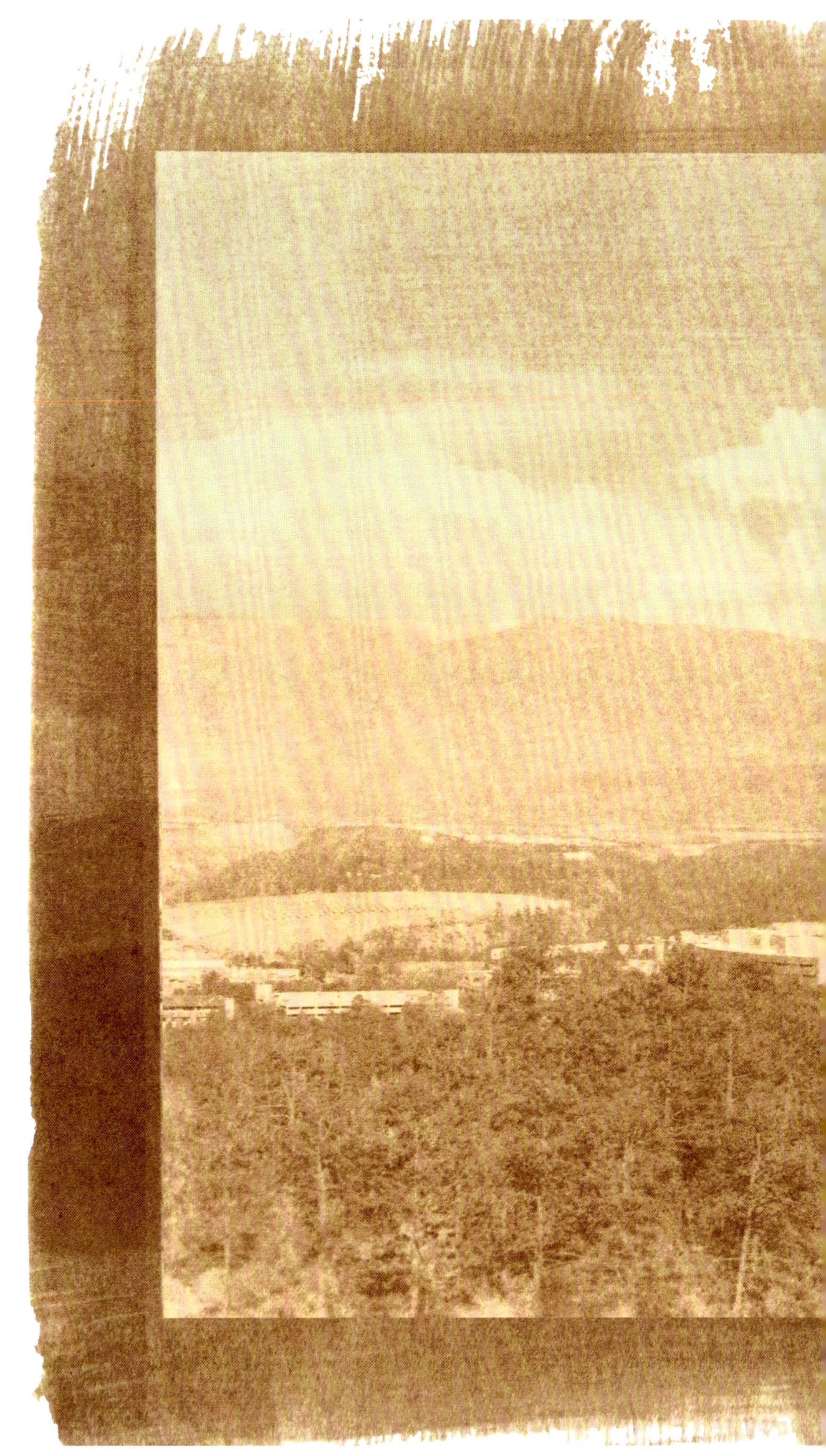

**Los Alamos
National Laboratory,**
New Mexico.

Radioactive waste
shipped to WIPP:
2,574,261 gallons.

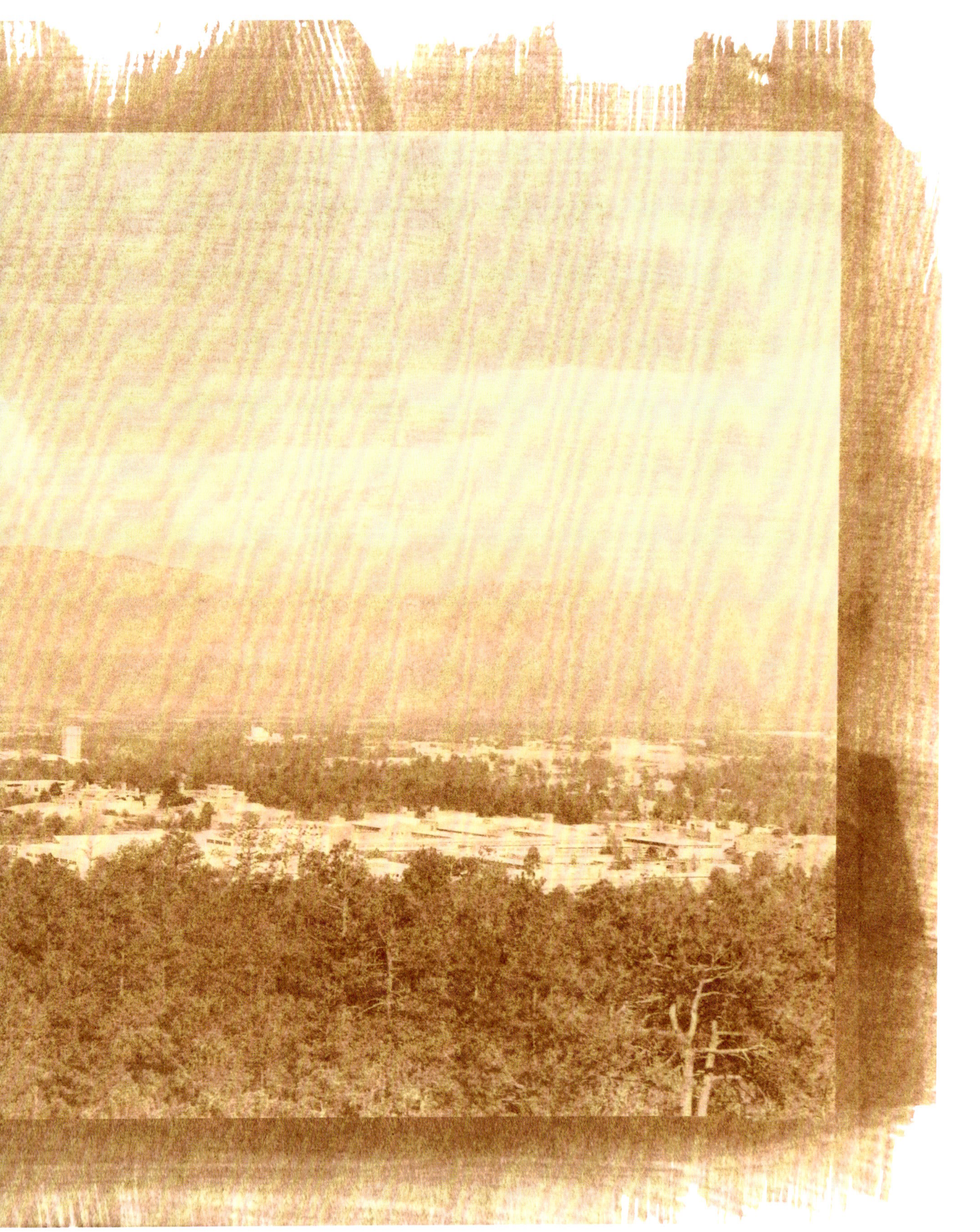

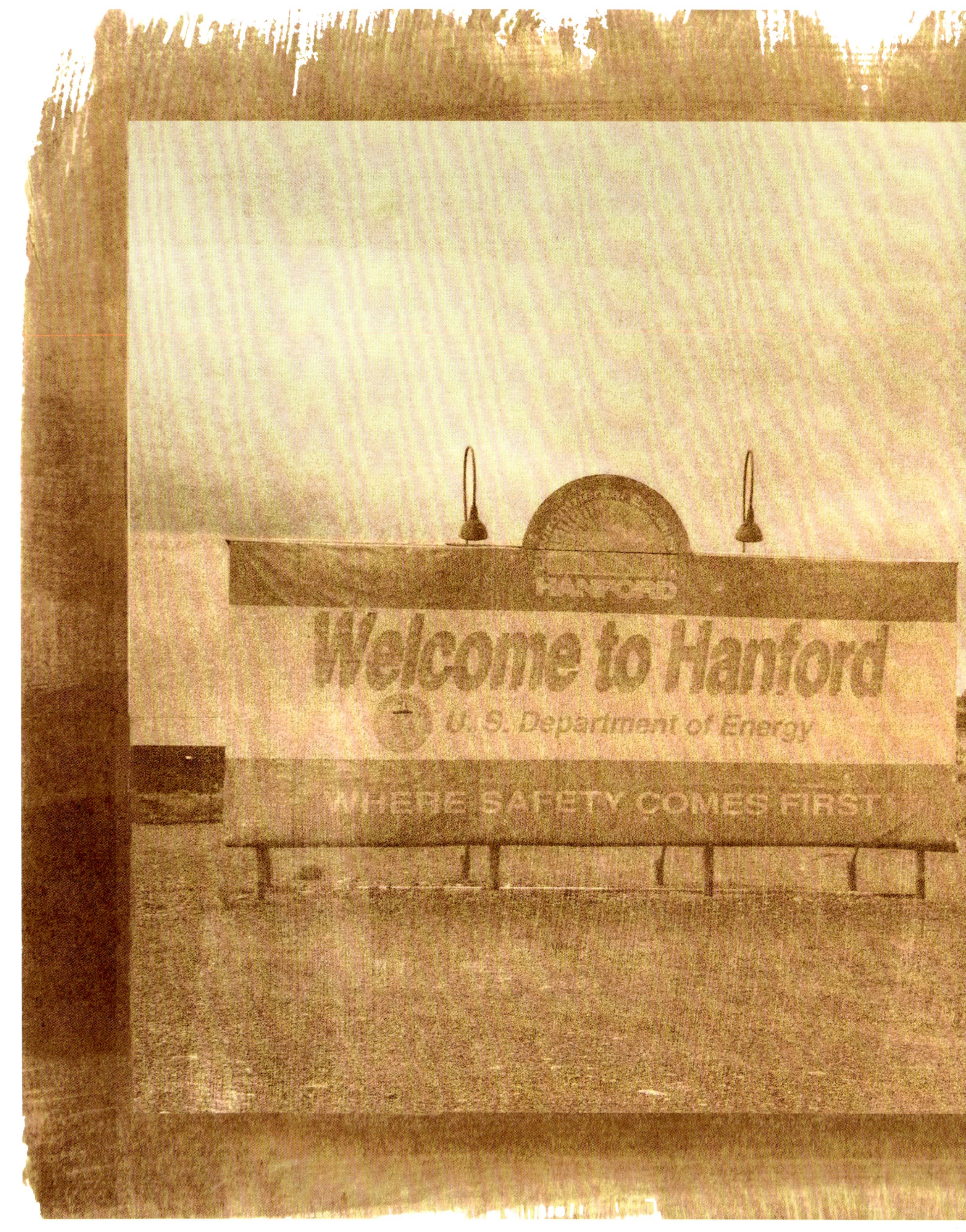
HANFORD
Welcome to Hanford
U. S. Department of Energy
WHERE SAFETY COMES FIRST

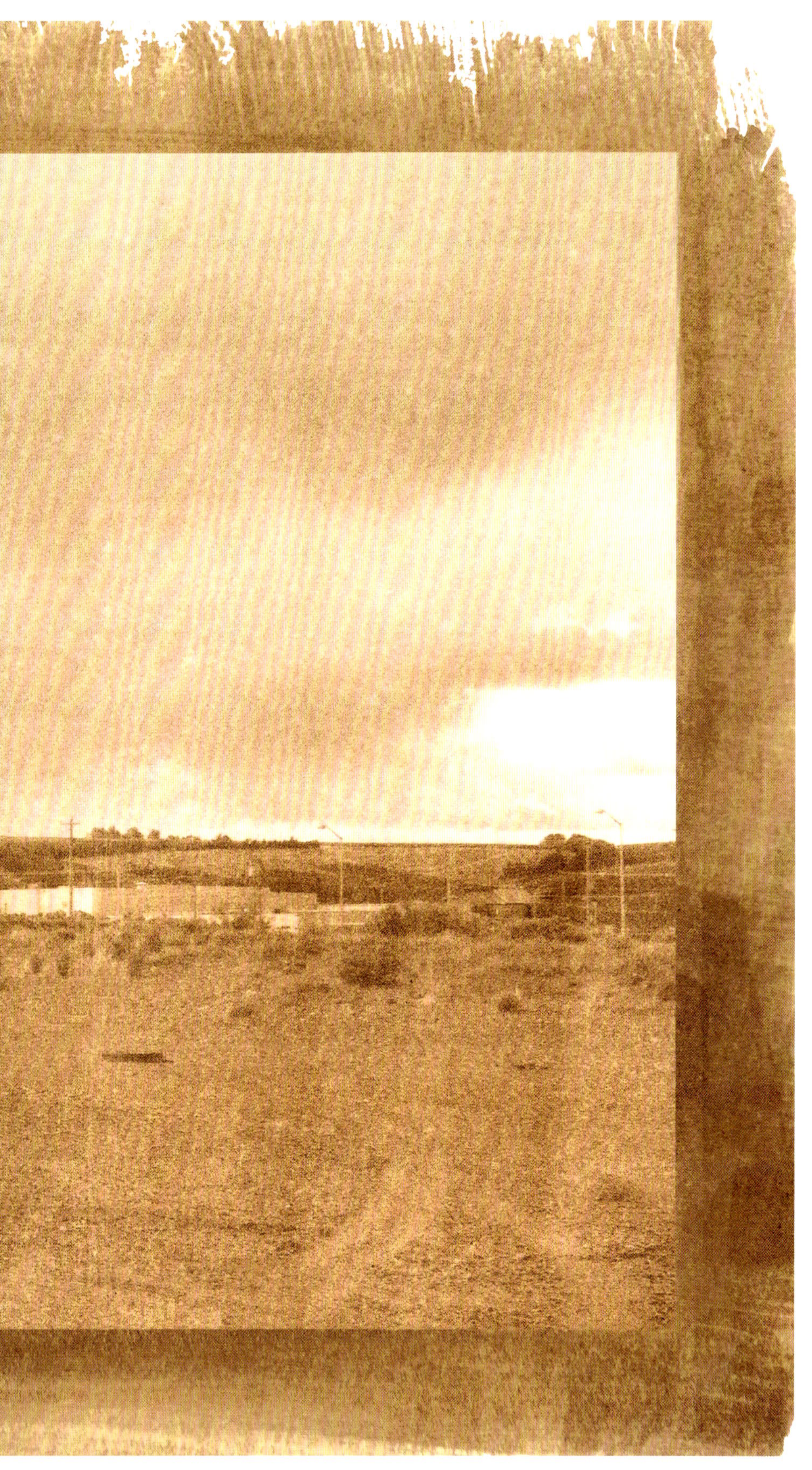

Hanford Site 2,
Hanford, Washington.

Radioactive waste shipped
to WIPP:
1,336,919 gallons.

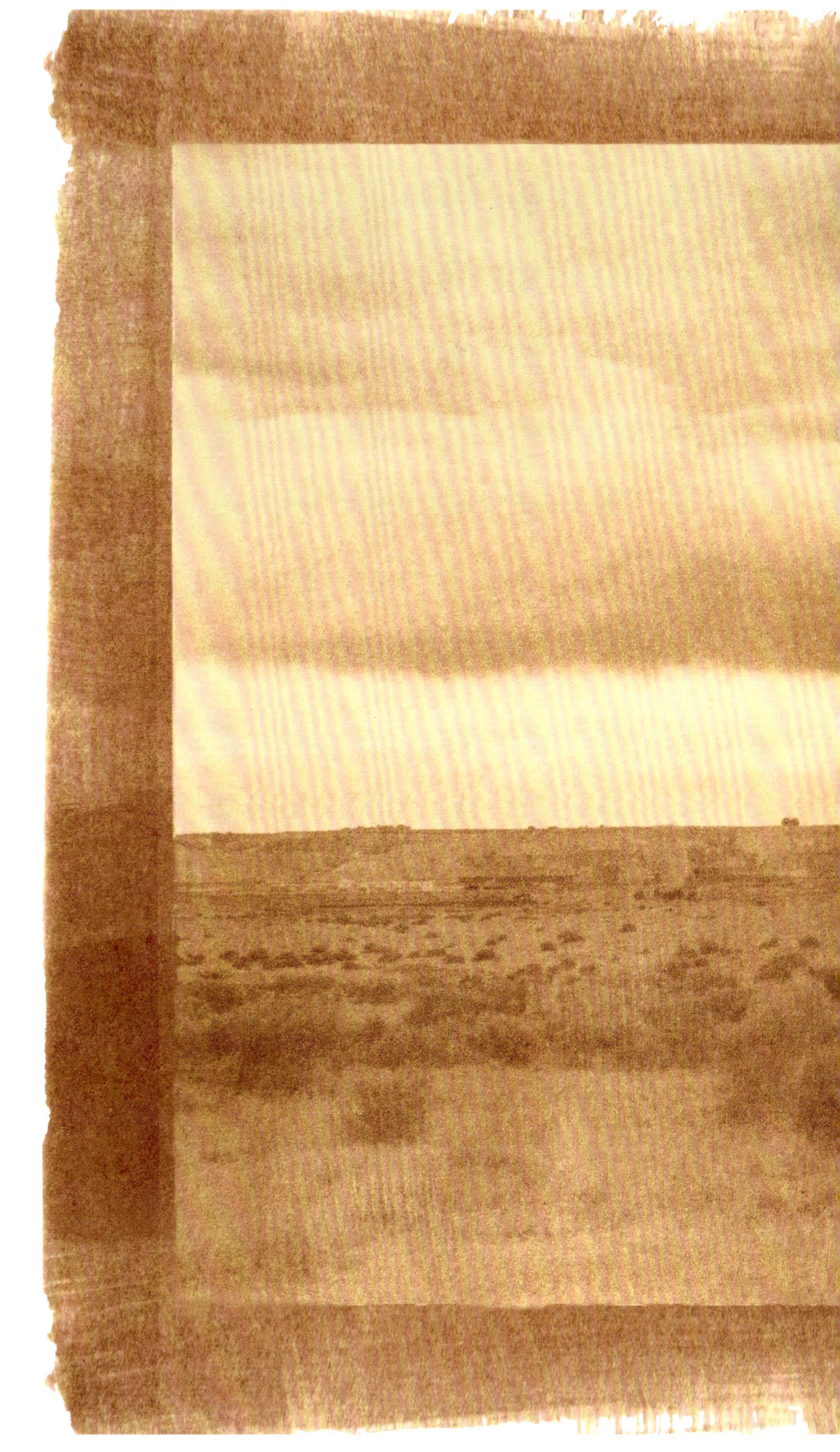

**Columbia
Generating Station,**
Hanford, Washington.

Radioactive waste
shipped to WIPP:
1,336,919 gallons.

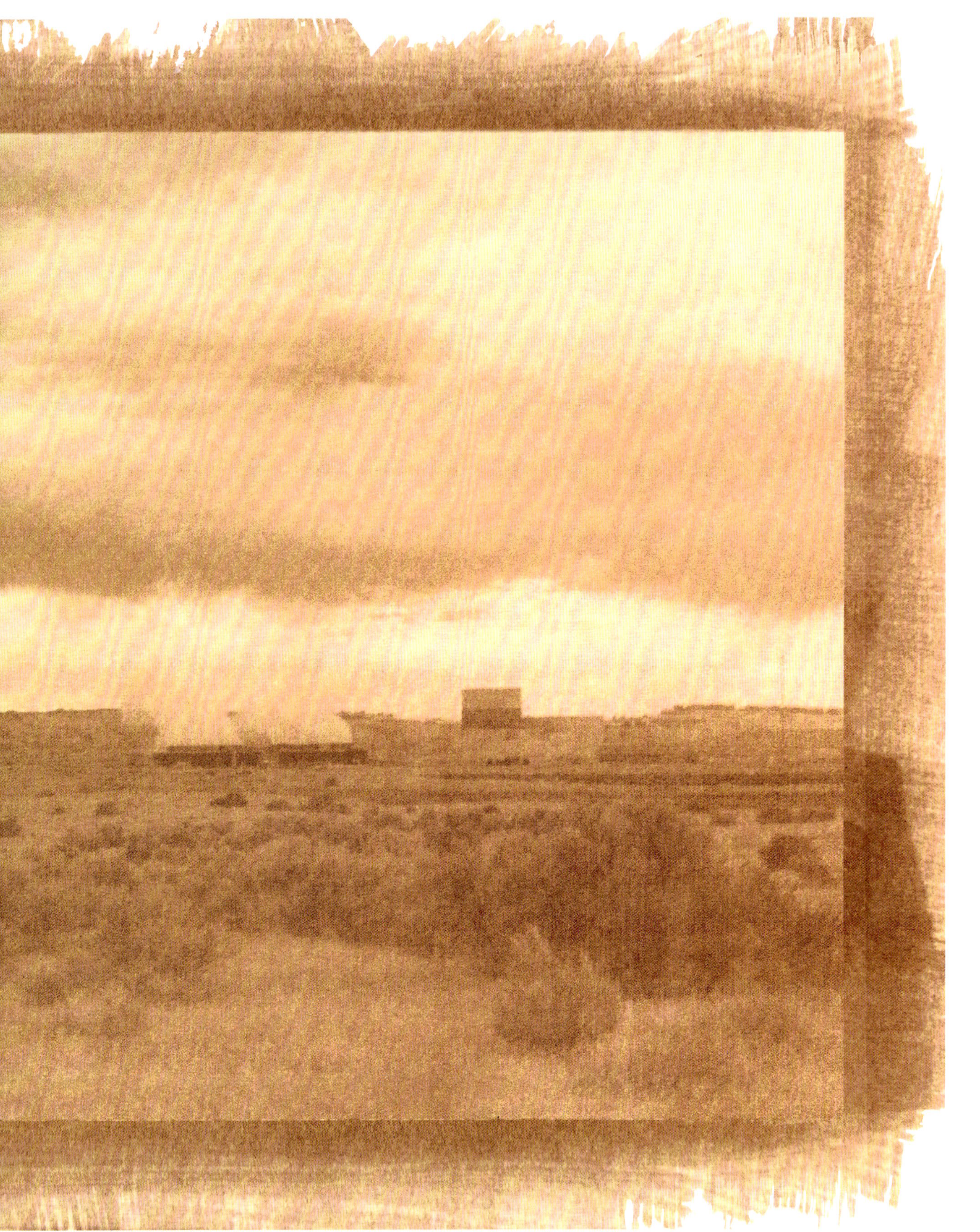

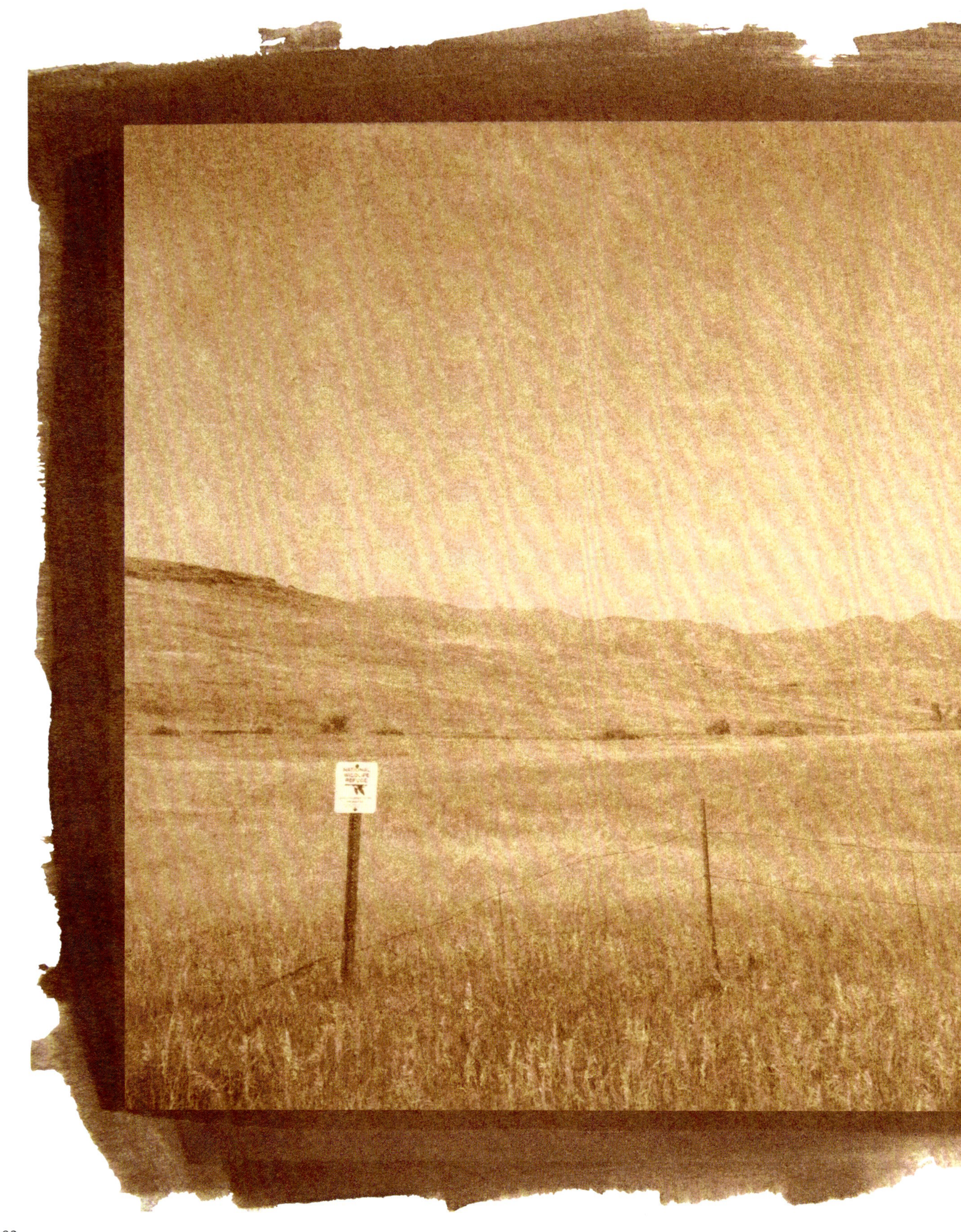

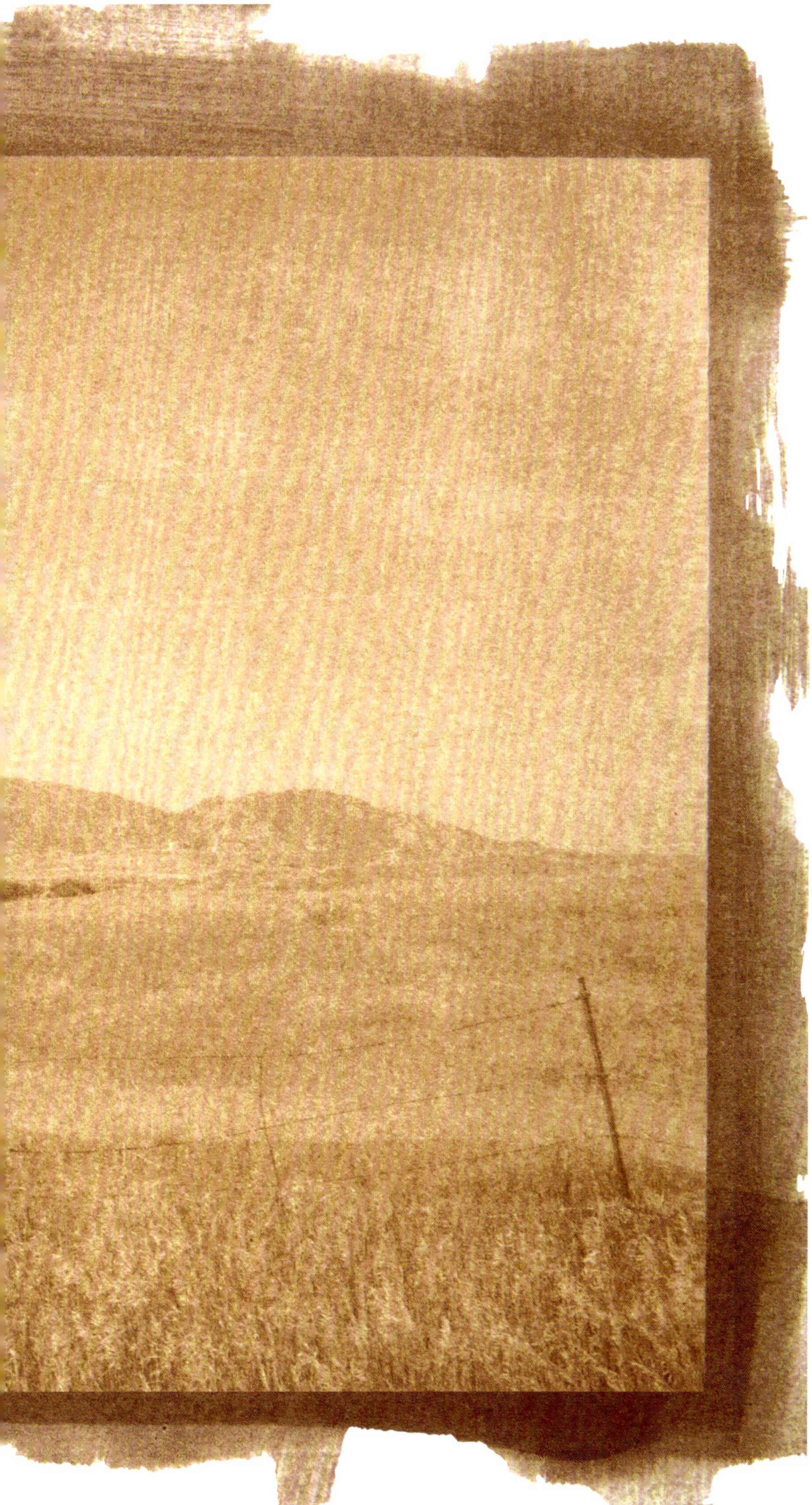

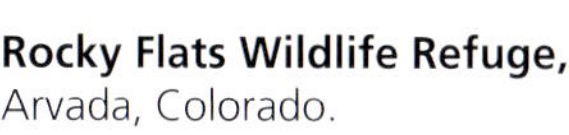

Rocky Flats Wildlife Refuge,
Arvada, Colorado.

Radioactive waste shipped
to WIPP:
3,978,943 gallons.

Hanford Site 1,
Hanford, Washington.

Radioactive waste
shipped to WIPP:
1,336,919 gallons.

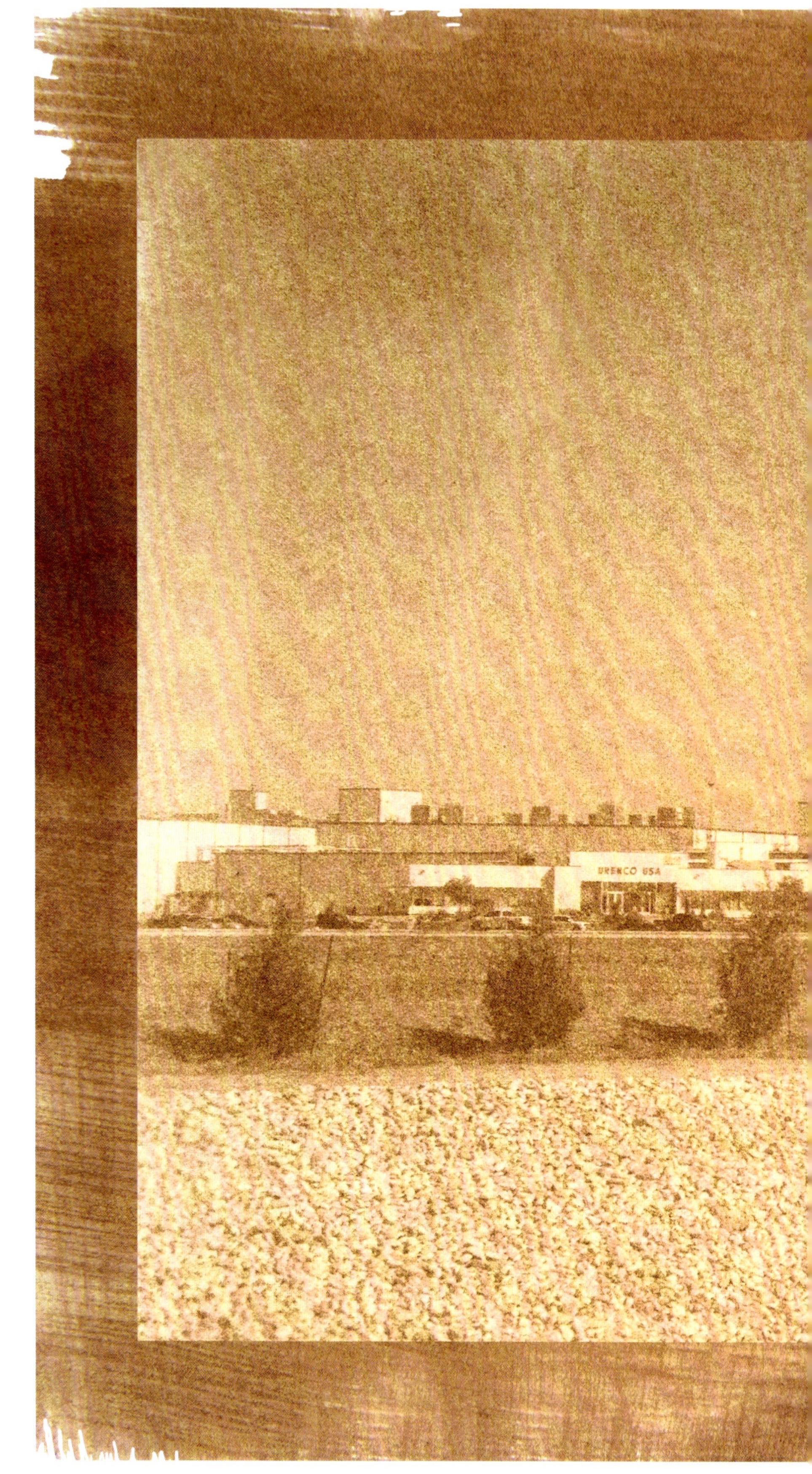

**Urenco Uranium
Enrichment Plant,**
Eunice, New Mexico.

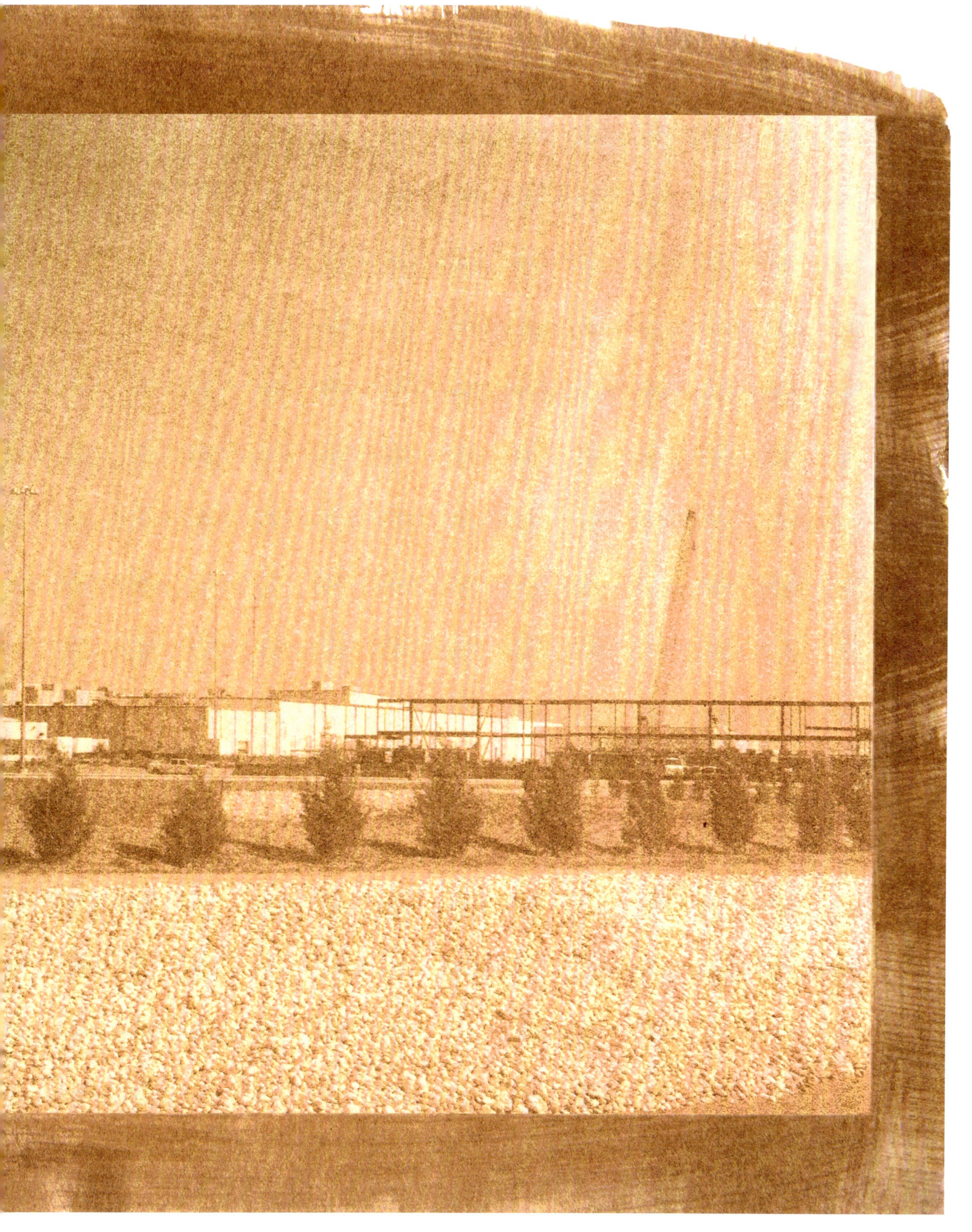

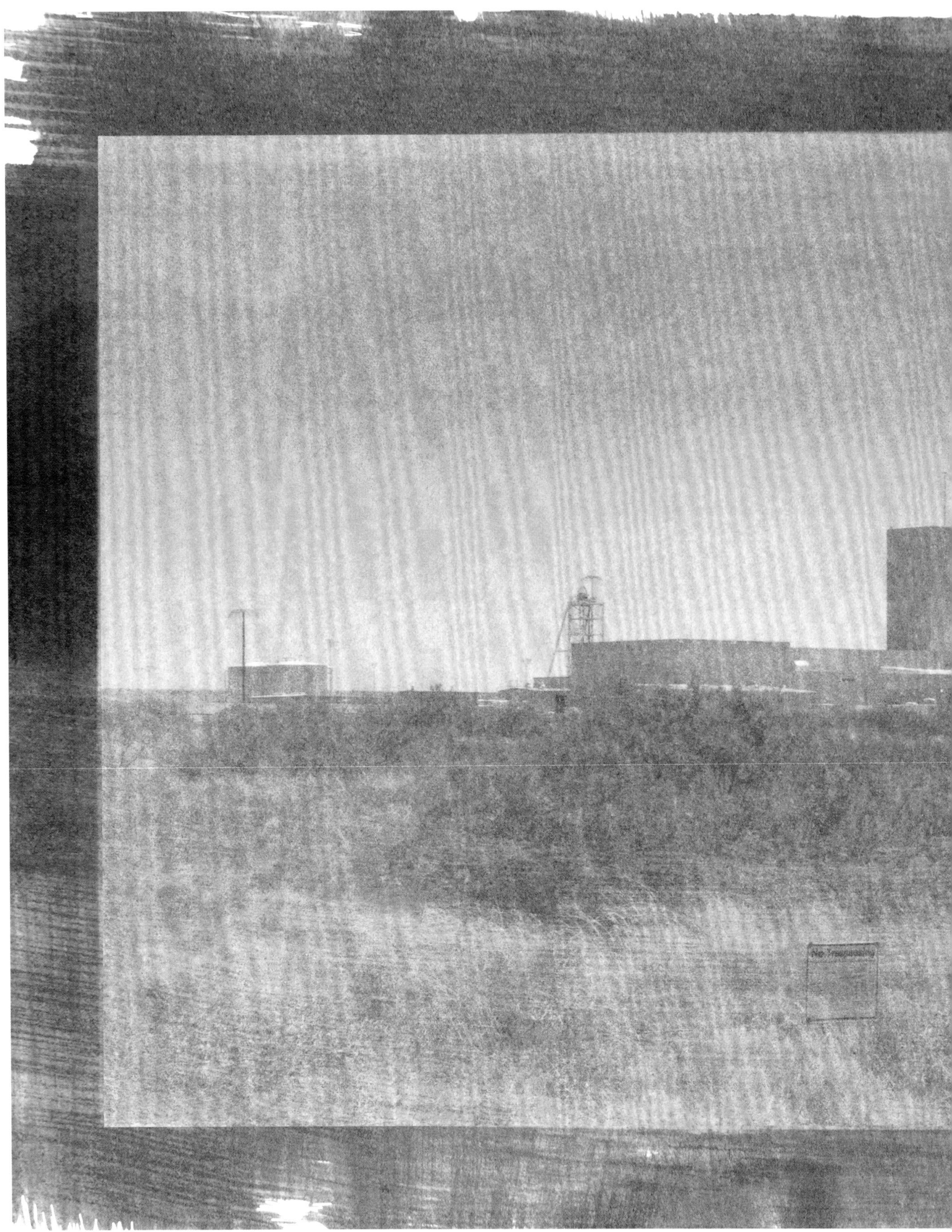
No Trespassing

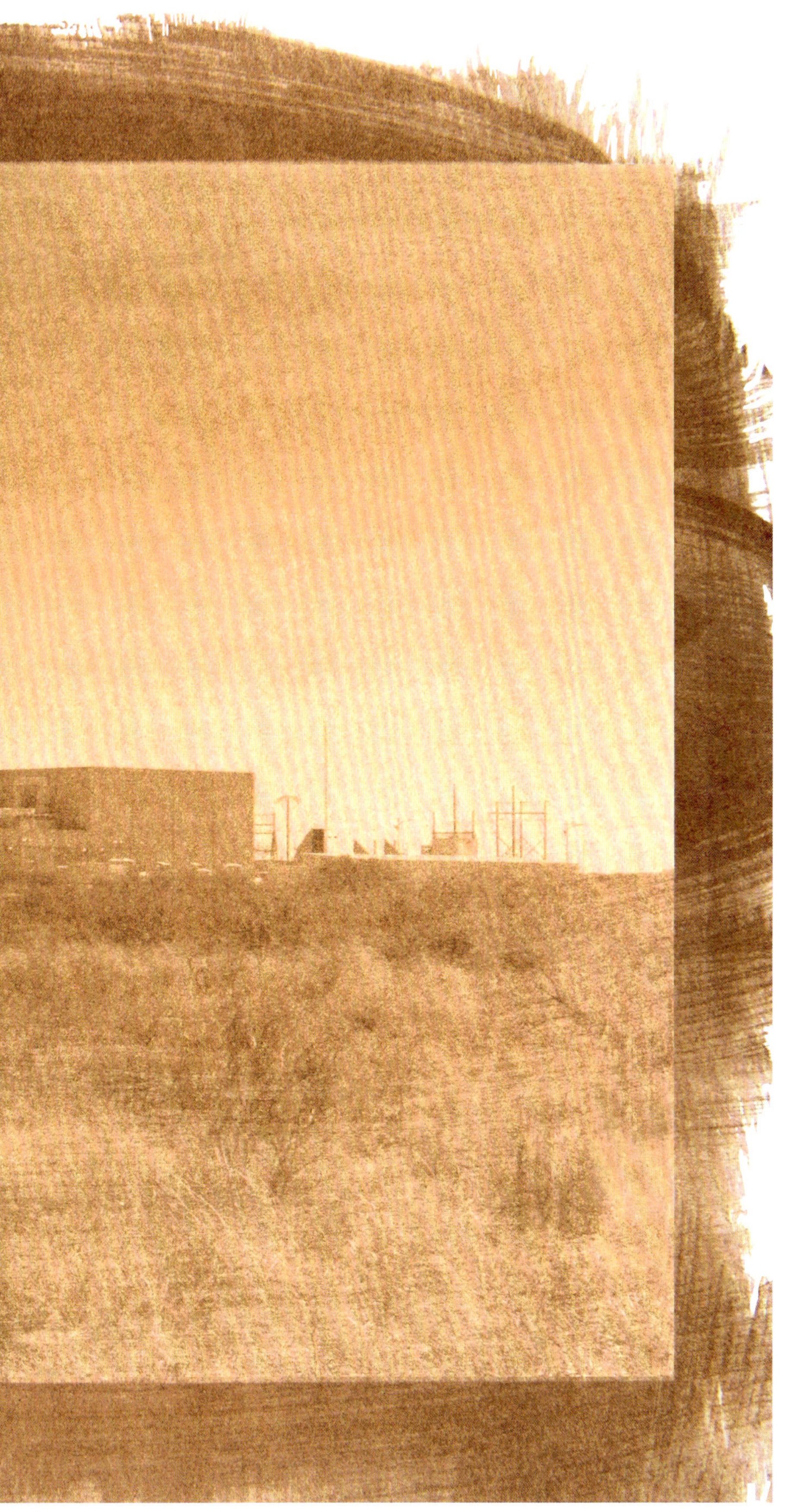

Waste Isolation Pilot Plant 1,
Carlsbad, New Mexico.

Amount of waste
emplaced to date:
25,857,295 gallons.

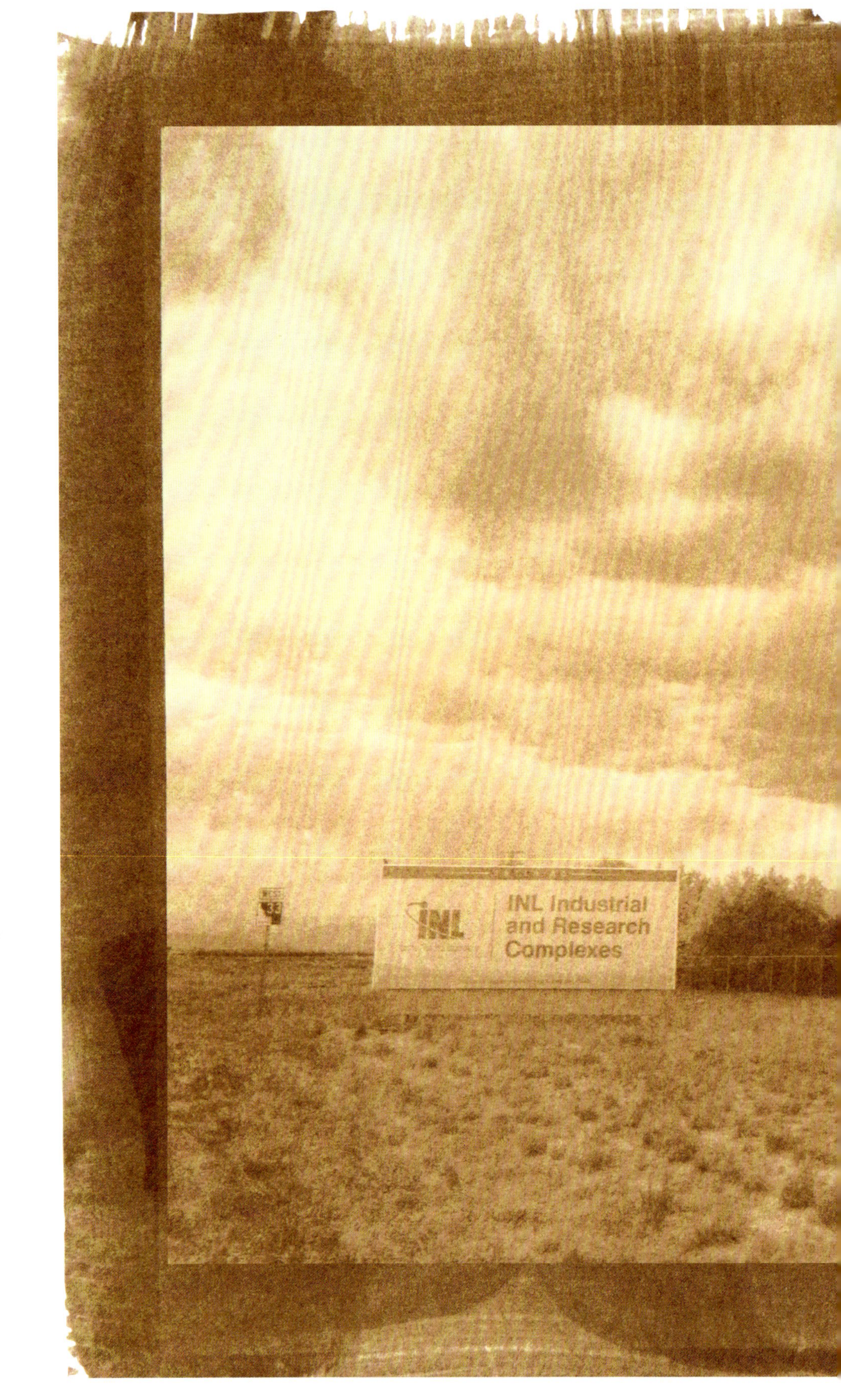

Idaho National Labs,
Idaho Falls, Idaho.

Radioactive waste
shipped to WIPP:
12,721,416 gallons.

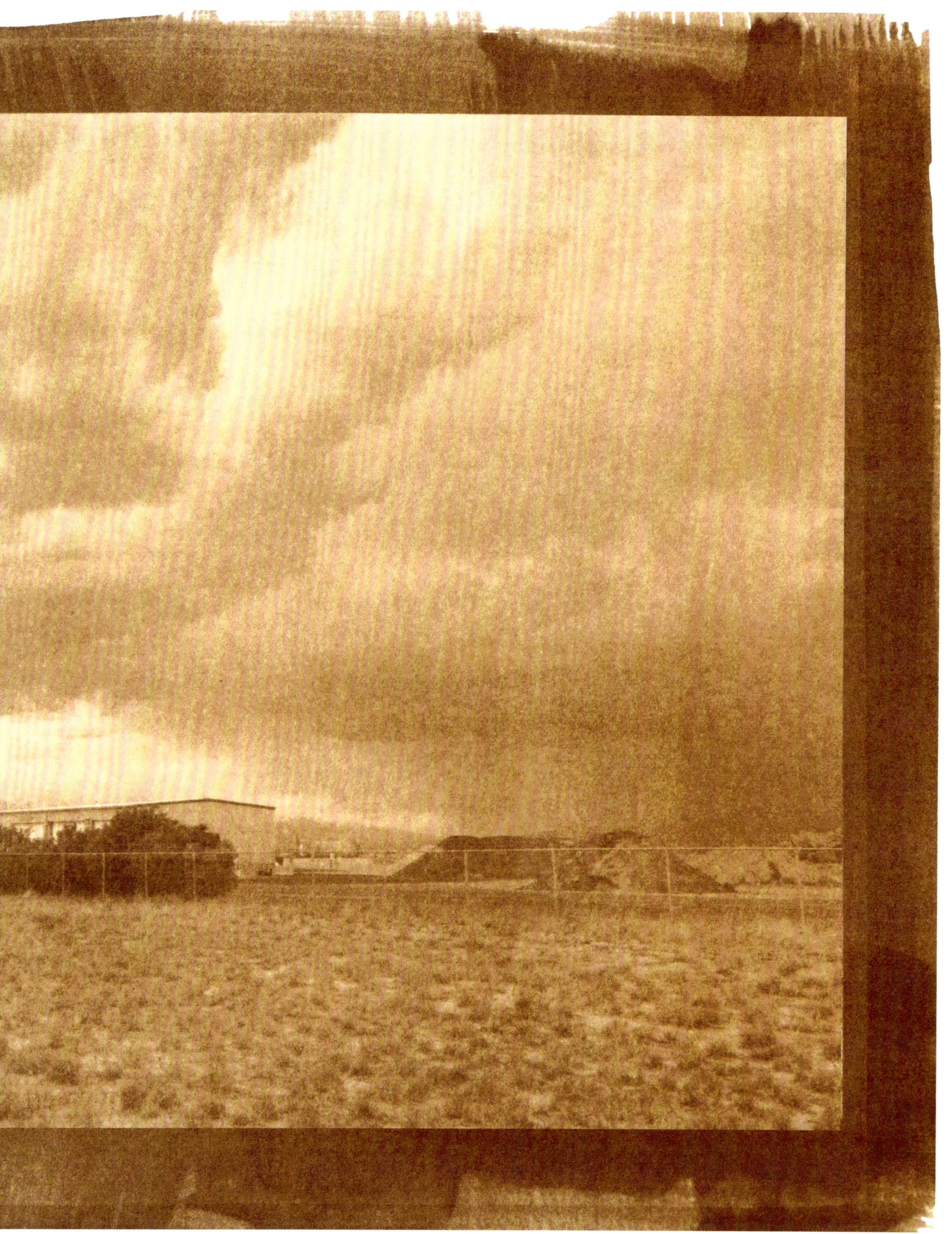

PART

VI

SCARS ON THE LANDSCAPE

*archival pigment prints and stills
from video, 2012*

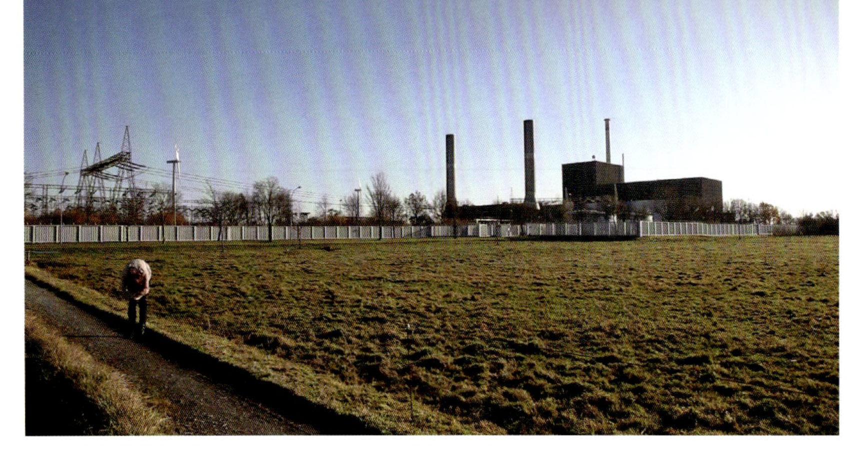

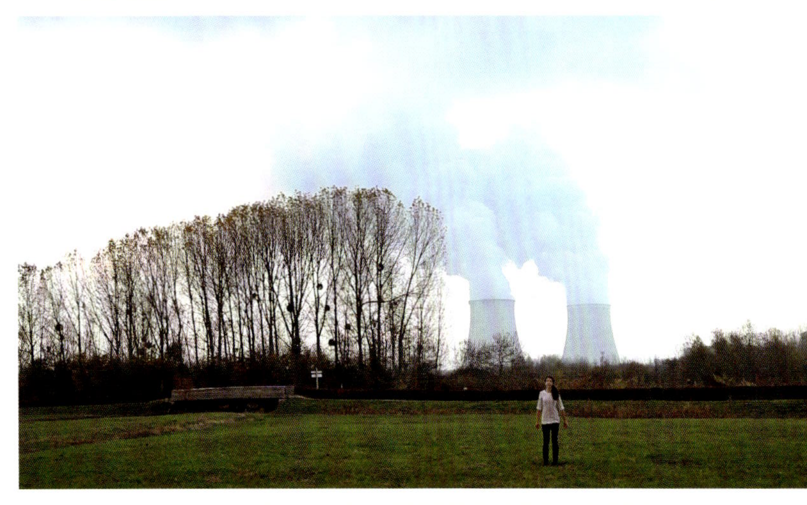

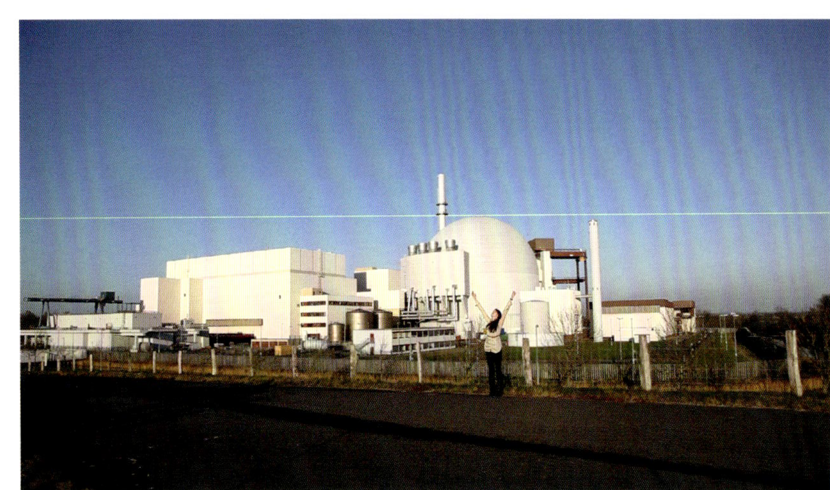

*Scars on the
Landscape,*
stills from video,
dimensions
variable, 00:48
seconds (silent)

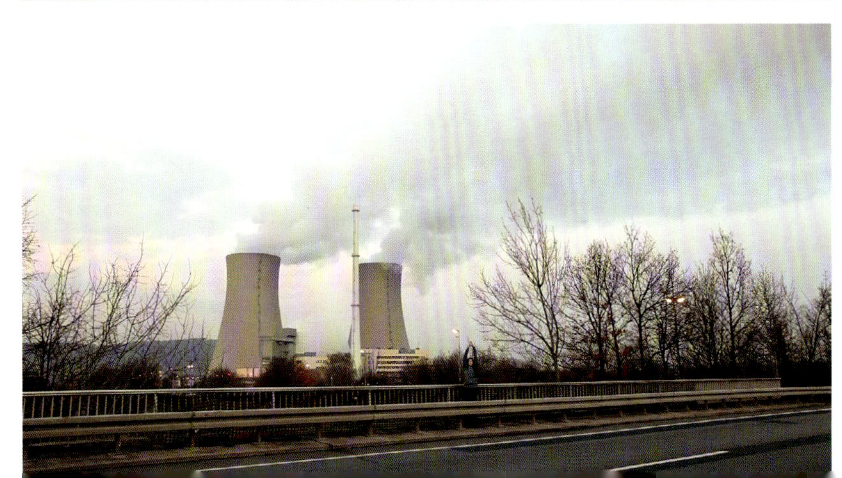

SCARS ON THE LANDSCAPE

Following the 2011 tsunami and nuclear meltdown in Fukushima, Japan, public outcry in Germany immediately resulted in the closure of eight German nuclear plants with all remaining nuclear facilities to be closed by 2022.[1] Outside of Japan, no other country responded to the Fukushima disaster as dramatically as Germany. Conversely, the neighboring country France continues to be the most nuclear energy-dependent nation in the world.[2] In 2012, I traveled by train for two weeks to active and decommissioned nuclear power facilities throughout Germany and France. Using my body in a performance-like gesture, I created a mark in time in the landscape surrounding the building as it was active or in flux between active and abandoned. The massive decommissioned monuments in Germany sit in a strange state: inoperable but not dead, technologically impotent but also powerfully dangerous. They tower above the rolling hills, sit between the rivers and windy air, and rest as scars on the landscape.

Platelist:

---

1   Judy Dempsey and Jack Ewing, "Germany, in Reversal, Will Close Nuclear Plants by 2022," May 30, 2011, accessed Sept. 18, 2020, https://www.nytimes.com/2011/05/31/world/europe/31germany.html.
2   "Nuclear Share Figures, 2009–2019," World Nuclear, May 2020, https://www.world-nuclear.org/information-library/facts-and-figures/nuclear-generation-by-country.aspx.

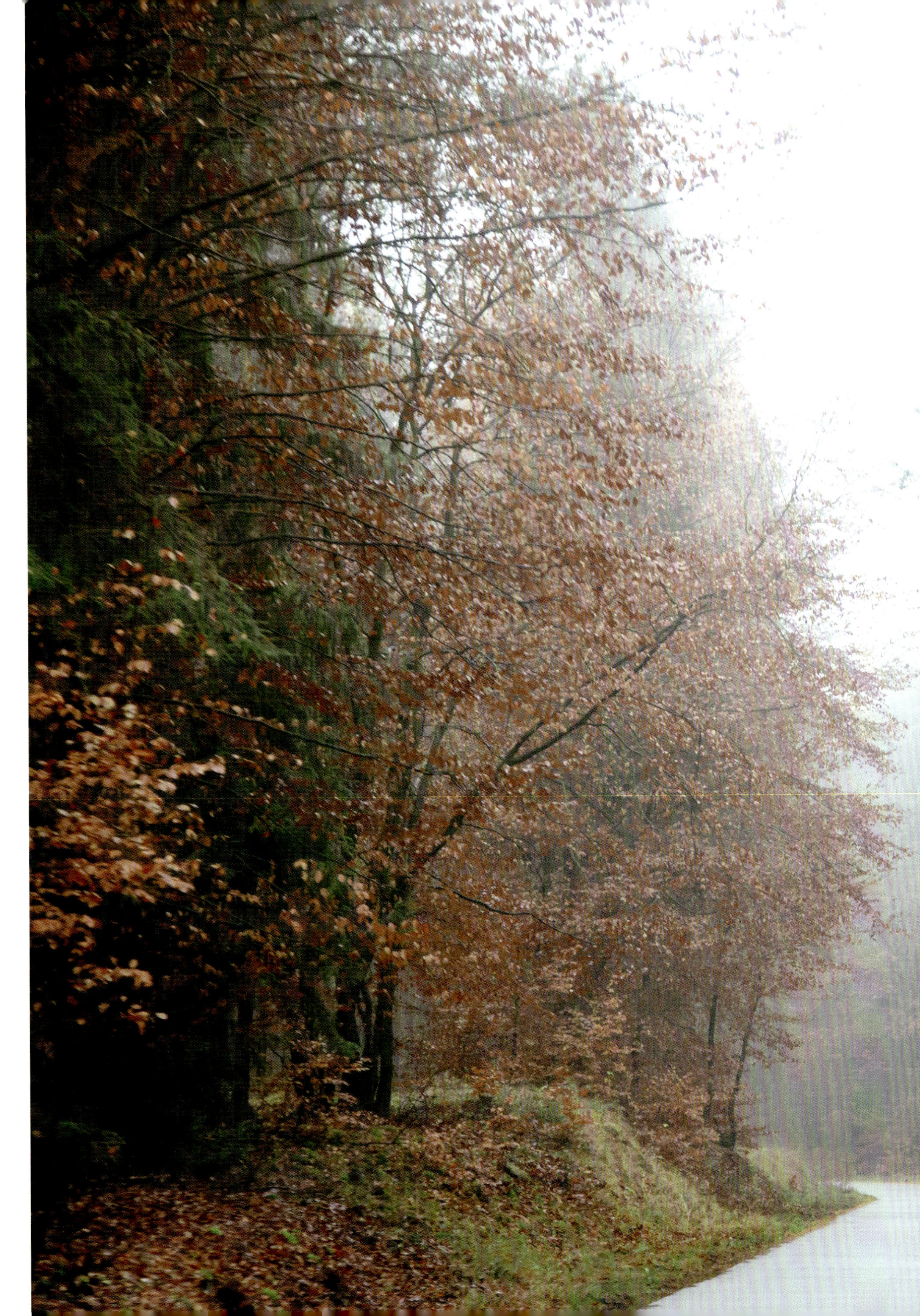

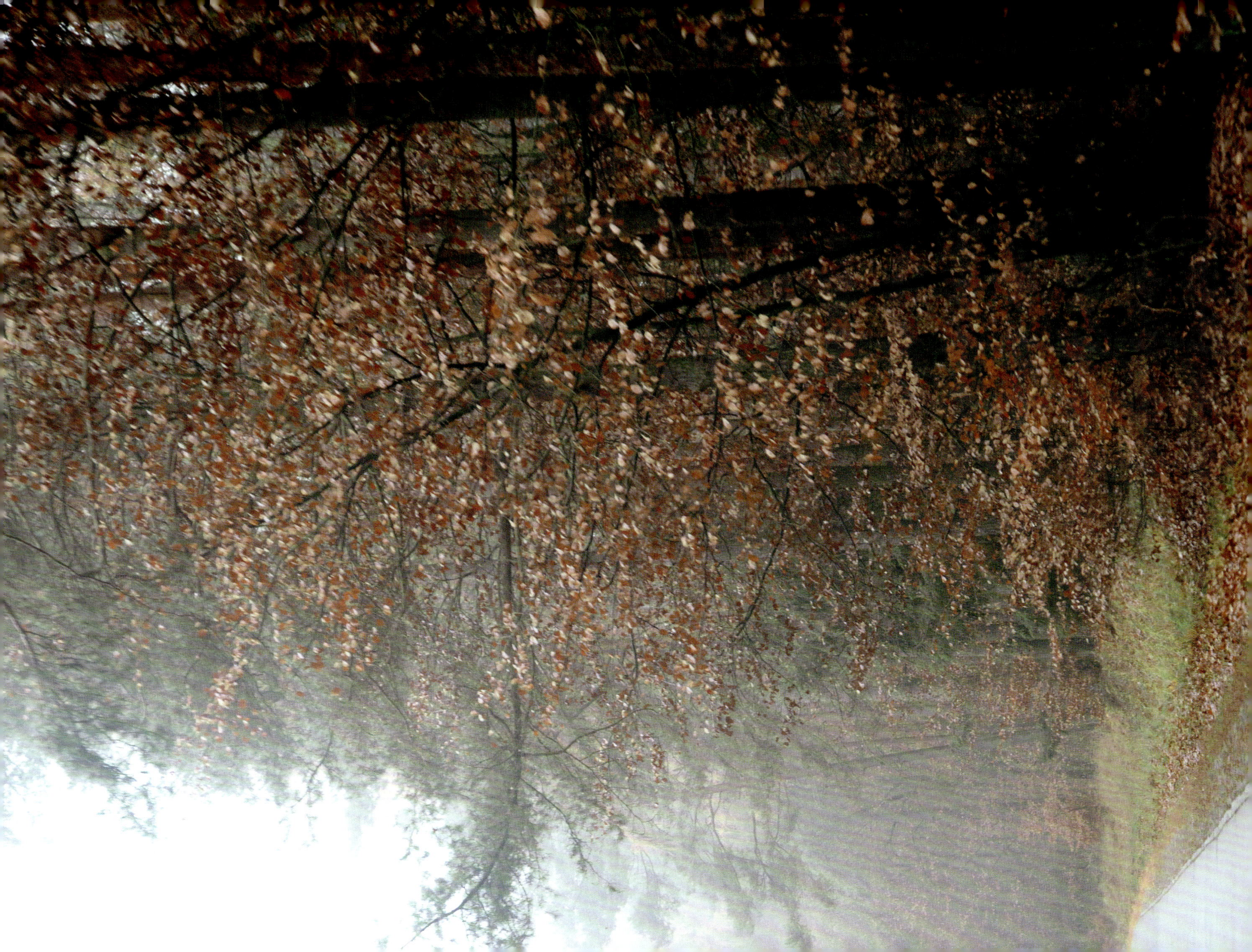

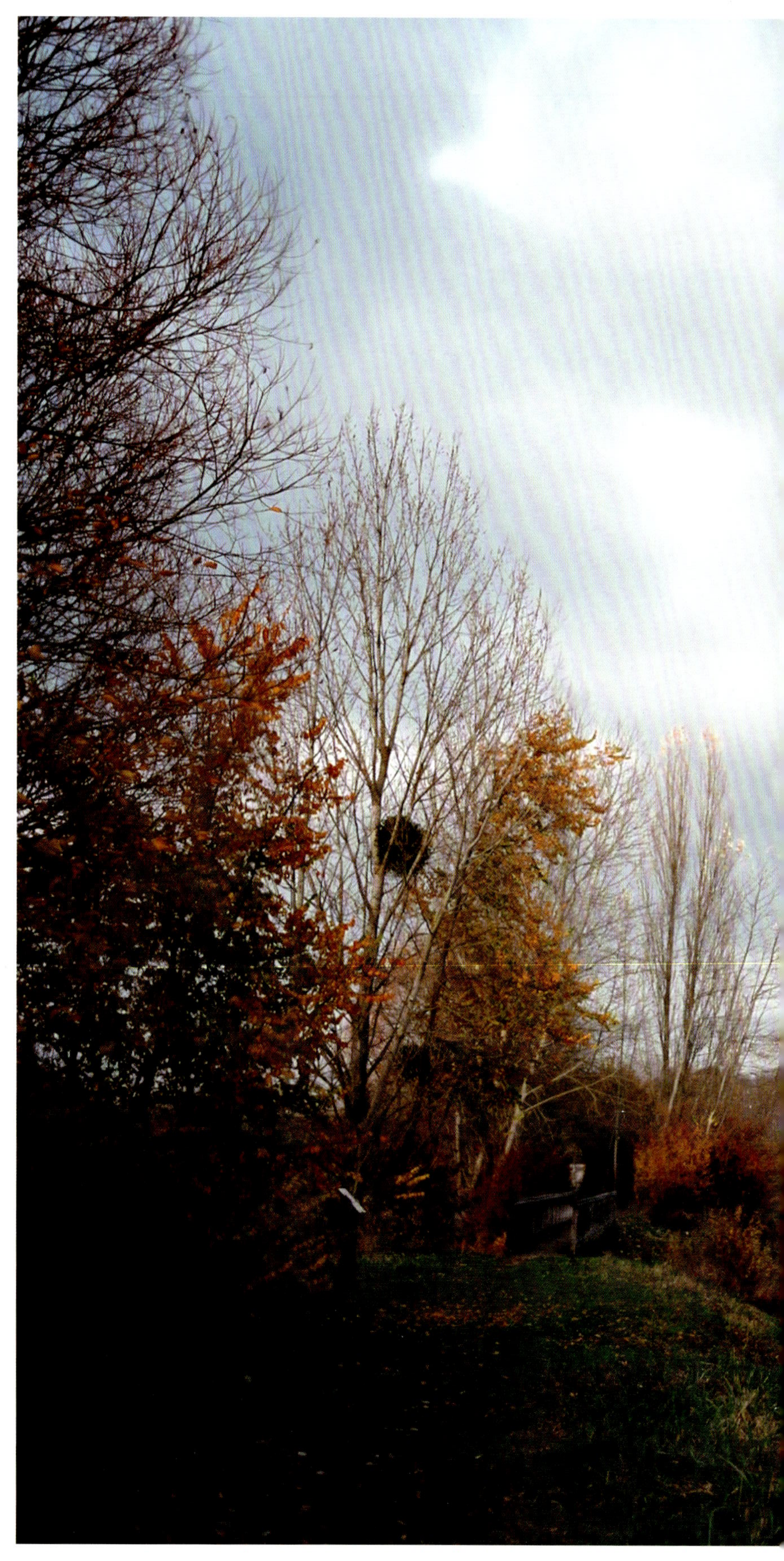

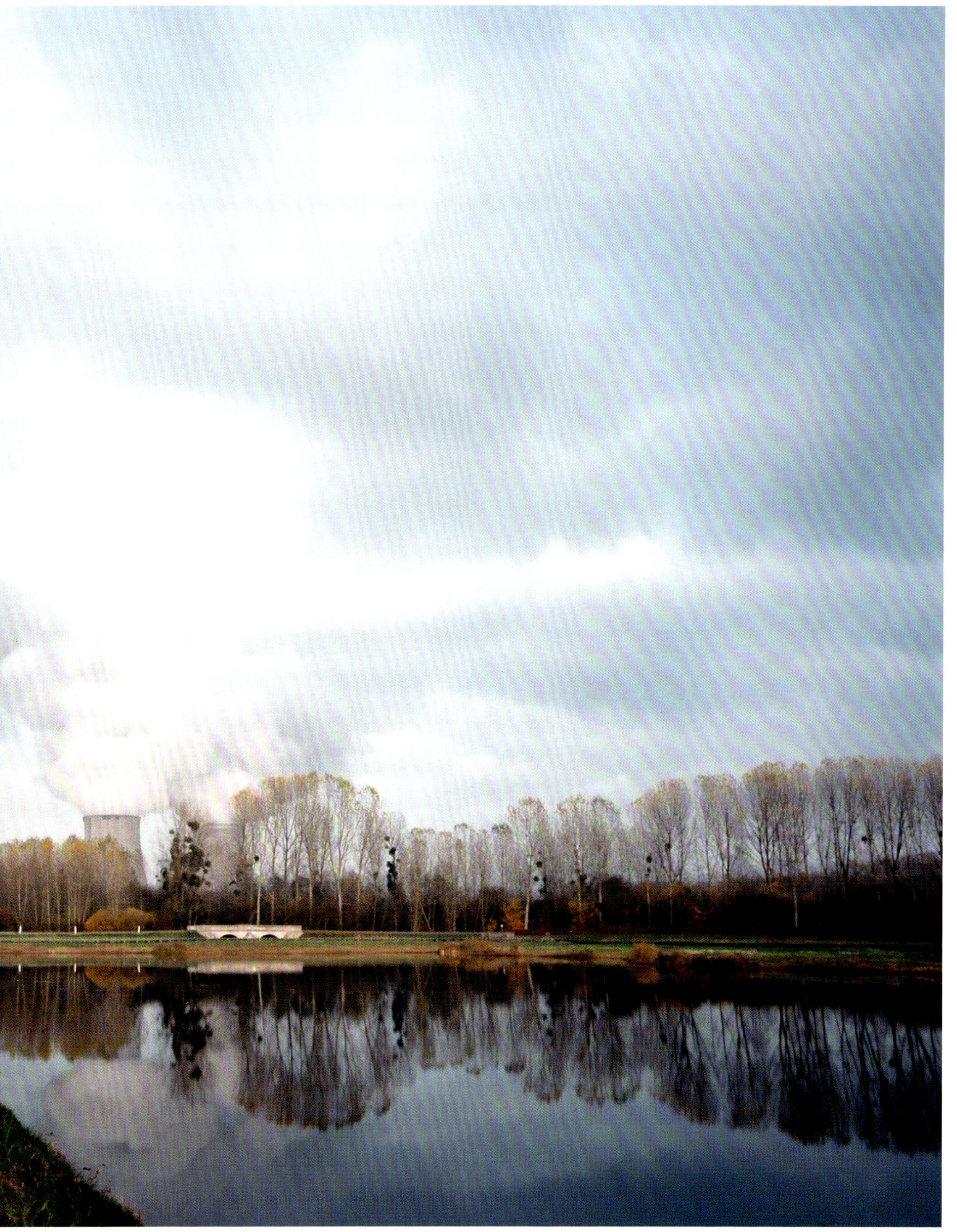

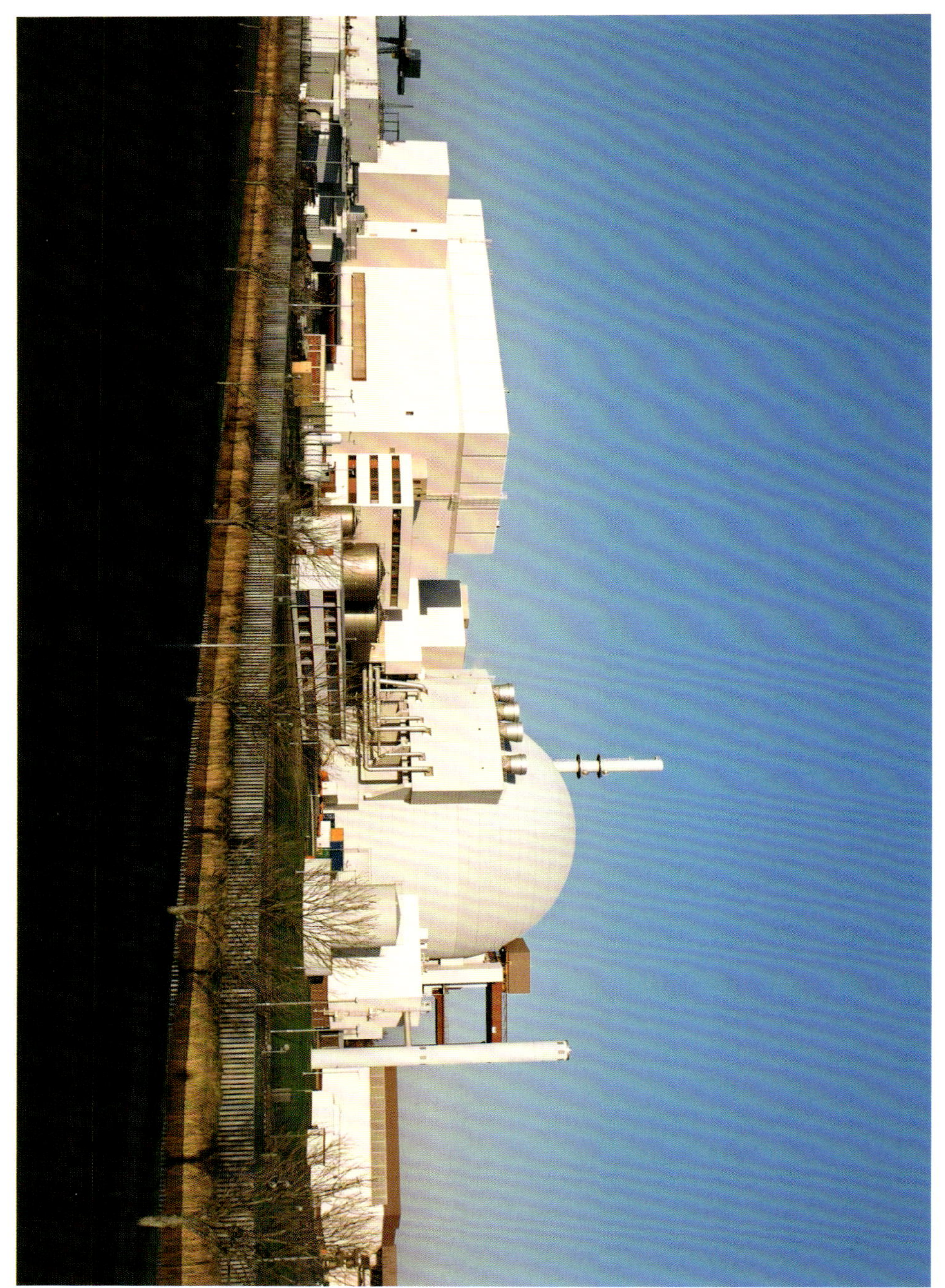

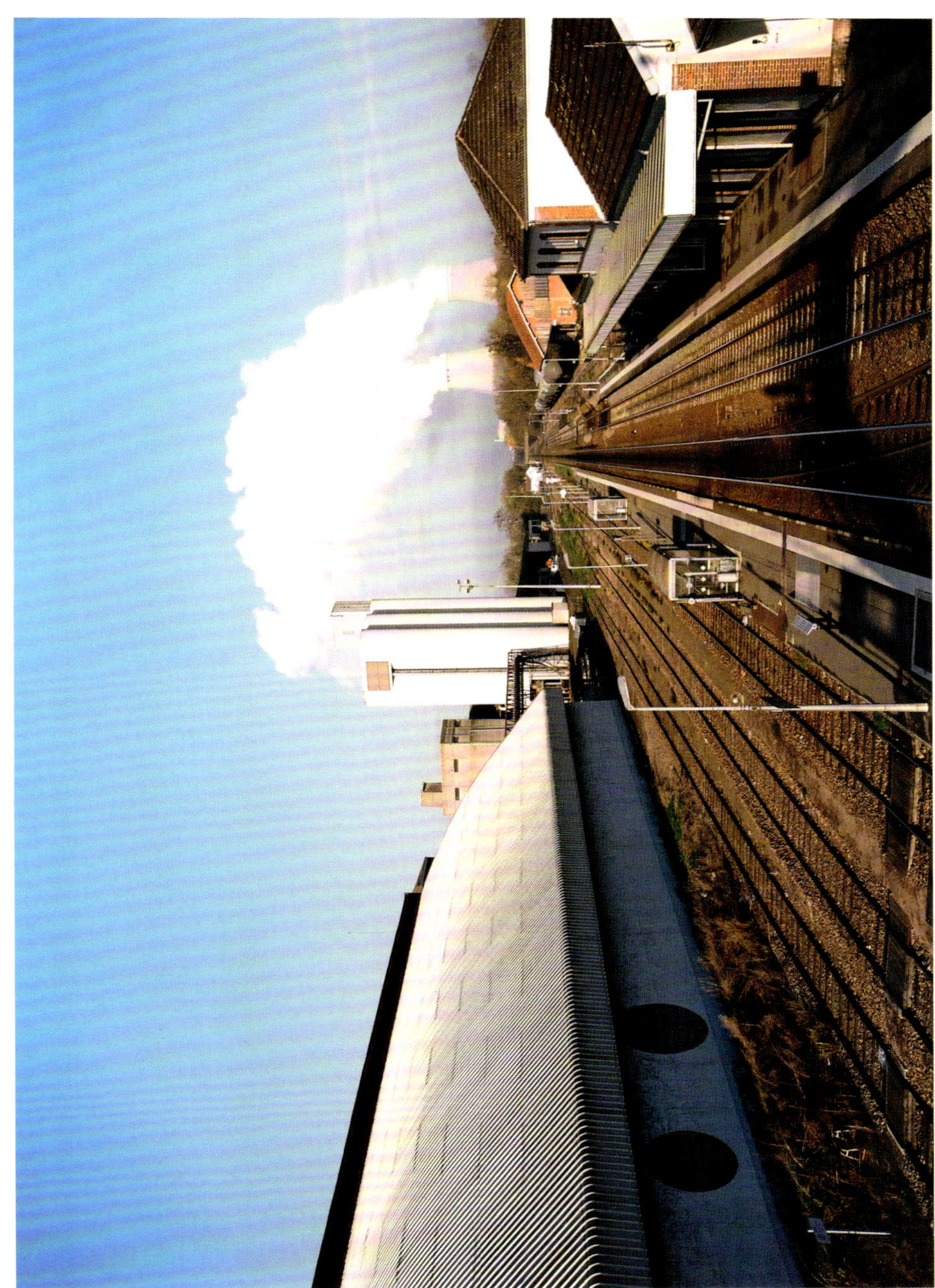

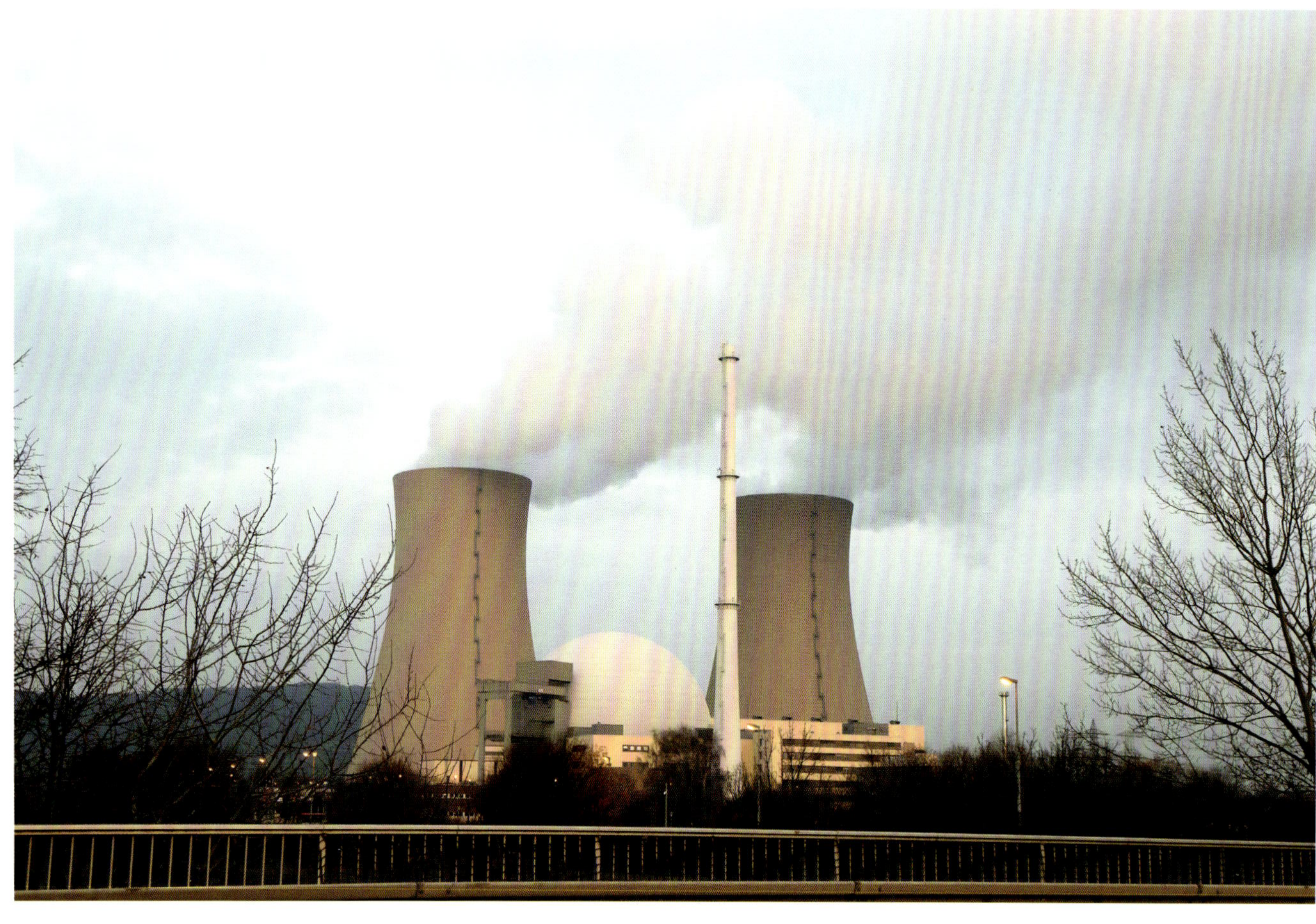

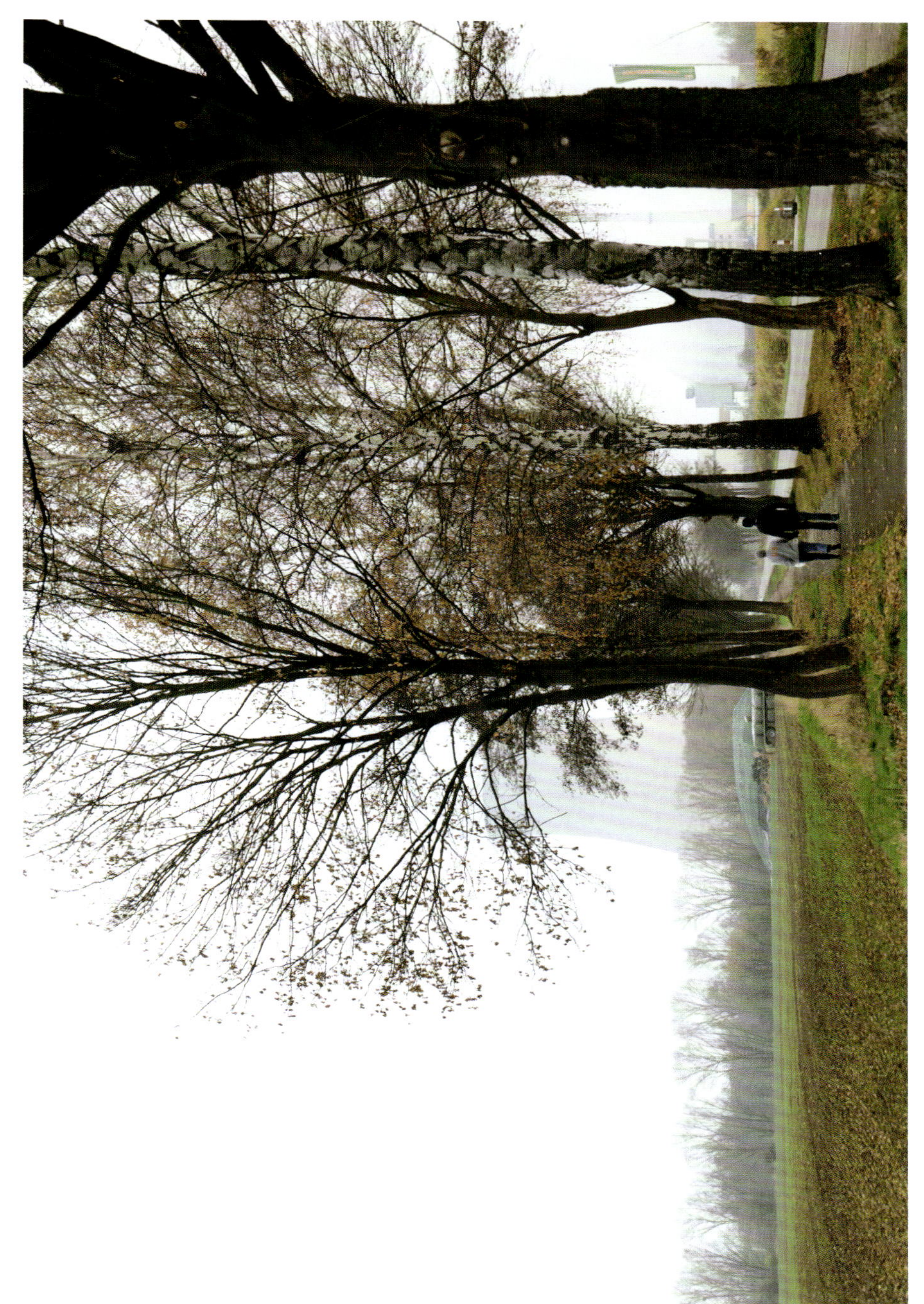

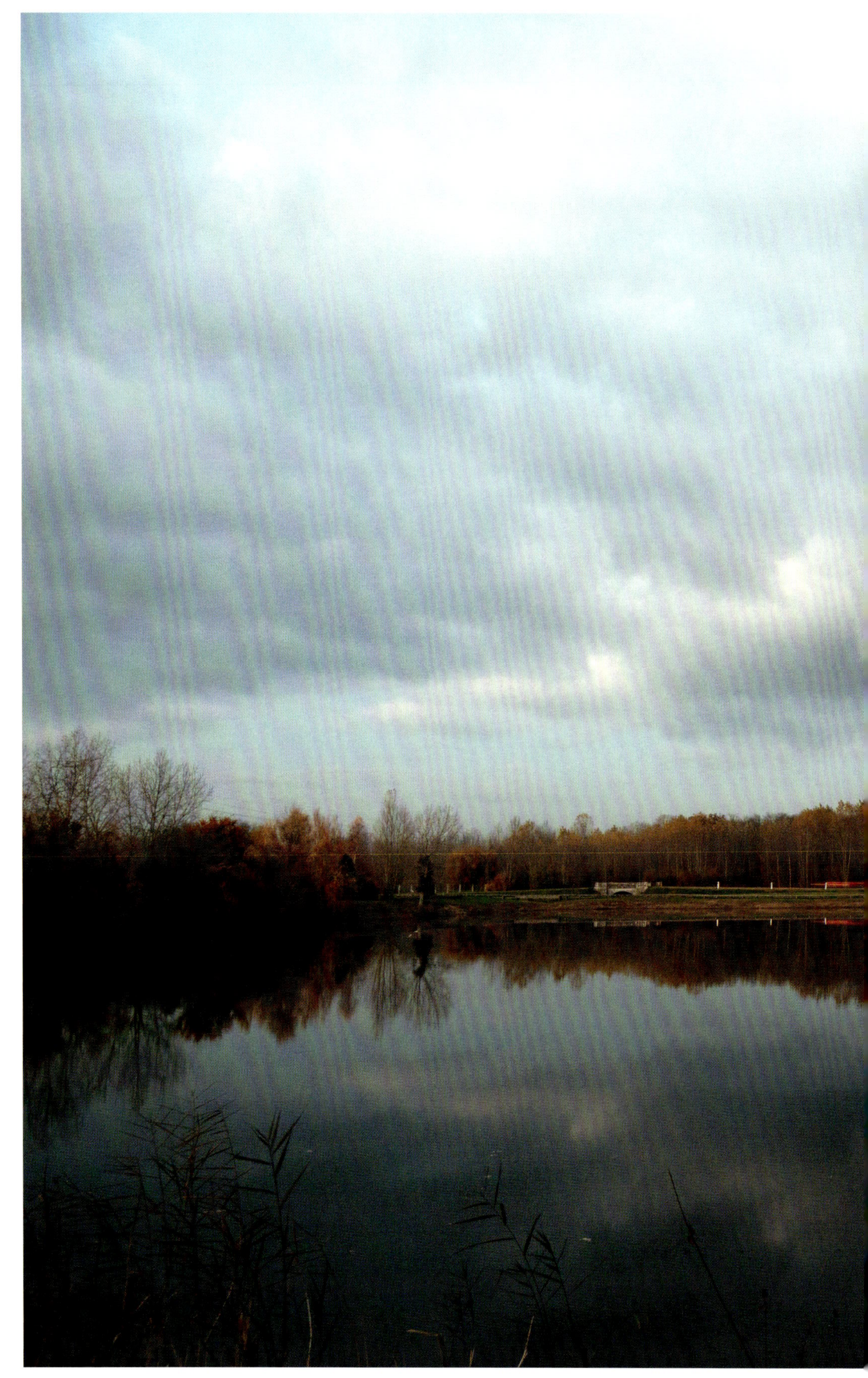

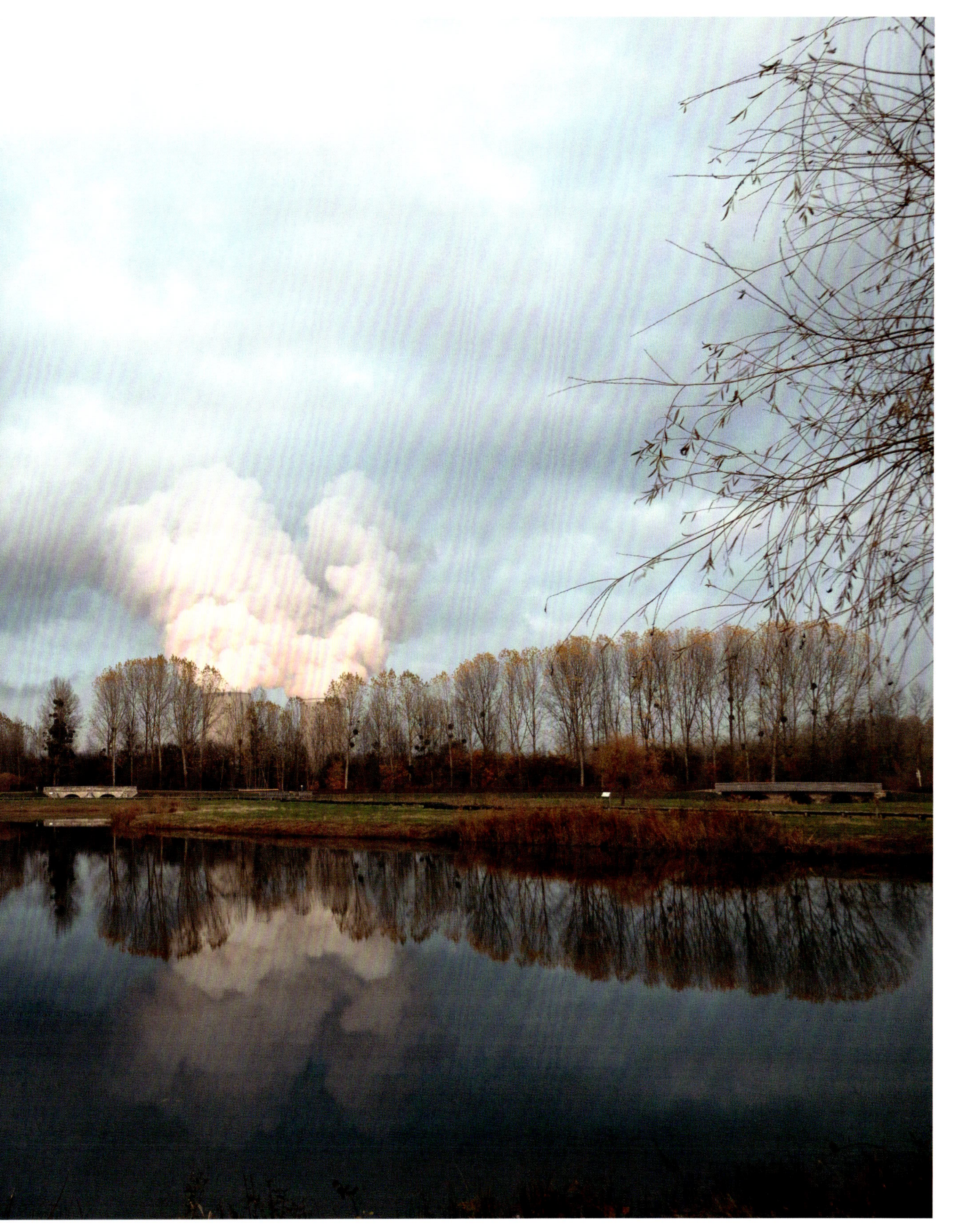

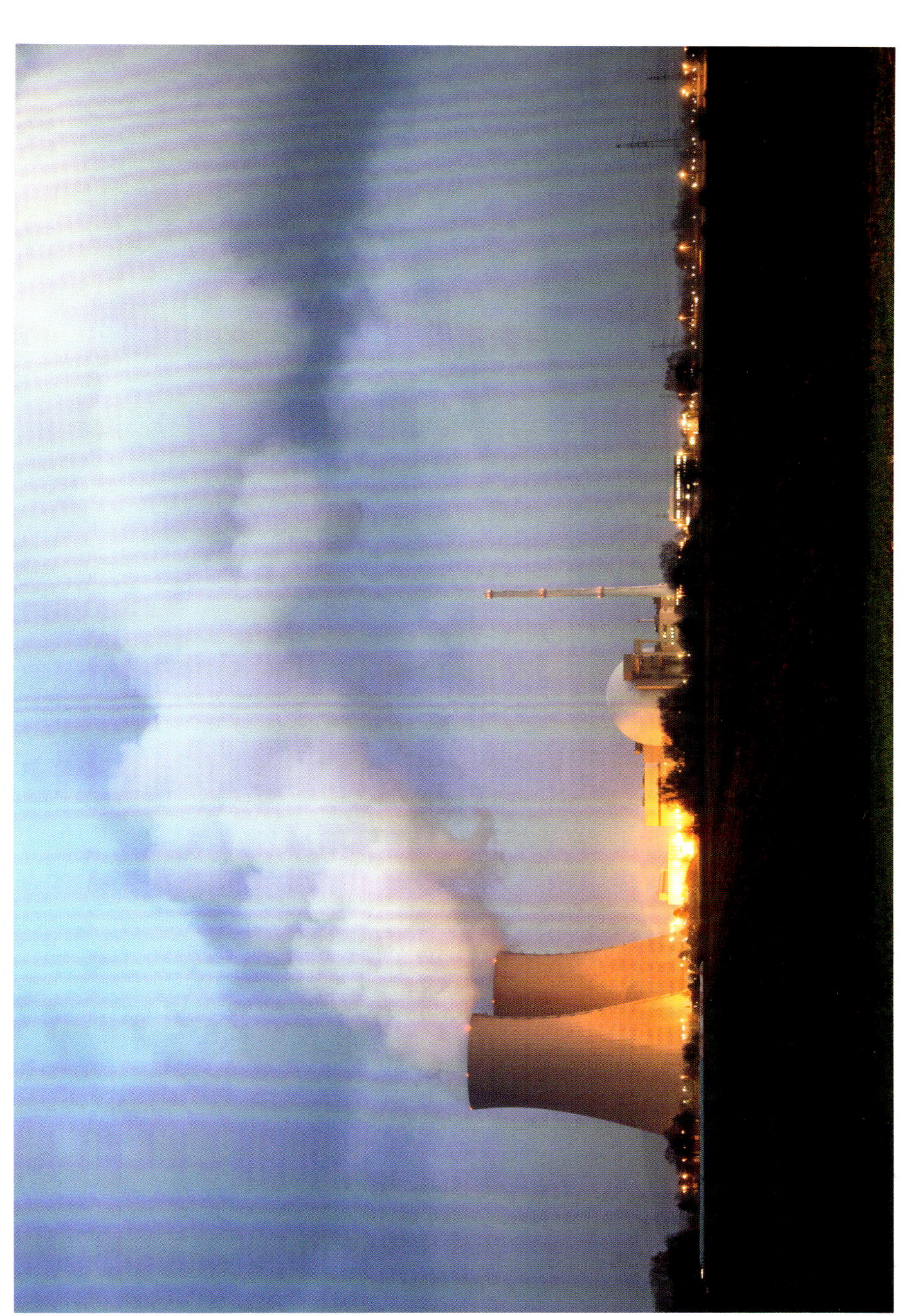

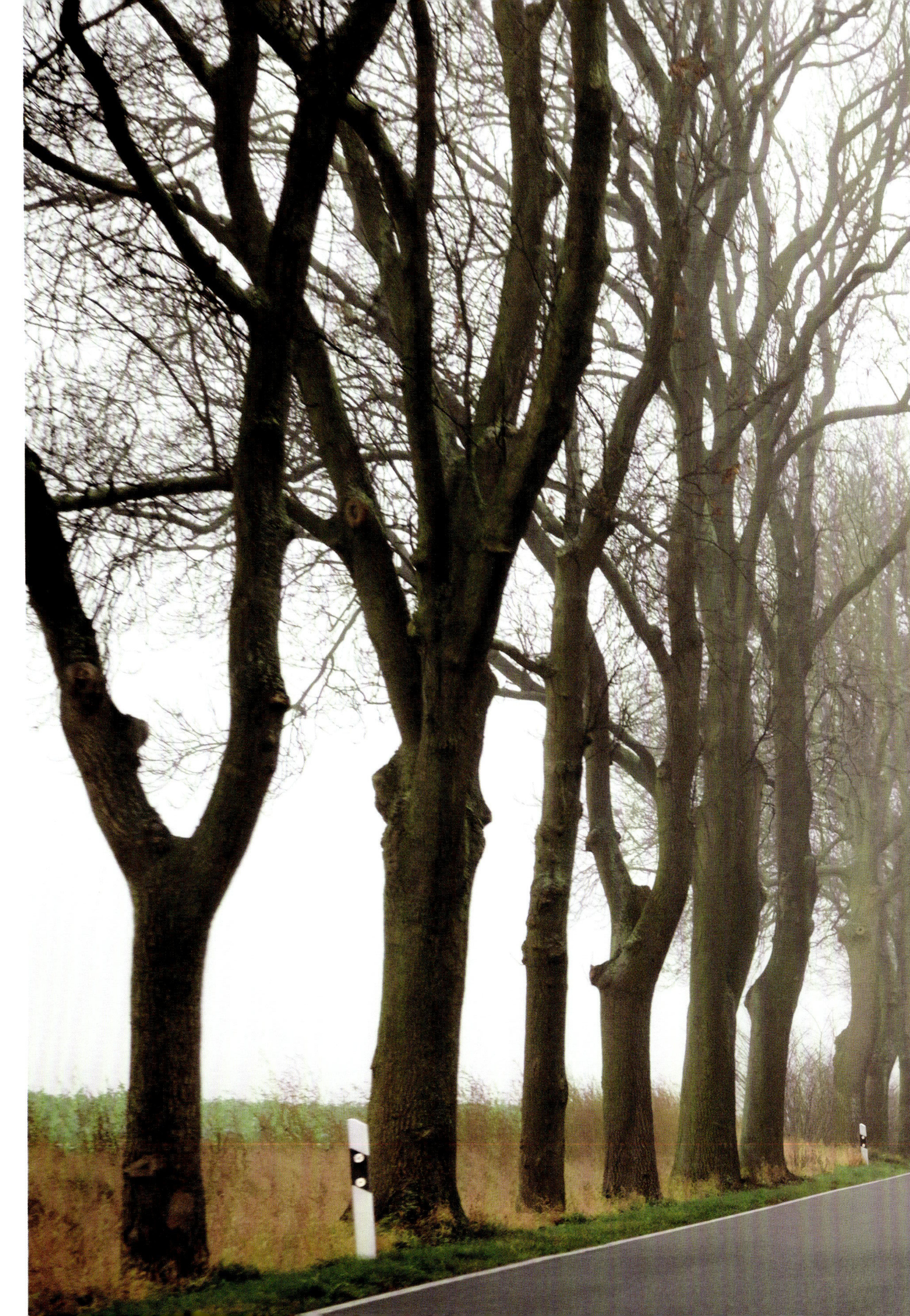

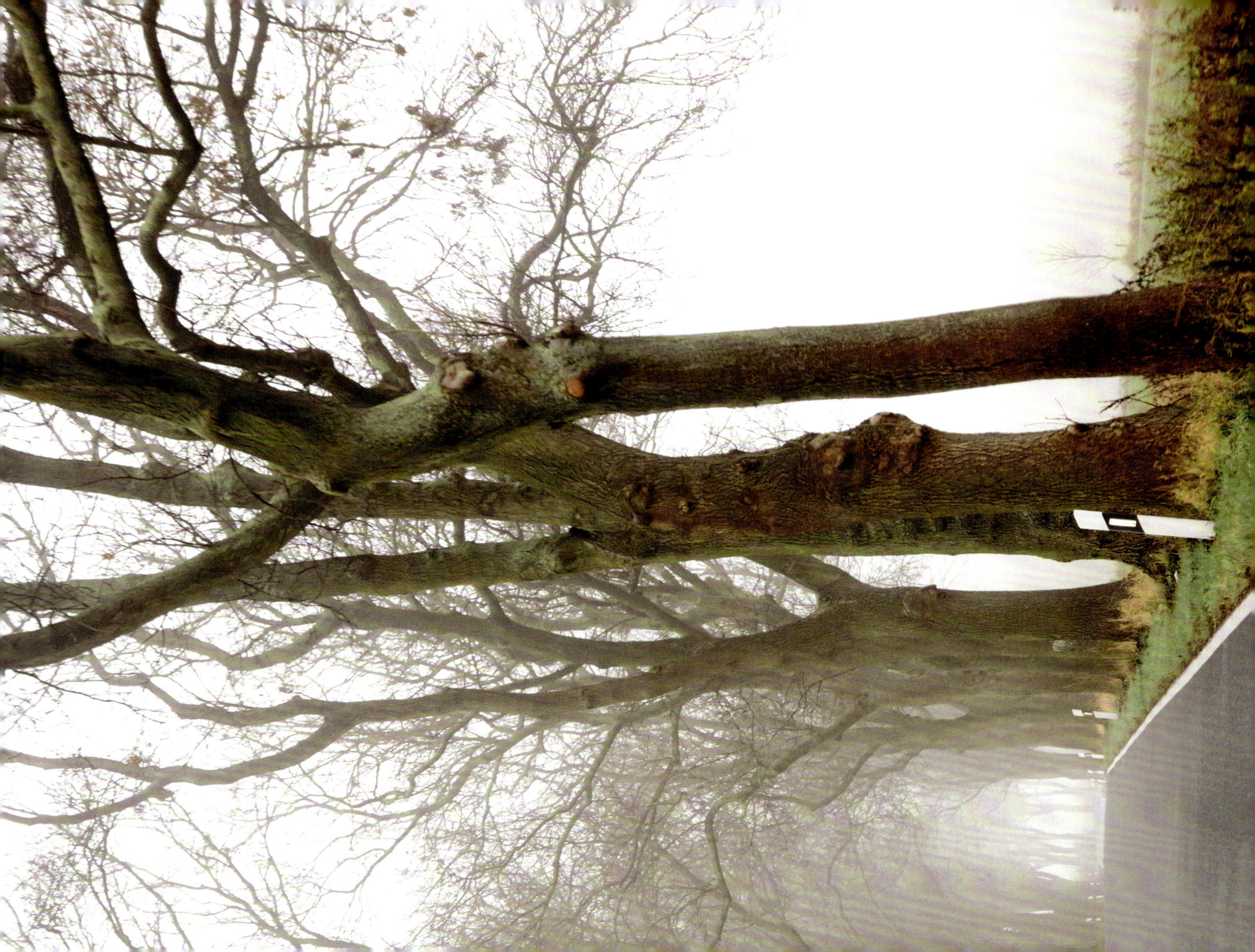

PART

VII

CONTROL ROOM

archival pigment prints, 2015

CONTROL ROOM

Plant Vogtle in Waynesboro, Georgia, has been called the site of the nuclear renaissance. Here, commercial nuclear energy reactors have been under construction for the first time in the United States since the 1979 partial meltdown at Three Mile Island in Dauphin County, Pennsylvania. Like the boomtowns that emerged from rapid industrial expansion, Waynesboro's population increase will be short-lived. Workers come from across the country for temporary jobs such as welding and running power lines from the new cooling towers. While some residents embrace the plant, others have fought against it since the 1980s when the first two reactors were built and they witnessed health and economic decline. Most recently, a community of activists has risen up against what they see as the nuclear industry using health as currency in exchange for temporary jobs. Other groups and individuals view nuclear energy as a solution in the climate change battle. Reactors 3 and 4 are set to go online in 2021 and 2022.[1]

Interested in the town of Waynesboro and Plant Vogtle, I spent a number of years researching the area. While visiting Waynesboro, I spent time with members of the community as well as Plant Vogtle workers. Eventually I gained access to Plant Vogtle and began interviewing town residents about the plant's history and the way it has affected the community.

---

1   "5 Things You Should Know About Plant Vogtle," Energy.gov, April 18, 2019, accessed Sept. 16, 2020, https://www.energy.gov/ne/articles/5-things-you-should-know-about-plant-vogtle-0.

Platelist:

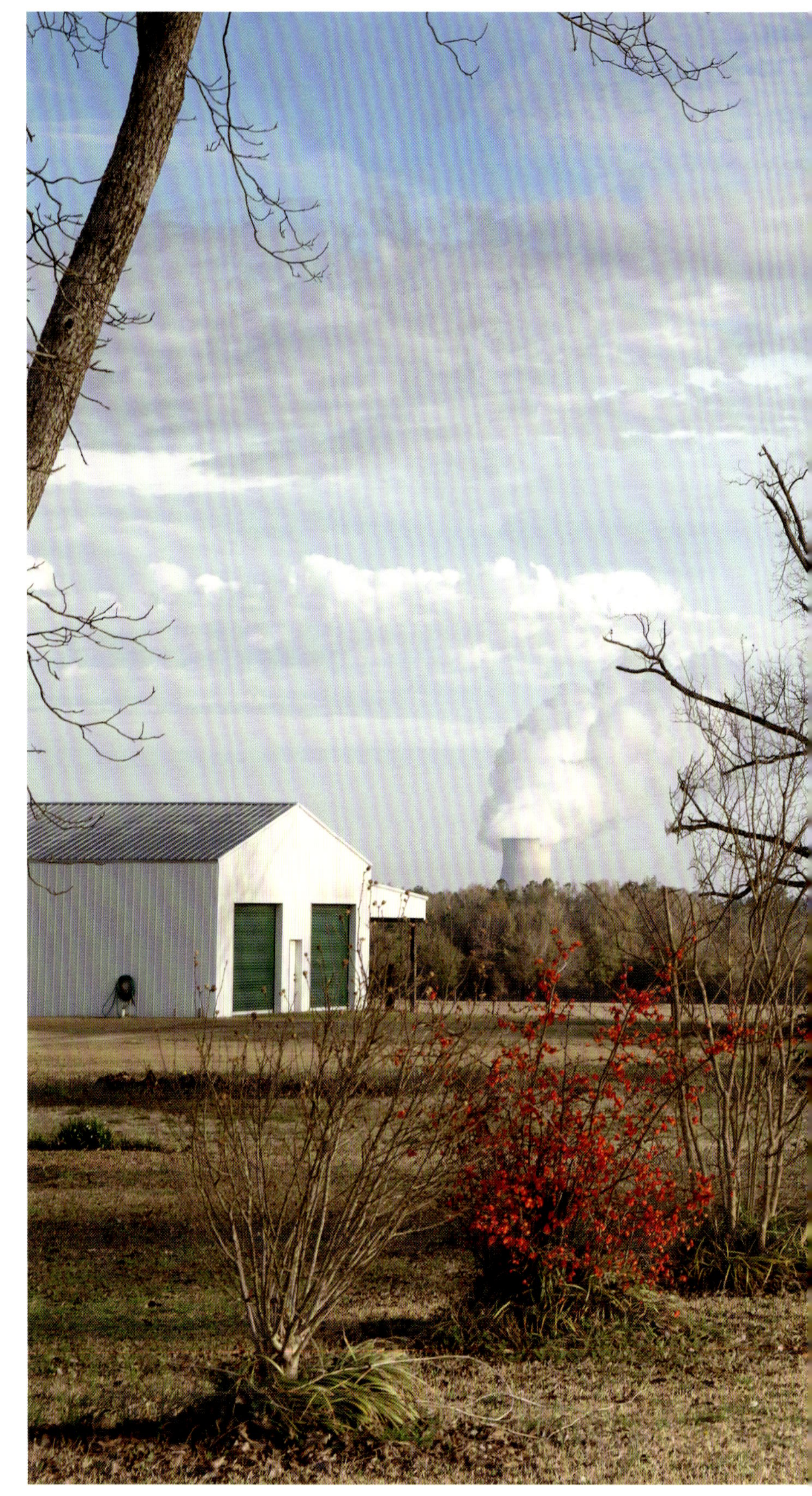

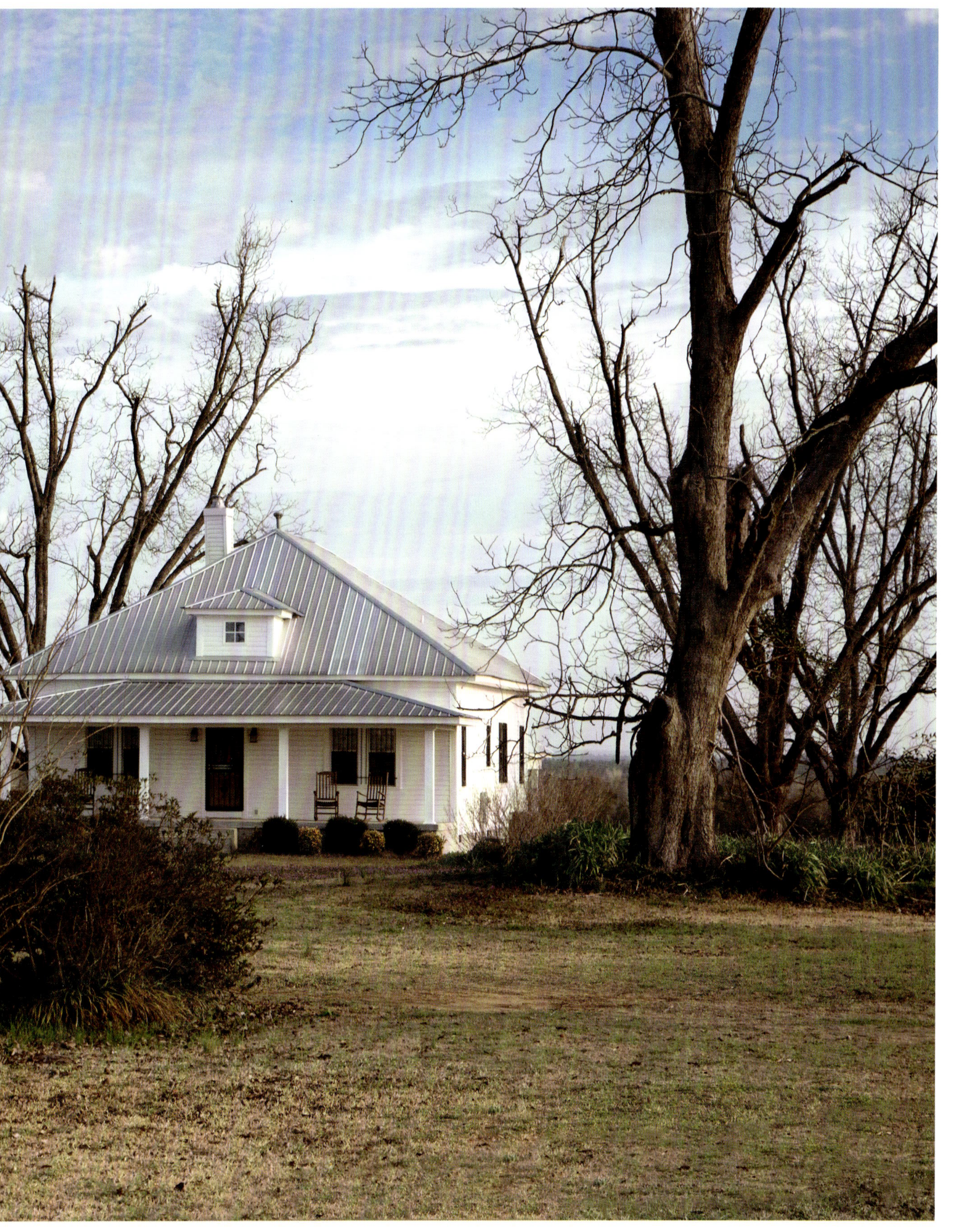

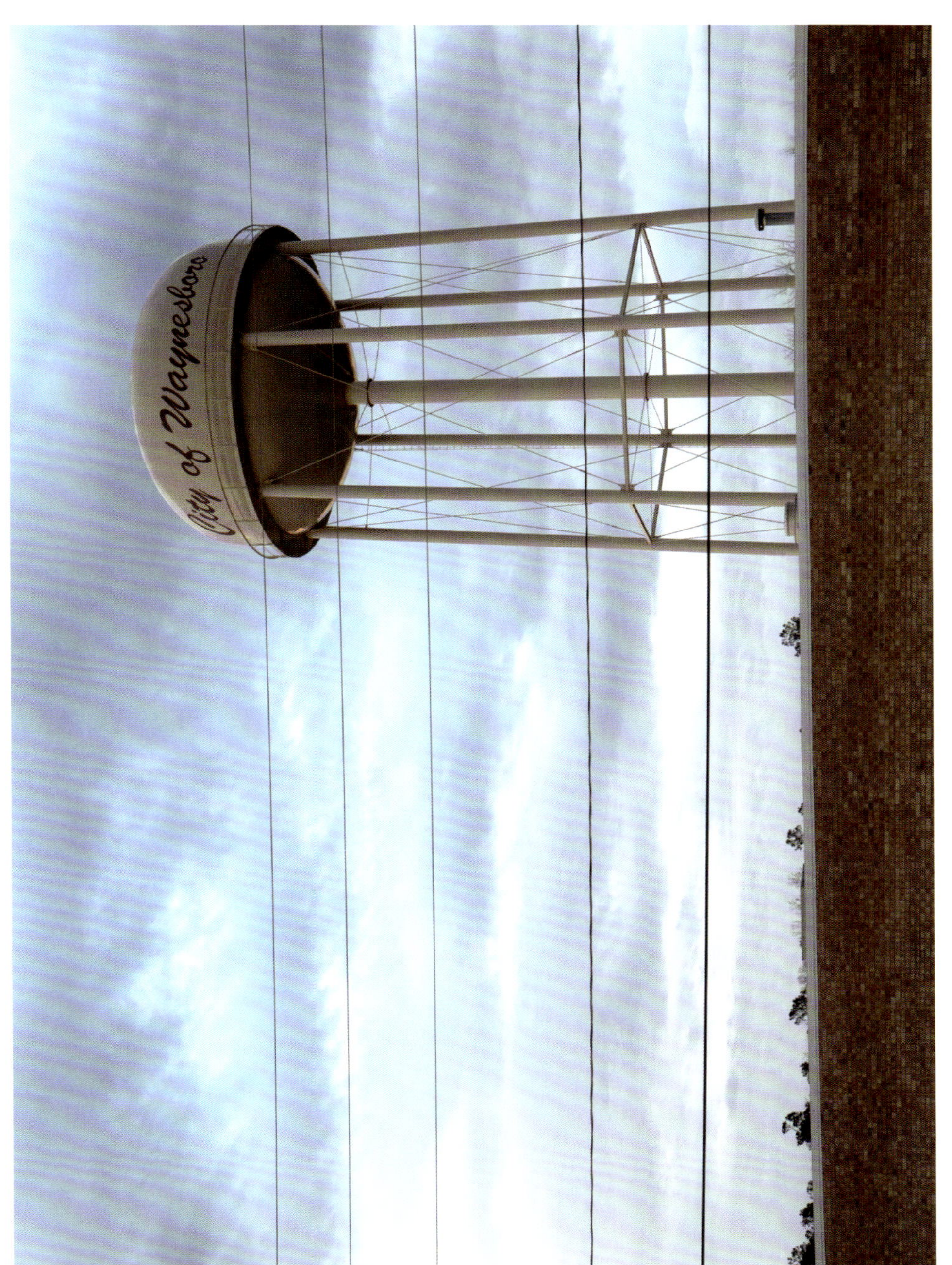
City of Waynesboro

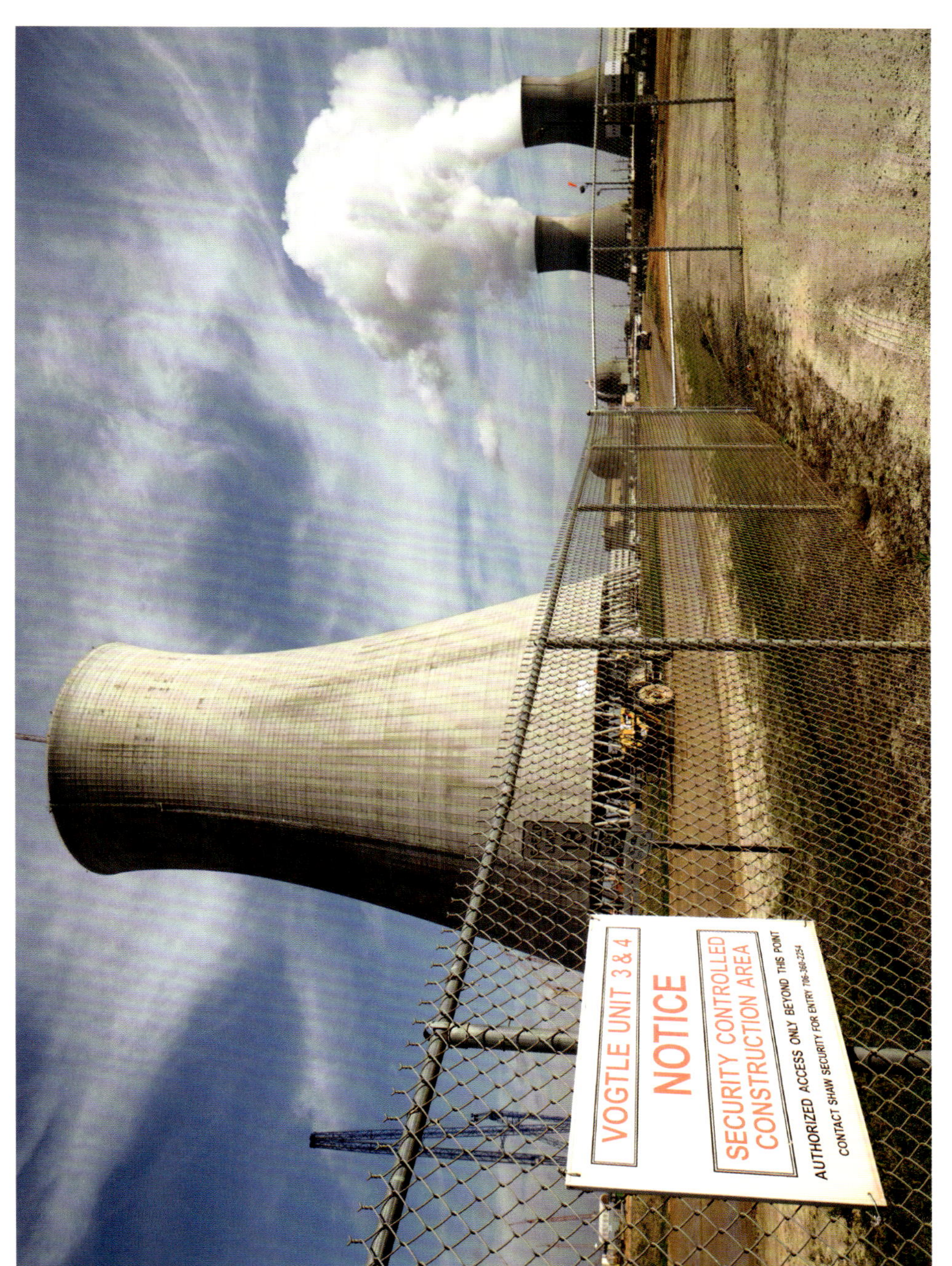
VOGTLE UNIT 3 & 4
NOTICE
SECURITY CONTROLLED
CONSTRUCTION AREA
AUTHORIZED ACCESS ONLY BEYOND THIS POINT
CONTACT SHAW SECURITY FOR ENTRY 706-360-2254

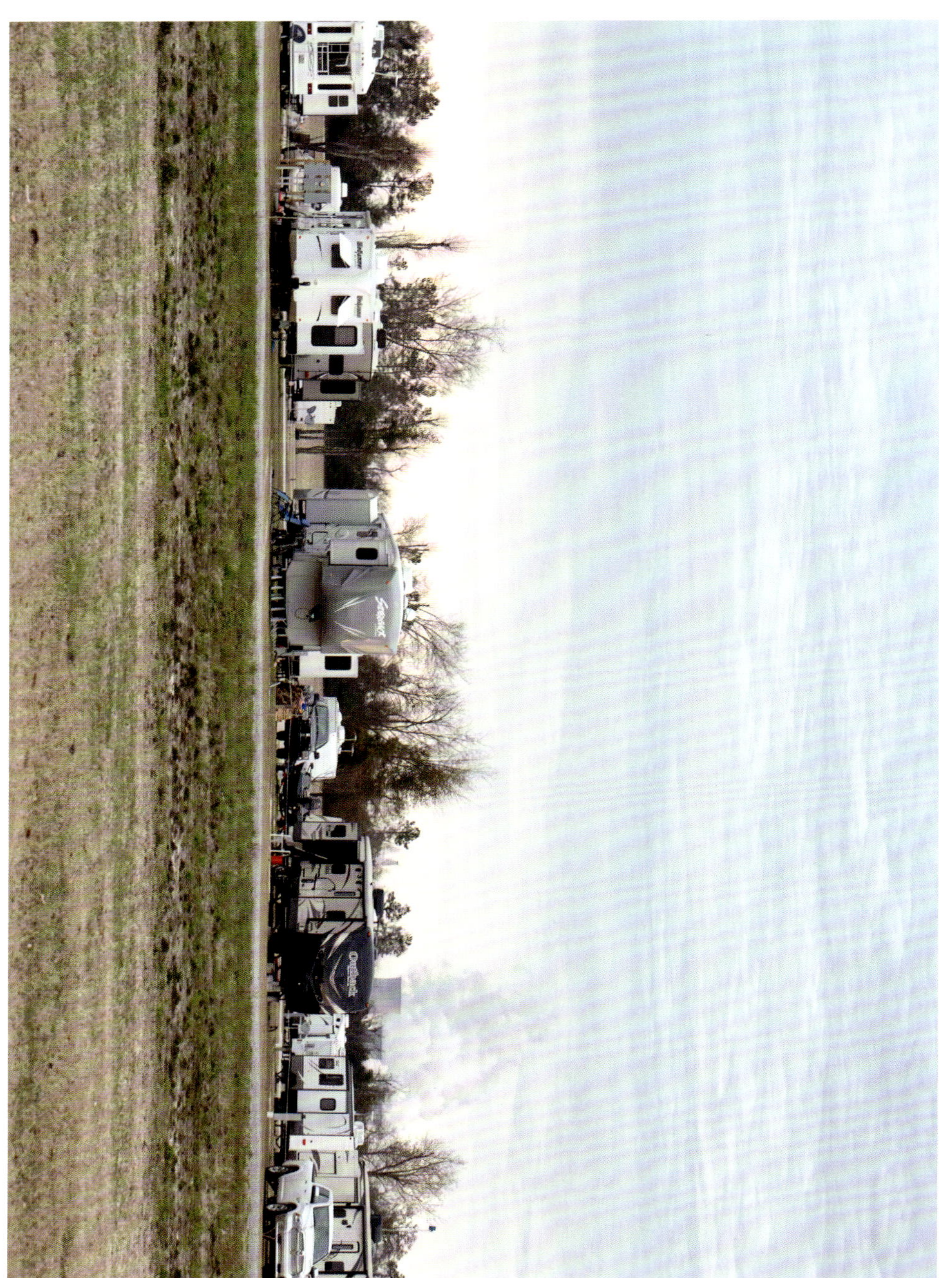

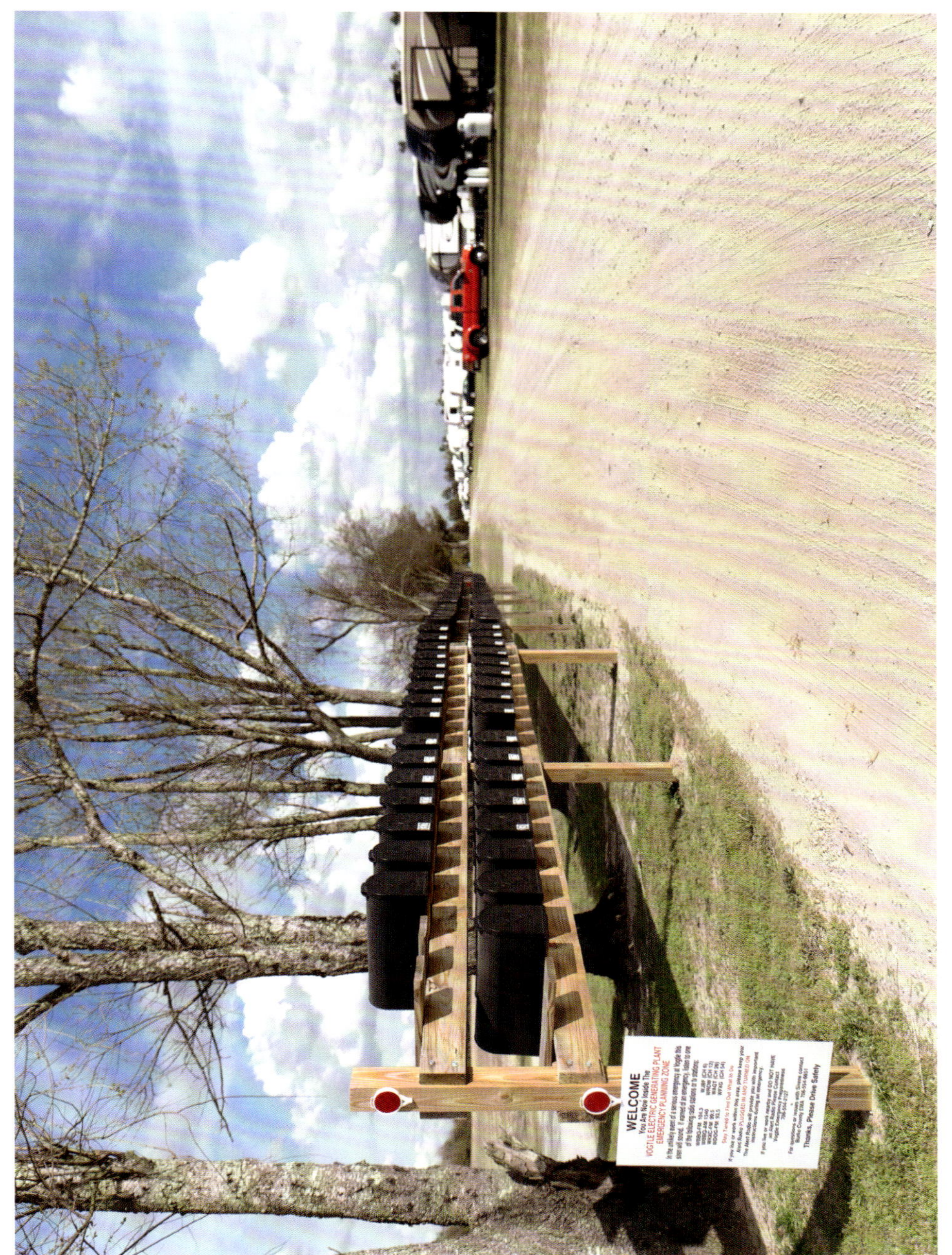

WELCOME
You Are Now Inside The
VOGTLE ELECTRIC GENERATING PLANT
EMERGENCY PLANNING ZONE
Thanks, Please Drive Safely

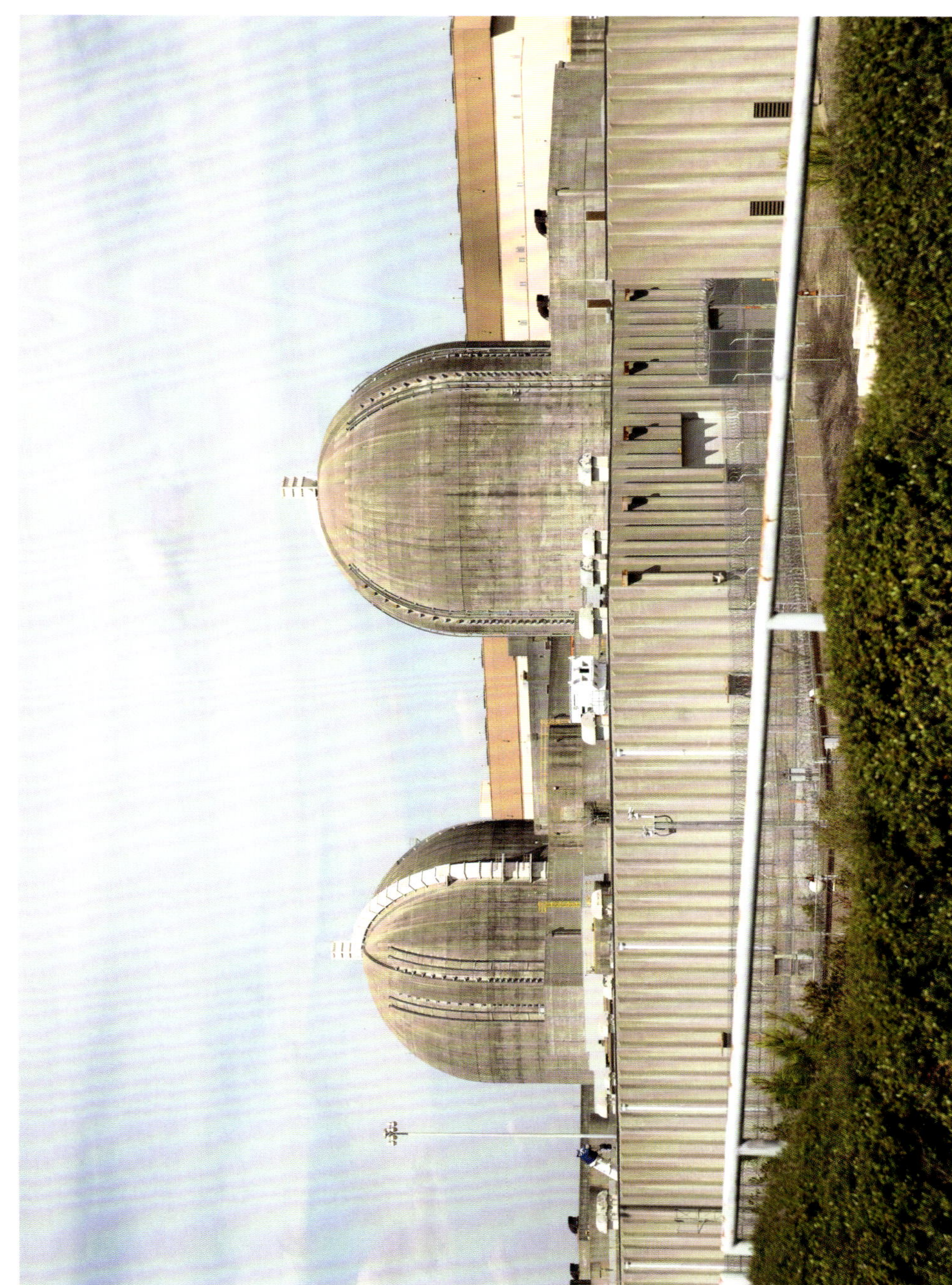

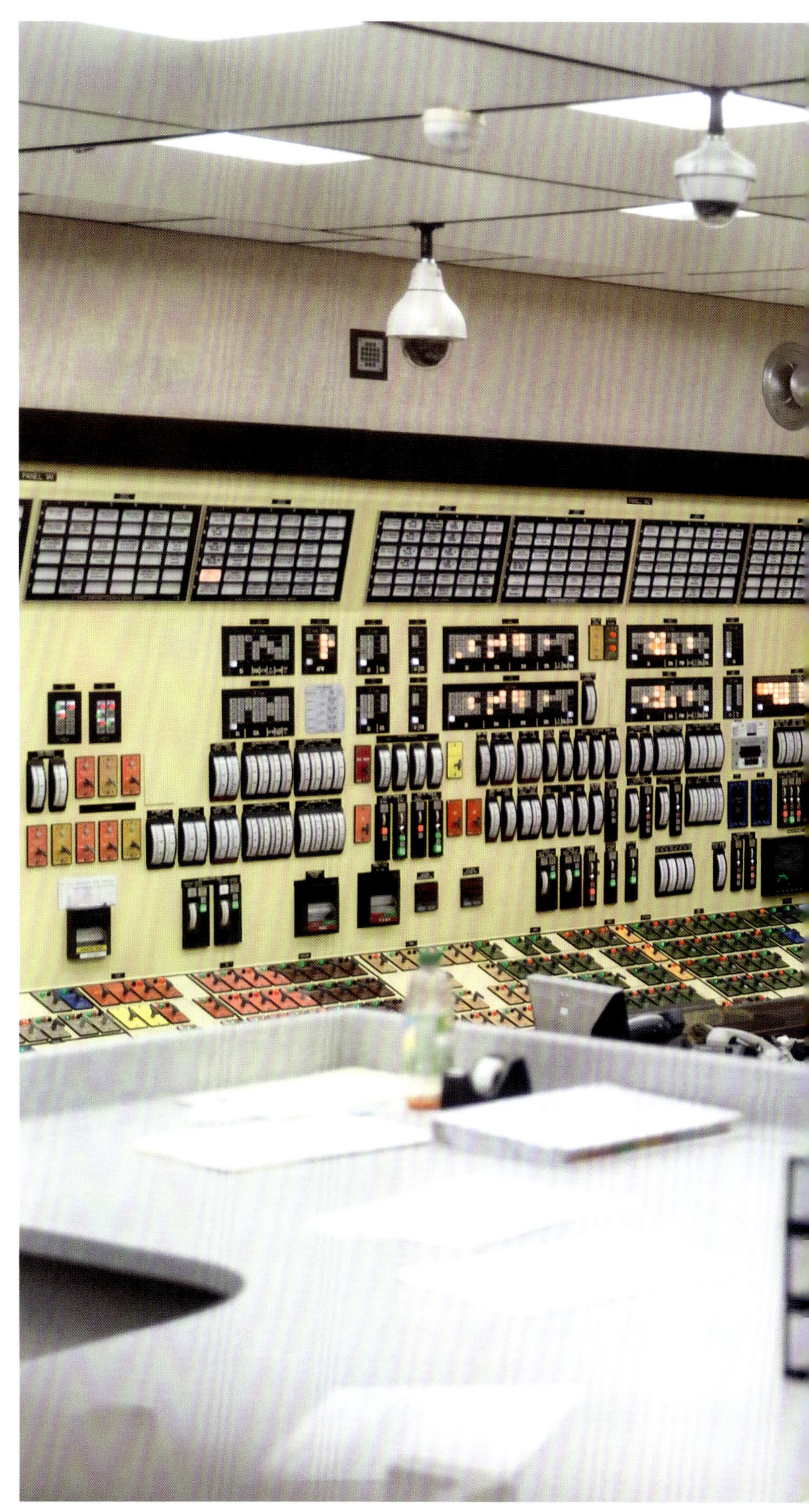

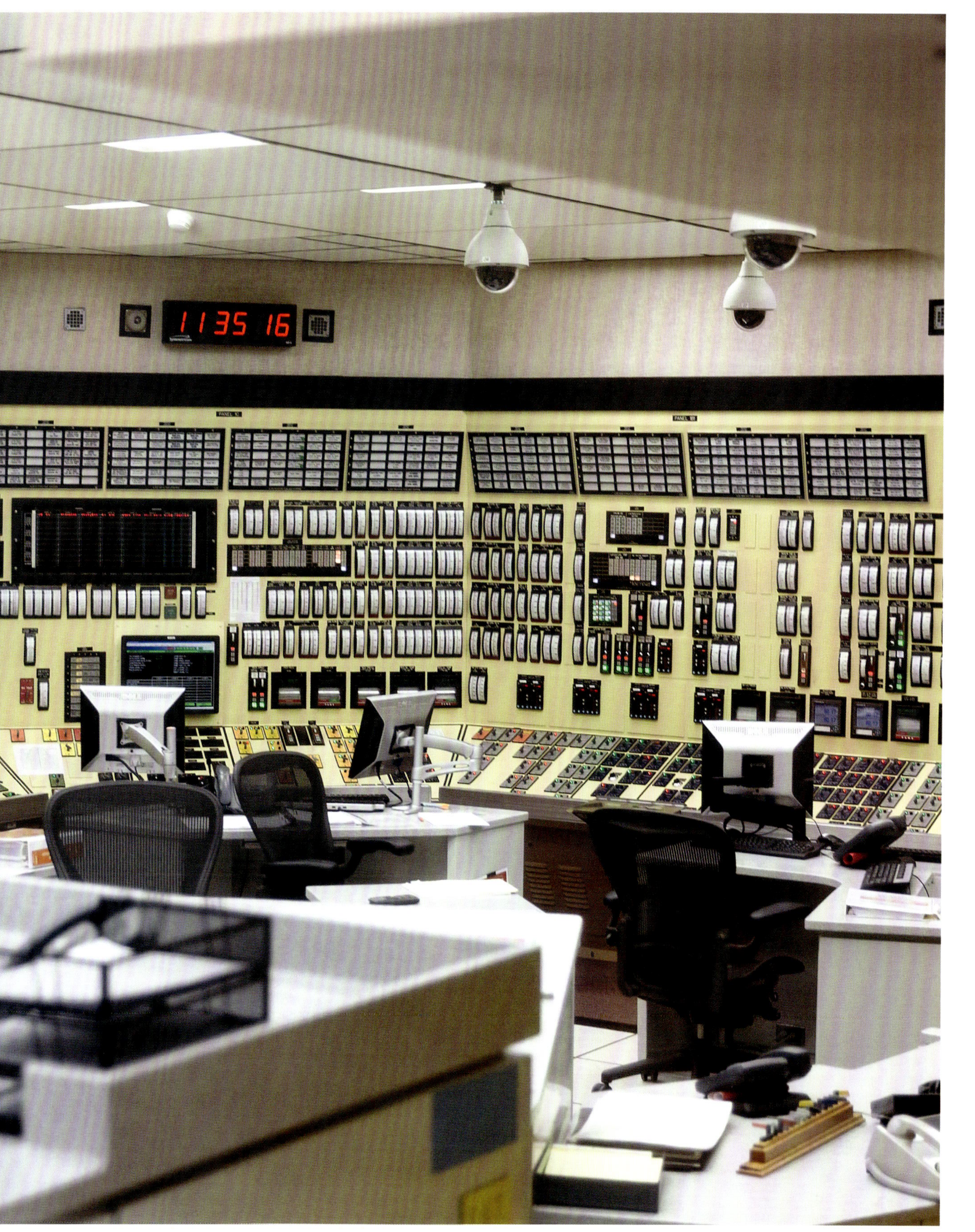

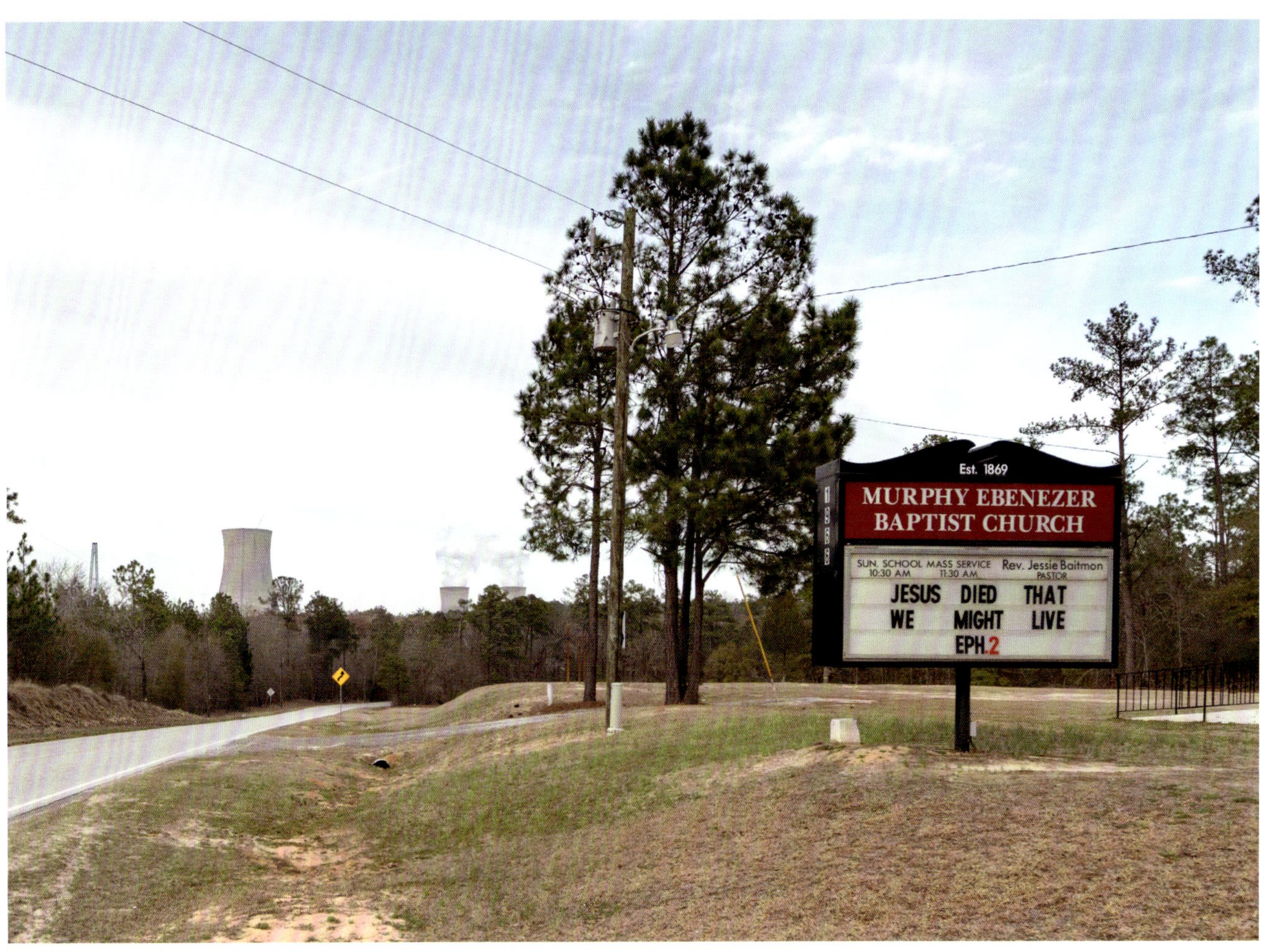

Est. 1869
MURPHY EBENEZER
BAPTIST CHURCH
SUN. SCHOOL   MASS SERVICE   Rev. Jessie Baitmon
10:30 AM   11:30 AM   PASTOR
JESUS   DIED   THAT
WE   MIGHT   LIVE
EPH. 2

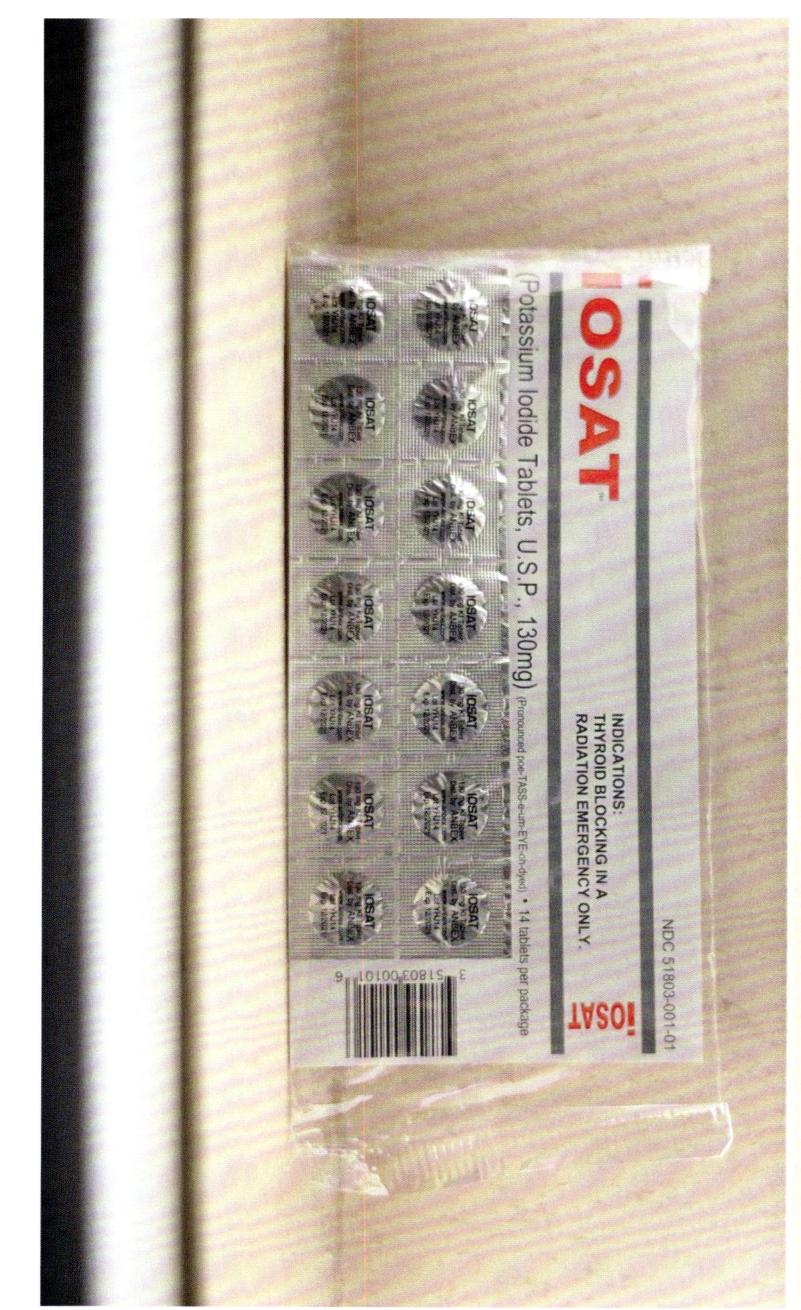
IOSAT
(Potassium Iodide Tablets, U.S.P., 130mg)
INDICATIONS:
THYROID BLOCKING IN A
RADIATION EMERGENCY ONLY.
NDC 51803-001-01
IOSAT
(Pronounced poe-TASS-e-um-EYE-oh-dyed) • 14 tablets per package

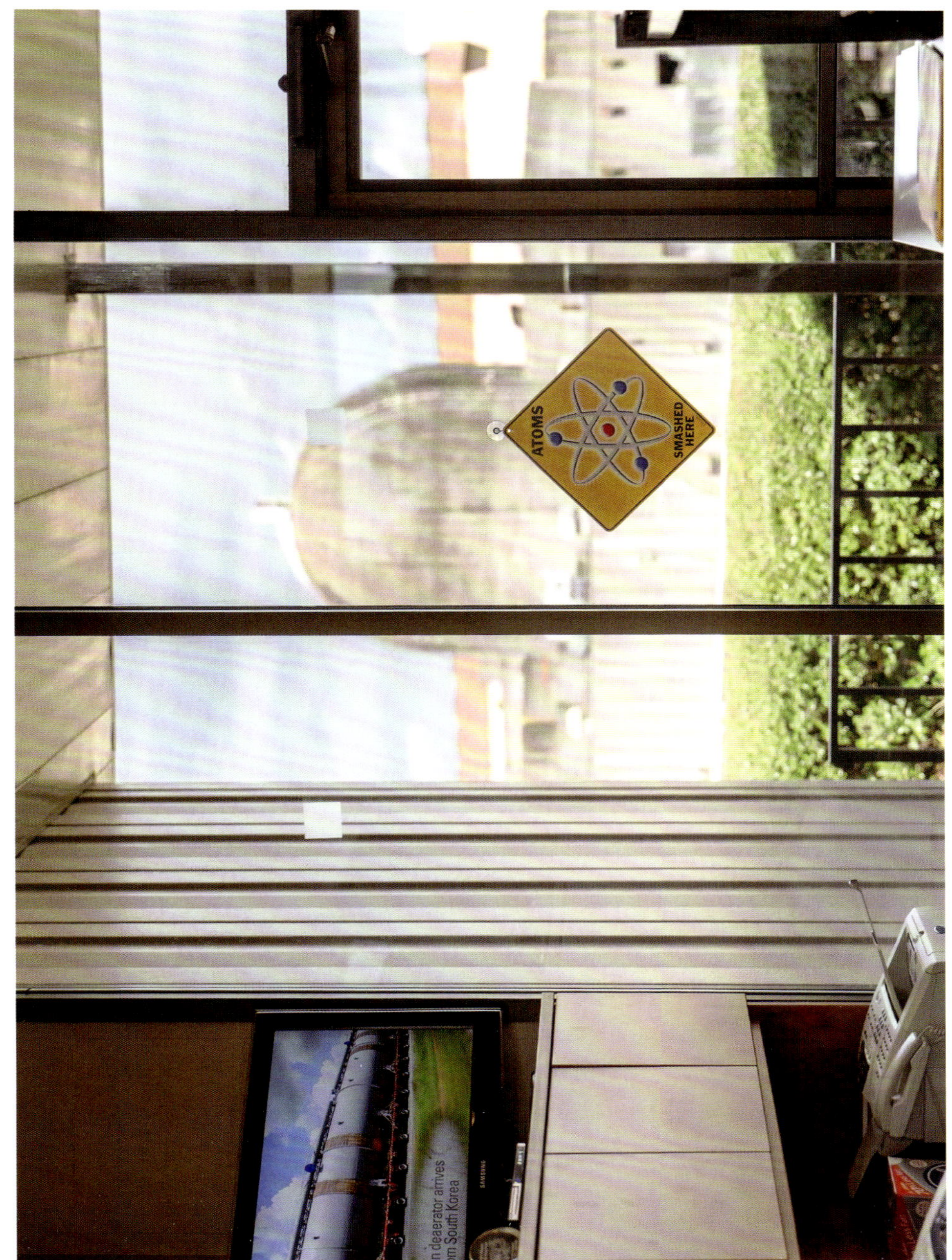
ATOMS
SMASHED
HERE

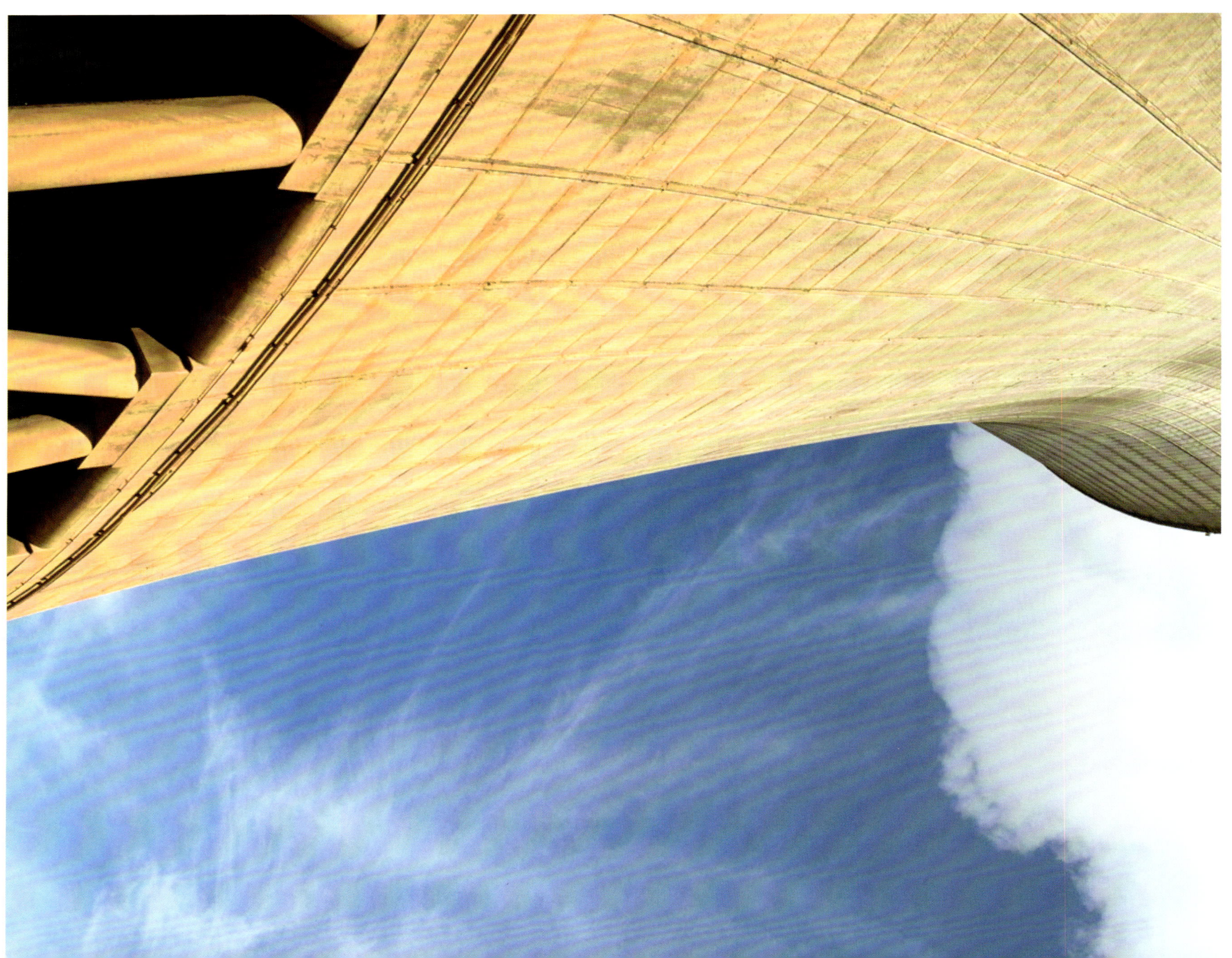

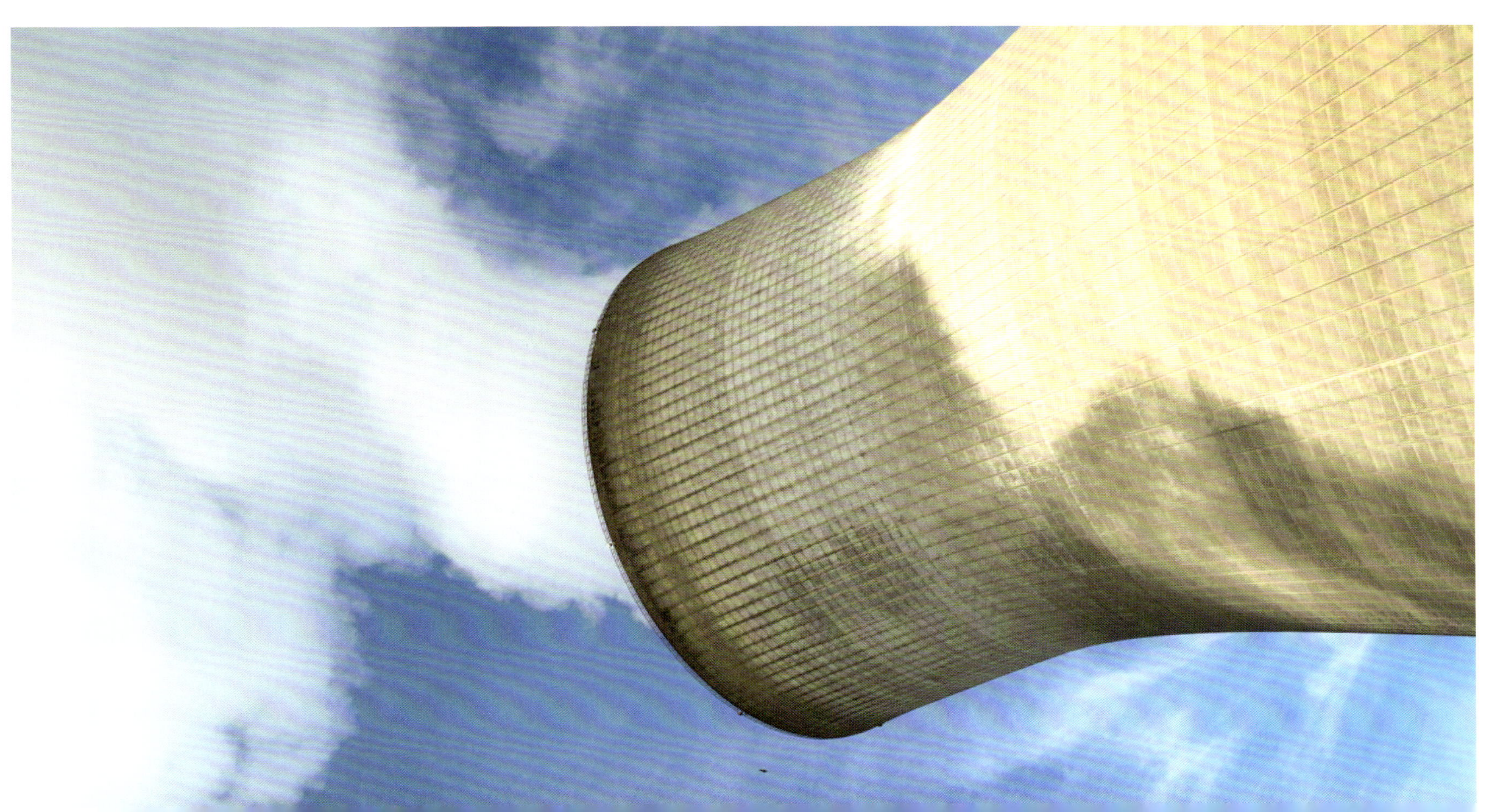

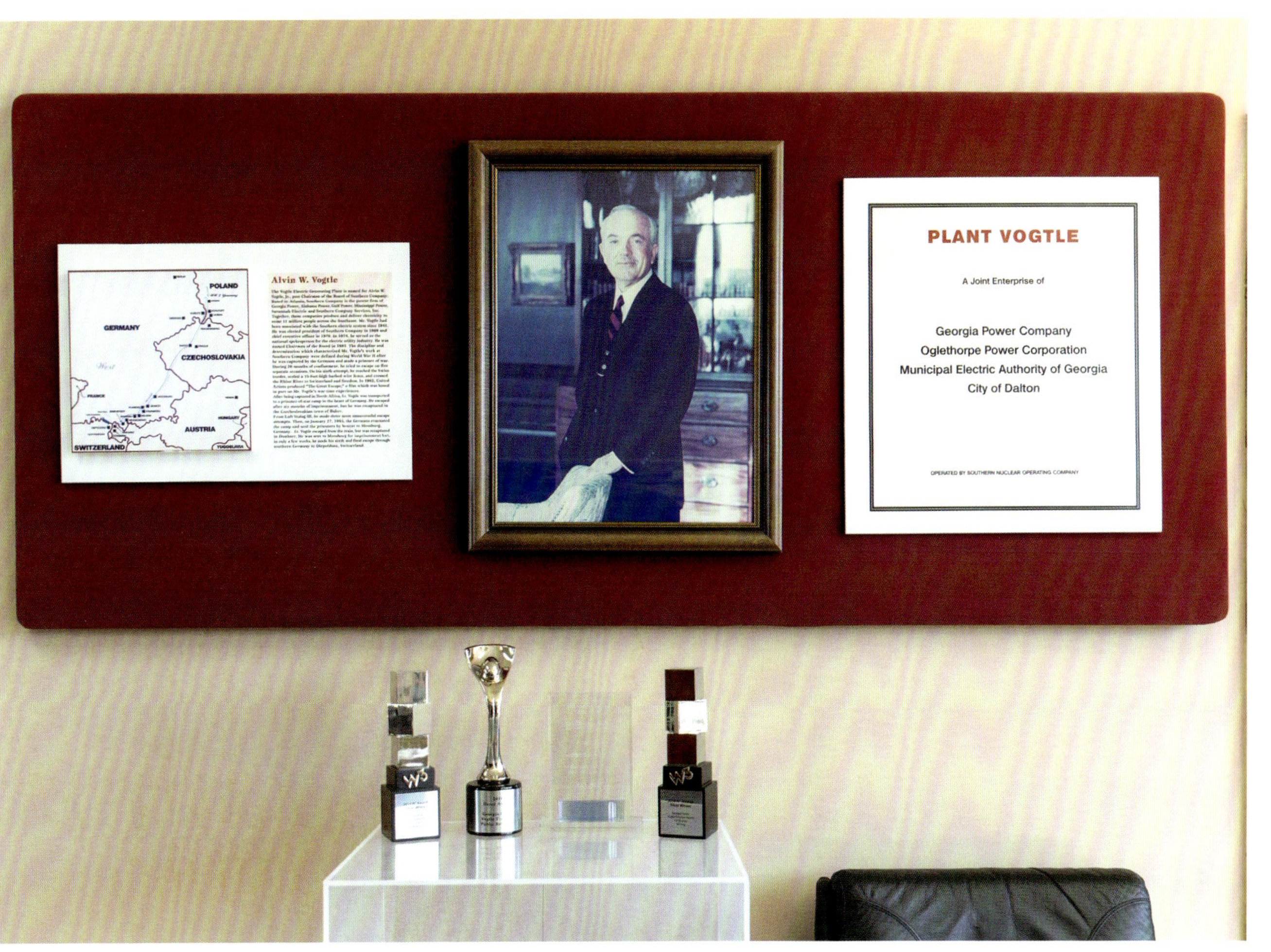

Alvin W. Vogtle

The Vogtle Electric Generating Plant is named for Alvin W. Vogtle, Jr., past Chairman of the Board of Southern Company. Based in Atlanta, Southern Company is the parent firm of Georgia Power, Alabama Power, Gulf Power, Mississippi Power, Savannah Electric and Southern Company Services, Inc. Together, these companies produce and deliver electricity to some 11 million people across the Southeast. Mr. Vogtle had been associated with the Southern electric system since 1941. He was elected president of Southern Company in 1969 and chief executive officer in 1970. In 1974, he served as the national spokesperson for the electric utility industry. He was named Chairman of the Board in 1983. The discipline and determination which characterized Mr. Vogtle's work at Southern Company were defined during World War II after he was captured by the Germans and made a prisoner of war. During 20 months of confinement, he tried to escape on five separate occasions. On his sixth attempt, he reached the Swiss border, scaled a 15-foot-high barbed wire fence, and crossed the Rhine River to Switzerland and freedom. In 1963, United Artists produced "The Great Escape," a film which was based in part on Mr. Vogtle's war time experiences.
After being captured in North Africa, Lt. Vogtle was transported to a prisoner of war camp in the heart of Germany. He escaped after six months of imprisonment, but he was recaptured in the Czechoslovakian town of Buboc.
From Luft Stalag III, he made three more unsuccessful escape attempts. Then, on January 27, 1945, the Germans evacuated the camp and sent the prisoners by boxcar to Moosburg, Germany. Lt. Vogtle escaped from the train, but was recaptured in Deathurt. He was sent to Moosburg for imprisonment but, in only a few weeks, he made his sixth and final escape through southern Germany to Diepoldsau, Switzerland.

POLAND
GERMANY
CZECHOSLOVAKIA
FRANCE
AUSTRIA
HUNGARY
SWITZERLAND
YUGOSLAVIA
West

PLANT VOGTLE
A Joint Enterprise of
Georgia Power Company
Oglethorpe Power Corporation
Municipal Electric Authority of Georgia
City of Dalton
OPERATED BY SOUTHERN NUCLEAR OPERATING COMPANY

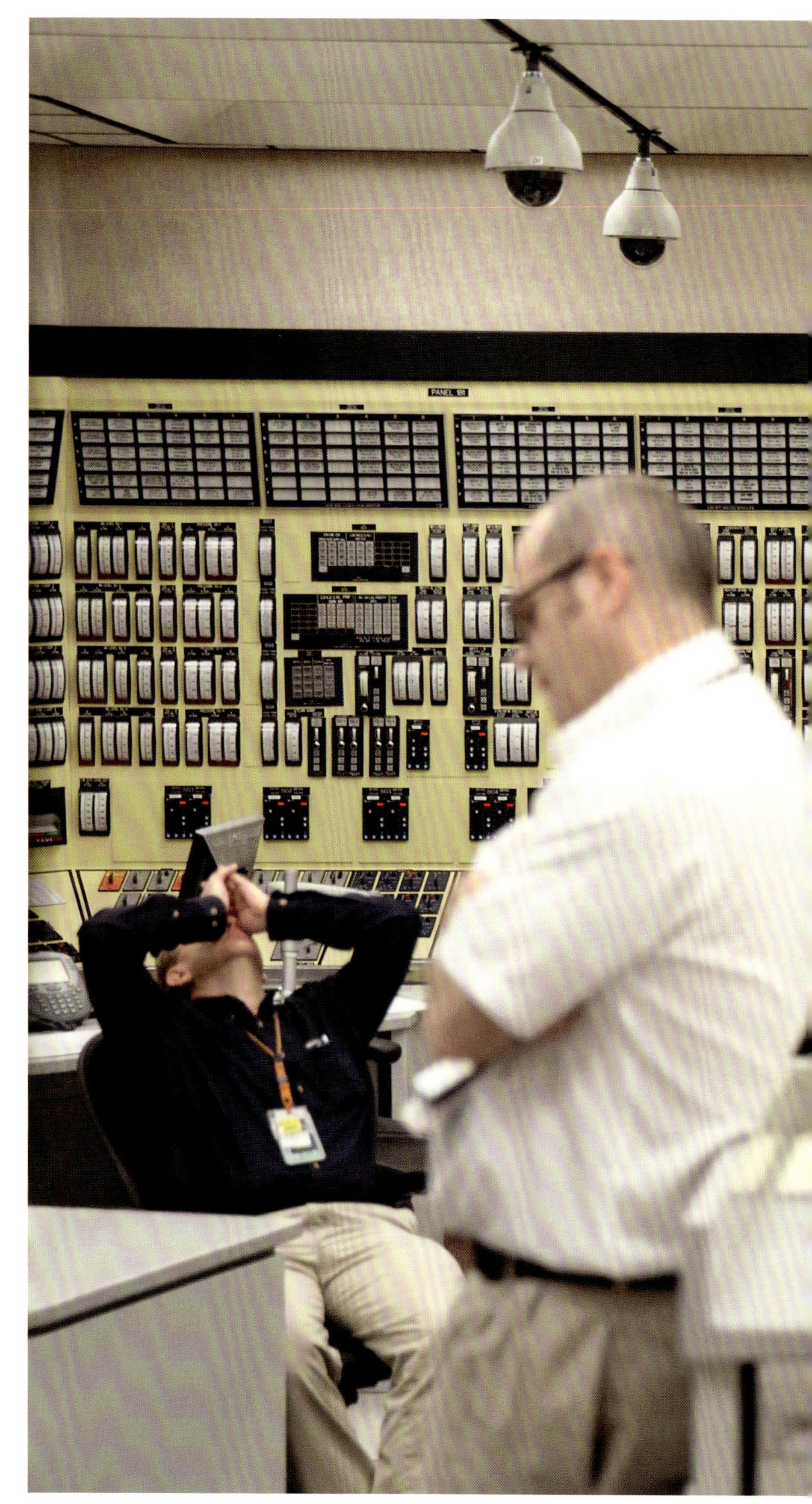

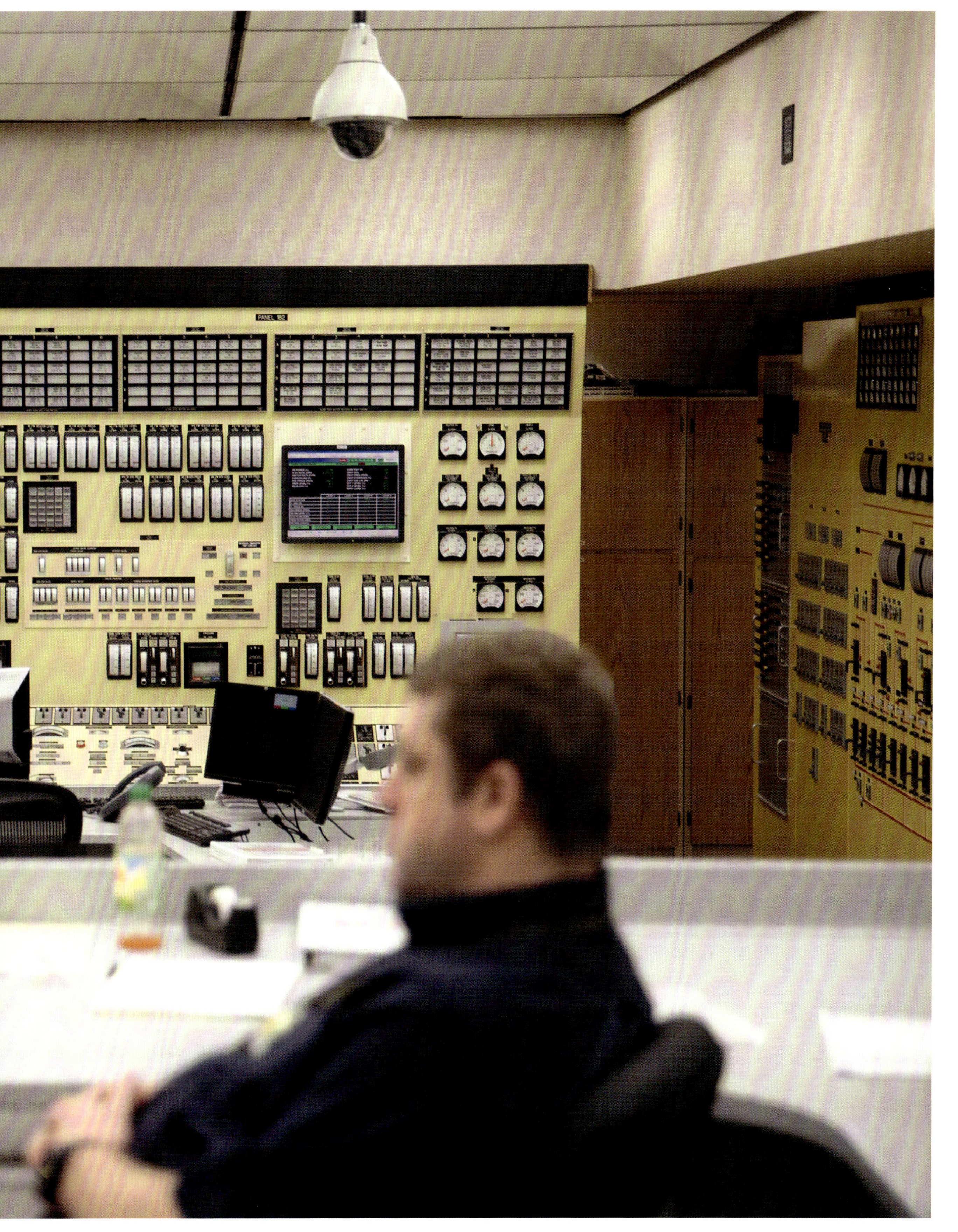

MADE YOU LOOK:
THE POLITICAL AESTHETICS OF ABBEY HEPNER

By Kirsten Pai Buick

At what point do we become "authentic" to our purpose? I ask because if one's vocation is perceived as arriving "too early" in one's development, then one is tasked with double the labor—learning all there is to know about the subject while beating back skepticism and active discouragement. Such doubling of labor exposes the purpose of "authenticity"—misunderstood as explanatory of "the real" while in fact put into operation as a strategy of either legitimation or de-legitimation, a weapon that seeks to persuade rather than describe and wielded by outsiders who have little or no conception of one's journey thus far. Such were the trials of Abbey Hepner, whose interests lie in the nuclear industry and who grew up between the Nevada Test Site, where the United States tested nearly one thousand nuclear weapons, and Idaho National Laboratory, an 890-square-mile section of desert used for reactor experimentation. Let me be clear, however: I do not invoke the place where she grew up as in any way "authenticating" her labors. Rather, the place where she grew up and grew into her work can only stop the chatter around authenticity if one believes that such experiences certify one's curiosity and that those experiences must be preemptively or defensively invoked to stop such questions around "rights"—the right to look, the right to know, the right to represent. On the contrary, her rights reside in those privileges bound to the individual whom the philosopher Jacques Rancière identifies as "the spectator." "The question of the spectator," he argues, [is] "at the heart of the discussion of the relations between art and politics."[1]

I. THE RIGHT TO LOOK

The nuclear industry is inextricably bound to politics—local, national, and global. And in Hepner's quest to understand its details, its totality, and its interconnectedness she has traveled to places as a spectator where, as a perceivable outsider (whether through gender, race, or nationality), she was often in danger of becoming the spectacle. Brilliantly, she learned to shift the attention to a spectacle of her making and regain her agency as spectator. The concepts of "agency" and "spectator" might at first seem oppositional, but as Rancière reminds us, "the spectator also acts" and the right to look inheres in the right to act. "Emancipation begins when we challenge the opposition between viewing and acting; when we understand that the self-evident facts that structure the relations between saying, seeing and doing themselves belong to the structure of domination and subjection. It begins when we understand that viewing is also an action that confirms or transforms this distribution of positions. The spectator also acts, like the pupil or scholar. She observes, selects, compares, interprets. She links what she sees to a host of other things that she has seen on other stages, in other kinds of place [*sic*]. She composes her own poem with the elements of the poem before her."[2] One such example is Hepner's time in Japan. According to the artist,

> Each of Japan's nuclear plants has its own mascot character. Until the 2011 Fukushima nuclear disaster, Japan had an amusement park called Atom World with mascots like Plutonium Kun

---

1 Jacques Rancière, *The Emancipated Spectator*, translated by Gregory Elliott (London and New York: Verso, 2011), p. 2.
2 Rancière, *The Emancipated Spectator*, p. 13.

and Denko Chan to explain why nuclear power is good for the world. The use of nuclear energy propaganda began in the United States as part of President Dwight D. Eisenhower's 1953 Atoms for Peace program. In order to shift negative attitudes away from the dropping of the atomic bomb, this program helped Japan develop a nuclear power industry, thereby promoting the peaceful use of nuclear technology.

While living in Japan and volunteering in the disaster zone left by the 2011 tsunami, I created *Nuclear Mascot* by photographing a fictional character with references to nuclear history and current concerns in Japan and the United States. For the final image in the series, I purchased advertisement space on a digital billboard in Shibuya Crossing, the busiest pedestrian crossing in the world with over one million people each day, and screened an image of the character for fifteen seconds every hour. This public art intervention replaced six minutes of commercial advertising with my nuclear mascot, raising a question about the role of media and propaganda in human-made disasters.[3]

Hepner's fictional nuclear mascot makes us look. It is a monumental, towering yellow figure with a cartoon face and eyebrows made up of stylized lightning bolts (i.e., symbols of energy). She photographs it overlooking the *Nuclear Neighborhood*; in a modern Japanese kitchen pouring contaminated *Milk* into a sink; removing mysteriously originated black hairs while sitting on a toilet in *Shaving Away Astro Boy* (the character of Astro Boy was also known as Mighty Atom, the robot boy who was written and illustrated in 1952 by Osamu Tezuka) and thus shedding its associations to a nuclear world and how it makes slaves of us all; walking the streets in *Northern Japan*; eating while watching a television whose screen reflects onto the cartoon face *170,000 Nuclear Protestors in Tokyo*. The mascot peers from inside an *Abandoned Elementary School* and sits disconsolately outside a *Northern Japan Elementary School*; and it towers in the landscape in *Moonlit* and crouches on the floor of a bamboo forest in its endeavor as a *Mushroom Collector*. As it goes about its business in the nuclear landscape, its environs animate it. And in a final photograph before it makes its appearance on the digital billboard at Shibuya Crossing, it seems to reject its complicity in nuclear propaganda as it sits angrily in a paved space that extols the virtues (the *Propaganda*) of the nuclear industry.

The final appearance of Hepner's fictional nuclear mascot is in response to the 170,000 nuclear protestors in Tokyo. Hepner subverts its fictional purpose as a symbol normalizing and celebrating the nuclear industry into one that acts against such propaganda and undermines advertising—it transforms the distribution of positions. The mascot is now also an emancipated spectator as Hepner projects its image on the digital billboard at Shibuya Crossing in Tokyo (the busiest pedestrian crossing in the world) to display the mascot as it points at us and then at itself with the caption "Dear Manmade, From All Of Us." Hepner timed it so that it was projected for the thousands of people who gathered to protest the betrayal of the Japanese Restoration Project, which, once voted into power, reversed its anti-nuclear position disappointing more that 80% of Japanese people who wanted nuclear power eliminated. Pointing out into the crowd, the indicting gesture echoes a photograph from a press release produced by the artist Kota Tekeuchi in 2011 in which the artist blames both the Tokyo Electric Power Company

---

3 Abbey Hepner, artist's website [http://abbey-hepner.com/#/work/nuclear-mascot]. The titles of the photographs that Hepner made of her fictional nuclear mascot are embedded in the text and available on the artist's website.

and the Japanese people for the manmade disaster at Fukushima Daiichi. Hepner, who was living in Japan at the time, characterizes the press release and the pointing gesture in particular as now belonging to her "social event memory" around the nuclear meltdown.[4]

II. DISMANTLING THE LABORING BODY / DISMANTLING THE AUTHENTIC

Hepner's interest and vocation around the politics of the nuclear industry accelerated while in graduate school at the University of New Mexico, where she was a student in the small but prestigious photo studio program. I have long been impressed by her strong sense of ethics and her belief in the transformative power of art. She is both clear-eyed and compassionate; these qualities shine through and engender confidence in her subjects—confidence that she will not betray the trust that they put in her and confidence that she will, to the best of her ability, represent them fairly. It is not often that someone is given five hours of supervised access to a nuclear control center, for example (more about that below). She also demonstrates unparalleled confidence in her subject matter. In addition to photography, Hepner has an incredible arsenal of expressive materials—from electronic music and film to performance and costuming to biological experimentation and work with uranium to make prints. As a conceptual artist, she marshals her subjects and subject matter to create thoughtful, thought-provoking, and aesthetic encounters between a broadly defined conception of art and audience. I have found her work ethic to be without equal both in terms of creating and participating in national and international residencies, exhibitions, and publishing opportunities. For Hepner, art is about aesthetics as well as communication. She is a true citizen of the world, having worked on nuclear projects in Kobe, Japan, as well as locations across the United States including New Mexico and Georgia. She truly strives to understand the larger picture and those technologies that link us all. Because communication is so important to her, she is a maker who is not restricted to one medium. She has the ability to make us look.

The significance of Hepner's work as a spectator/artist can be further illuminated by Jacques Rancière, who noted that the original meaning the word "emancipation" was "emergence from a state of minority." In this state, laboring bodies had singular tasks at which only they were good. These artisans, perforce, spent all of their time at their tasks and in their place because "work does not wait." Moreover, there was a harmonious relationship "between an occupation and an equipment; between the fact of being in a specific time and place, practicing particular occupations there, and being equipped with the capacities for feeling, saying and doing appropriate to those activities."[5] Rancière distinguishes this Platonic sense of "emancipation" from "social emancipation," which "signified breaking this fit between an 'occupation' and a 'capacity.' It signified dismantling the labouring body adapted to the occupation of an artisan who knows that work does not wait and whose senses are adapted to this 'absence of time.' Emancipation workers fashioned in the here and now a different body and a different 'soul' for this body—the body and soul of those who are not adapted to any specific occupation; who employ capacities for feeling and speaking, thinking and acting, that do not

---

4 Abbey Hepner, unpublished Qualifying Paper written in partial fulfillment for the MFA degree in Art Studio, on file at The University of New Mexico Libraries (Fall 2014), pp. 9–12.
5 Rancière, *The Emancipated Spectator*, p. 42.

belong to any particular class, but which belong to anyone and everyone."[6] Hepner also functions as an emancipation worker whose practices refuse the borders and boundaries of "the authentic," whether it is medium, material, or geography. She follows the poem wherever it may lead.

This leads me to the second set of objects that I think reveal the importance of her work—the dyadic relationship between *Control Room* and her various bodies of landscape representations such as *Transuranic*, *Scars on the Landscape*, *Palinopsia*, and *Bomb Pulse*, for example. Hepner notes:

> Plant Vogtle in Waynesboro, Georgia, is the site of the nuclear renaissance. Here, commercial nuclear energy reactors have been under construction for the first time in the United States since the 1979 partial meltdown at Three Mile Island in Dauphin County, Pennsylvania. Like the boomtowns that emerged from rapid industrial expansion, Waynesboro's population increase will be short-lived. Workers come from across the country for temporary jobs such as welding and running power lines from the new cooling towers. While some residents embrace the plant, others have fought against it since the 1980s when the first two reactors were built and they witnessed health and economic decline. Most recently, a community of activists has risen up against what they see as the nuclear industry using health as a currency in exchange for temporary jobs. Other groups and individuals view nuclear energy as a solution in the climate change battle. Reactors 3 and 4 are set to go online in 2021 and 2022.[7]

Control Room is filled with gauges, switches, computers, and lights all set into a yellow panel and framed by a room hopelessly stuck in the '70s. The cameras on the ceiling provide 360-degree views of what happens in that room. Hepner was inspired to create her image after having seen Thomas Demand's *Control Room* while living in Japan—the difference is that Demand's image is a reconstruction of the Fukushima Daiichi power plant after its evacuation, while her image is of the control room simulator at Plant Vogtle in Waynesboro, Georgia.[8] Given the potential for failure and the untold consequences of even one disaster, *Control Room* is an ironic title. Ironies accrue. The results of nuclear "control" are abundantly written on the land. There is no great and powerful Oz at work, just the mundane tasks that circumscribe the functioning of a nuclear plant. Meanwhile, the auditory and visual experiences to be had in the installation *Transuranic* at first give us the sense of rather mundane and even boring landscapes, but strangely hued. And then we hear the Geiger counter as it registers the nuclear material that went into creating the uranotypes. And then we see the maps that inform us of the infection that spreads across the continental United States. In *Scars on the Landscape*, Hepner creates archival prints that chronicle her travels to active and decommissioned nuclear power plants in Germany and France, where she used her body to create "a mark in time in the landscape surrounding the building as it was active or in flux." In accord with her nuanced approach to medium, Hepner uses X-ray film (X-rays and gamma rays are known cancer-causing agents) to create the images for *Palinopsia*. *Bomb Pulse* is particularly evocative—it is landscape no longer an external and externalized experience; instead, it is landscape written on the bone. A series of cyanotype on bone, the series is

6   Rancière, *The Emancipated Spectator*, p. 43.
7   Abbey Hepner, artist's website [https://abbey-hepner.com/#/work/control-room/].
8   Abbey Hepner, unpublished Qualifying Paper, p. 8.

initially reminiscent of Georgia O'Keeffe's encounters with the New Mexico desert and her collecting of cow skulls. However, upon closer inspection, Hepner has created a series of cyanotype on bone to reference radiocarbon dating and the existence of carbon-14 that "naturally exists in the air, plants, animals, and our bodies."

Hepner's installations and photographs multiply the sense of mundane danger, of the imperiled commonplace. The sum of her work on the nuclear industry are, in the words of Rancière, "scenes of dissensus" while the *Control Room* is an apt metaphor for her hope that we can change course; it is the inside that can hopefully be "cracked open." Rancière: "What 'dissensus' means is an organization of the sensible where there is neither a reality concealed behind appearances nor a single regime of presentation and interpretation of the given imposing its obviousness on all. It means that every situation can be cracked open from the inside, reconfigured in a different regime of perception and signification. To reconfigure the landscape of what can be seen and what can be thought is to alter the field of the possible and the distribution of capacities and incapacities."[9] In allowing her into the control room where she made photographs, Hepner extends spectatorship to her audience; she extends to us the possibility of agency and therefore change.

III. THE AESTHETIC EFFECT

I have relied heavily on two sources throughout this essay—Abbey Hepner, whom I was fortunate enough to mentor throughout her graduate studies, and Jacques Rancière, who taught at the University of Paris VIII, France, from 1969 until 2000 and who held the Chair of Aesthetics and Politics from 1990 until his retirement. As an art historian who works in a department where art studio, art history, and art education are joined, I often encounter the blunderbuss of authenticity. In Hepner's case and defense, almost a decade later Rancière has allowed me to answer her questions and concerns more fully and to hopefully provide students who are fortunate enough to encounter her work with the conceptual tools to think through their particular callings—what does it mean to act as an emancipated spectator rather than be narrowly defined and forced to act within the authentic?

As an emancipated spectator, Hepner lays it all before us because she understands that technology creates exactly such opportunities for dissensus—not to reveal a "reality hidden behind appearances" but instead to show us what is there and to leave it up to us what to make of it. For example, in the series *Monument Plinth*, an ugly and ironic inverse of the ancient burial mounds constructed by indigenous people, Hepner uses aerial images to represent the mounds built as uranium disposal cells that are our toxic contribution to the landscape. In *Uravan*, she "unearths" the town of Uravan, Colorado, founded in 1912 but buried by the EPA in 1986 under layers of clay, soil, and rock because it was contaminated by radioactive chemicals. Such opportunities created by Hepner coincide with Rancière's assertion that there is no "normative idea of what art has to do. I really don't think that there is a good practice of art. The relation between the consensual image and subversive images is constantly shifting so that you have to, at each moment, displace the displacement itself."[10]

9 Rancière, The Emancipated Spectator, pp. 48–49.
10 Jacques Rancière, *The Politics of Aesthetics: The Distribution of the Sensible*, edited and translated by Gabriel Rockhill (London: Bloomsbury Academic, 2004), p. 79.

Hepner is now a professor. Nevertheless, like all of my best students, she still questions; her questions make her a better teacher and mentor for her own students even as her questions remain with me and prod me to question. Recently, in an e-mail exchange, she expressed the following:

> There are times when I think that art has served as a vessel of communication for me—something that could transcend a once broken voice. But also, photographs don't say anything without context. They can't free me from my responsibility.[11]

And once more, I can suggest some resolution in the work of Rancière. In an interview with Gabriel Rockhill titled "Farewell to Artistic and Political Impotence," Rockhill posed the question to Rancière: "What is the role of the critic, the interpreter, the theorist in drawing out or highlighting the political elements in works of art or artistic endeavors? I know that you've been very critical of certain conceptions of committed art or politicized art that try to reduce the political dimension of art to the artist's intention. What, then, is the role at the opposite end of the spectrum, i.e., not with the producer of works of art but with their reception by the interpreter, the theorist, the active spectator if you will. Do they play a role in articulating the political power of works of art? Or is this power somehow inherent in works as they stand?" To some extent, Rockhill's question is also Hepner's and reflects her concerns around image making. Rancière's response is actually the inspiration for my subtitle, "The Political Aesthetics of Abbey Hepner." Powerfully, he answers, "No, I don't think that the power is inherent in the work as it stands because for me the problem is that **there is no politics of art; there is a politics of aesthetics**. This means that what is important is not the idea that the work can have this or that effect. In fact, the work is an implementation of an idea of the artist, which means that the work is an implementation of the relation of an artist to politics." (Emphasis mine.) The next part of his answer is the source for the third subheading of this essay: "But this does not mean at all that the artist can anticipate political effects of the work. **Thus, the effect, the aesthetic effect, is not the effect of a work in the sense that a work should produce this energy for action or this particular form of deliberation about the situation. It's about creating forms of perception, forms of interpretation."**[12] (Emphasis mine.) Indeed, photographs cannot free us from our responsibilities, but Hepner's generosity means that she shares with us the right to look. In emancipating herself as a spectator, she frees us all.

11 Author e-mail correspondence with the artist (September 27, 2020).
12 Rancière, *The Politics of Aesthetics*, pp. 79–80.

ACKNOWLEDGMENTS

The Light at the End of History is made possible by the many individuals and communities who have embraced my curiosity and allowed me to learn from them and the lands they inhabit, including past residents of Uravan, Colorado; the Rimrocker Historical Society; residents of Waynesboro, Georgia; Plant Vogtle; EBR-I Atomic Museum; the National Atomic Testing Museum and Archive; Earl McBride and Kathy Owens; It's Not Just Mud volunteers; residents of Ishinomaki, Yokohama, and Yokosuka; residents of Hanford, Washington; and downwinders of Utah and Southern Idaho.

I am grateful for Nancy Zastudil for her early support and encouragement of my work and for her assistance with editing this book, as well as her friendship and keen insight. I thank Mark Finco for assisting me in obtaining the aerial images and Scott White for creating the beautiful maps based on a few ideas and many edits. I also thank George and Prudy Hepner for their support, assistance in collecting materials, and coordination with the maps and satellite images. Thank you Daylight Books, specifically Michael Itkoff for proposing the idea of a book and believing in it, and Ursula Damm for her design brilliance.

I am deeply indebted to Kirsten Pai Buick for writing the essay for this book. Her teachings have made an incredible impact on my life and her mentorship has helped me understand the gift and responsibility of my art practice. She is the kind of educator every student deserves to have, and the kind that I will spend my life striving to be.

For insight and guidance, and for always providing sound advice and encouragement, I thank Meggan Gould, Jim Stone, and Edward Bateman.

For supporting the creation of this book and the bodies of work within it, I thank the following individuals and institutions: Southern Illinois University Edwardsville; SIUE College of Arts and Sciences; the Society for Photographic Education; Joan Linder; Jennie Lamensdorf; the University of Buffalo Galleries; the University of New Mexico; Howard L. Franks Memorial Fellowship; the Puffin Foundation; Steffan Riebel and the Institut für Alles Mögliche; Ralph, Tina, and Sebastian Hold; Yaelle Amir; and SITE Santa Fe. Thank you to everyone who preordered a book and helped it come to fruition.

None of this would have been possible without my lifelong partner Evan Hepner, who moved across the country to support me and endured two long years apart so that I could follow my dream. He is my biggest advocate, one who listens to audiobooks about nuclear history and navigates as I seek out remote and secret corners of the world.

CONTRIBUTORS

Abbey Hepner is assistant professor of photography at Southern Illinois University Edwardsville. She holds a BFA in art and a BA in psychology from the University of Utah, and an MFA in photography from the University of New Mexico. Her work examines health, technology, and our relationship with place. She frequently works at the intersection of art and science, examining biopolitics and the use of health as a currency. Her work has been exhibited widely in such venues as the Mt. Rokko International Photography Festival, SITE Santa Fe, Krannert Art Museum, the University of Buffalo Art Galleries, and the Lianzhou Foto Festival.

Essay:

Kirsten Pai Buick is professor of art history at the University of New Mexico where she teaches in the areas of the visual culture of the first British Empire; US art to 1940; African American art; representations of the American landscape and representations of enslavement; and the history of women as patrons and collectors of the arts. She has published extensively on African American art and been the recipient of numerous awards and fellowships, including the Smithsonian American Art Museum's Pre-Doctoral Fellowship and the Charles Gaius Bolin Fellowship at Williams College. In 2015, she was chosen as the eleventh recipient of the David C. Driskell Prize for excellence in African American art. Her book *Child of the Fire: Mary Edmonia Lewis and the Problem of Art History's Black and Indian Subject* is published by Duke University Press. Her second book, *In Authenticity: Kara Walker and the Eidetics of Racism*, is in progress.

Copy editor:

Nancy Zastudil, owner of The Necessarian, LLC, is an independent editor working toward equitable representation in the arts. She regularly edits exhibition catalogs for individuals and organizations, and she contributes to local and national art publications. In addition, Zastudil participates in artist award juries and grant proposal reviews, most recently for the Fleishhacker Foundation, Creative Capital, and the Harpo Foundation. She received her MA in curatorial practice from California College of the Arts and her BFA in painting and drawing from the Ohio State University.

Maps:

Scott White is professor of geosciences at Fort Lewis College in Durango, Colorado. His degrees are in geology (BS and MS) from Tennessee Tech University and Texas Christian University, and geography (PhD) from the University of Utah. His teaching and research interests focus primarily on the use of Geographic Information System (GIS) software for natural and cultural resources management, as well as cartographic design. Recent projects include a study of late 1800s through mid-1900s tourist mapping for Yellowstone National Park by the National Park Service and mapping companies used by the passenger railway companies.

Images:

Mark Finco, PhD, is principal and senior scientist at RedCastle Resources, Inc., which specializes in the use of geospatial data—particularly remote sensing imagery—for forestry and natural resource management applications. He has worked in the United States and internationally in this field for over twenty-five years. His doctorate is in geography from the University of Utah, and his BS and MS are in engineering from Purdue University and Lehigh University, respectively. As a geographer, his interest runs deep in how "place" affects natural processes and human activities.

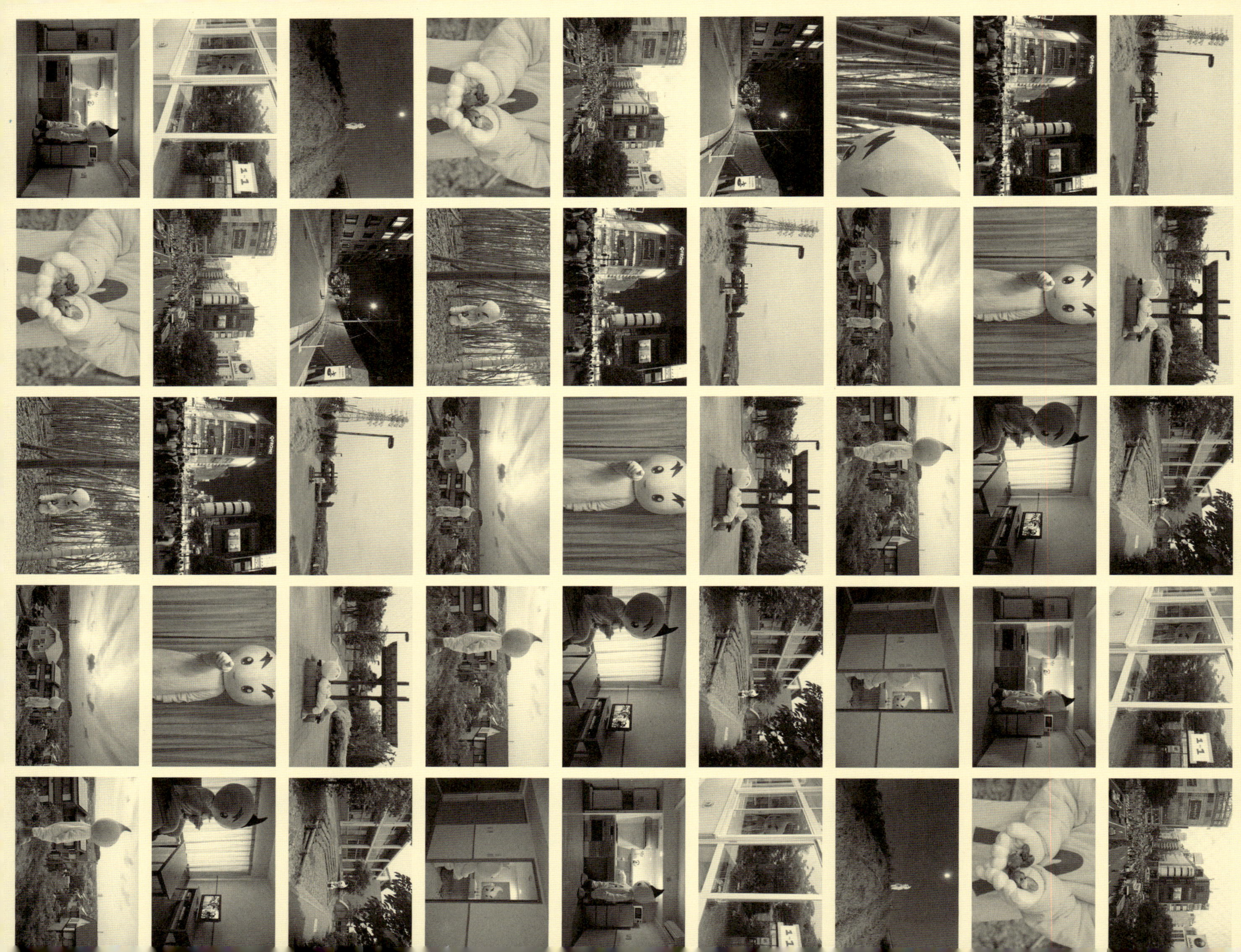